THE
RUNNING
OF THE
BULLS

THE
RUNNING
OF THE
BULLS

INSIDE THE CUTTHROAT RACE FROM
WHARTON TO WALL STREET

NICOLE RIDGWAY

GOTHAM BOOKS

GOTHAM BOOKS
Published by Penguin Group (USA) Inc.
375 Hudson Street, New York, New York 10014, U.S.A.
Penguin Group (Canada), 90 Eglinton Avenue East, Suite 700, Toronto, Ontario,
Canada M4P 2YE (a division of Pearson Penguin Canada Inc.); Penguin Books
Ltd, 80 Strand, London WC2R 0RL, England; Penguin Ireland, 25 St Stephen's
Green, Dublin 2, Ireland (a division of Penguin Books Ltd); Penguin Group
(Australia), 250 Camberwell Road, Camberwell, Victoria 3124, Australia
(a division of Pearson Australia Group Pty Ltd); Penguin Books India Pvt Ltd,
11 Community Centre, Panchsheel Park, New Delhi - 110 017, India; Penguin
Group (NZ), Cnr Airborne and Rosedale Roads, Albany, Auckland, New
Zealand (a division of Pearson New Zealand Ltd); Penguin Books (South Africa)
(Pty) Ltd, 24 Sturdee Avenue, Rosebank, Johannesburg 2196, South Africa

Penguin Books Ltd, Registered Offices: 80 Strand, London WC2R 0RL, England

Published by Gotham Books, a division of Penguin Group (USA) Inc.

First printing, August 2005
10 9 8 7 6 5 4 3 2 1

Copyright © Nicole Ridgway, 2005
All rights reserved

Gotham Books and the skyscraper logo are trademarks
of Penguin Group (USA) Inc.

Library of Congress Cataloging-in-Publication Data

Ridgway, Nicole.
The running of the bulls : inside the cutthroat race from Wharton to Wall Street
/ Nicole Ridgway.
    p.   cm.
ISBN 1-59240-125-2
1. Wharton School. 2. Finance–Vocational guidance–United States. I. Title.
HF1134.W4477R53 2005
330'.074811–dc22   2005008784

Printed in the United States of America
Set in Berthold Caslon Book BE
Designed by Daniel Lagin

For my mother, Connie,
and anyone who holds a passion—and pursues it

CONTENTS

CONTENTS

PROLOGUE

"Come on in! There's room." University of Pennsylvania career counselor Peggy Curchack is cheerfully ushering students into the Amado Recital Room in Irvine Auditorium, handing each a flyer as they pass by. With her salt-and-pepper hair, persistent smile and warm demeanor, Peggy emits more of a friendly, aunt-like air than that of a woman organizing a university-wide event in the midst of one of the most hectic times on Penn's campus. The latecomers to today's "Interviewing from the Corporate Employer's Perspective" workshop stake out places on the floor, many of them turning off cell phones as they unload their book-laden backpacks and take a seat. The students have come to hear the candid insights of recruiters, in hopes of learning what impresses and irks them the most before embarking on job interviews in the days and weeks ahead.

It's early October, the thick of the fall recruiting season for the Class of 2004, and recruiters—many of them hailing from Wall Street—have been migrating to Penn's campus for close to a month now to hunt for a new crop of young talent. Students enrolled in the university's business school—the Wharton School—are especially feeling the heat. Unlike many of their counterparts at Penn's other undergraduate schools, they have already been involved in recruiting since early September. They have "dropped" their resumes with investment banks, consulting firms, and some of the world's biggest corporations and are now waiting to hear back about whether or not they have been chosen for an interview. The seniors, who comprise about two-thirds of the eighty or so students in the room, are particularly anxious, because they are facing the prospect of fewer job opportunities than the seniors who graduated just four years earlier (as they were being accepted to the school). The rest of the attending students are juniors and a smattering of sophomores looking to get a leg up on internship recruiting in the coming spring.

Slated to give presentations at today's workshop are a recruiter from General Mills, one of the world's largest food makers, and a banker from Goldman Sachs, arguably the most prestigious of Wall Street's investment banks. Goldman is regarded highly–even revered–by many students at Penn, especially by those enrolled in Wharton. The competition to get a foot in the door at the bank is intense. Getting a job there is considered by many Whartonites to be a crowning achievement and a perfect complement to their business degree. It is no wonder the room is packed.

Joining Peggy at the front of the room is Misty, the recruiting manager from General Mills. With her mahogany hair tied back in a buoyant ponytail, Misty appears equally as wholesome and cheery in her red knitted crewneck sweater with the stark white-collar tips of her shirt folded neatly at the neck. The two women are ready to begin the workshop, but there is one major piece missing–the Goldman representative is nowhere to be found, causing several students to glance toward the door as if trying to summon her entrance.

Misty begins the session without her. After warming up the crowd with a few lighthearted icebreakers, she directs their attention to the flyer that they were handed at the beginning of the session. It is a list of interviewing "dos and don'ts" whimsically illustrated with General Mills' brand mascots, including the Pillsbury Doughboy, the Trix Rabbit, and the Lucky Charms Leprechaun. Referring to the list, Misty recommends that the students become well-versed in a company's brands and services before heading into their interviews.

"You students at Penn, this is one of the things you guys are *best* at," she praises the group emphatically. Misty then launches into some physical pointers: "Make sure you have good posture, that your back is not touching the back of the chair," she counsels. "Lean forward. Make eye contact."

This isn't exactly the inside advice that the upperclassmen in the room had been hoping for. A few students grow visibly listless, shifting in their seats. They have heard these tips hundreds of times before from their career counselors, and some of them begin to wonder what they are going to get out of this whole presentation.

General Mills, like many other companies recruiting on campus, conducts situational interviews in which a student is asked for an example of a difficult problem that they have encountered, what they did to deal with it and what the outcome was, continues Misty. "Don't be afraid to share a negative answer," she encourages the group. "Just show how you learned from it or put a positive spin on it." As Misty's twenty-minute time limit comes to an end, she delivers yet one more pep talk to bolster the students' resolve before they embark on their job interviews.

"The interview process is not designed to be a scary process. I know it can be a scary process, but it's not meant to be," she says with a reassuring smile. "Force yourself to take deep breaths. Just know it will be fine. It will all work out."

As Misty delivers her final remarks, the representative for Goldman Sachs enters the room and promptly takes Misty's place at center stage. Linda is Asian, and her shiny black hair is perfectly smoothed back in a tight bun. Wearing a dark-colored suit with a patterned scarf wound tightly around her neck, Linda's look is more rigid and corporate than Misty's. Right off the bat, the students can tell that Linda is a no-nonsense kind of woman. She looks serious, and she means business. The mood of the students changes visibly as she begins to speak. Her words—her insight—are what they are here for.

A train delay had caused Linda to run late, she explains. "I apologize for being late. The way to have a good interview is *not* to be late like I was."

Linda has been working at Goldman Sachs for three years now. She was a chemistry major in college and took a job as an analyst at a consulting firm for a couple of years before going to a top law school and eventually joining Goldman. Hers is a résumé worthy of an elite Goldman banker.

Looking around the room at the motley assortment of college students, Linda declares that dressing professionally for an interview is imperative. She recounts that early on in her career, she was told that there are only three appropriate colors for business attire: black, navy and gray. The only patterns: solids and pinstripes. "You want them to pay attention to *you* and what *you've* accomplished," she explains. "You don't want them to be paying attention to your tie."

Like Misty, Linda tells the crowd to research the company before interviewing with them. But she expands on the advice, telling the students not to rely solely on information from corporate Web sites because every candidate worth their salt does that. To gain that crucial edge over other candidates, they must dig deeper, she explains. Penn, and more importantly Wharton, has an alumni network teeming with people working on Wall Street. Students should use some initiative and networking skills to take advantage of those connections and set up informational interviews with their Penn brethren at the Goldmans and Morgan Stanleys of the world before they face recruiters.

As Linda makes it clear to the group that there's nothing more annoying to recruiters than an applicant who comes unprepared to an interview, her tone intensifies. "It's a waste of *their* time. It's a waste of *your* time," she says in a manner that indicates that this has happened to her one too many times before.

Taking a pregnant pause to let the severity of what she has just said sink in, Linda continues. Next topic: the résumé. Without exception, students *must* know their résumés "cold," because everything on it, including a potential hire's hobbies or interests, can become talking points for the interviewer.

"If you are interested in capital markets and you say you follow the markets, then me asking a question about the markets is fair game," Linda tells them. "Don't act like you're an expert if you're *not*."

Linda then brings up a common interviewing quandary, the "list-your-three-greatest-strengths-and-weaknesses" question. Figuring out the positive attributes to share about oneself shouldn't be that difficult, she says, but finding the appropriate negative things to say is something that students debate over time and again. To give the response that their faults include being a "workaholic" or a "perfectionist" is transparent and trite, she cautions; interviewers have heard these responses dozens of times before. Instead, they should think of something "not too negative" and explain how they are working on it.

All of this advice is good, but many of the students sitting in the room are wondering: *But what does it take to get a job at Goldman?* They're looking for some secret insight, something to make them a more viable candidate than the competition they are up against—many of whom are sitting in this very room, eagerly hanging onto Linda's every word just as they are.

What Linda says next only heightens their anxieties. She reiterates that the competition for jobs is so tough that they must watch their step. A student who doesn't know the answer to a technical or quantitative question or doesn't market himself to recruiters will likely lose all chances of getting a job offer, because there will always be another student who does know the answer, she explains.

"In your head you should have five selling points that you want to get across *no matter what*," she proclaims. "If you *don't* do this, you'll be at a disadvantage, because other students *are* doing this."

As Linda continues to dole out her no-nonsense interview advice, the warm optimism instilled by Misty has all but dissipated into a cold new reality for the students in the room. If they weren't already hyperaware of the multitude of fierce competition waiting to take the most coveted spots at the investment banks, they were now. Linda closes with a dictum heard more often on a salesroom floor than on a college campus. "*Always* sell yourself," she tells them. "Throughout the whole process, even after you have gotten the offer, you should *always be selling yourself.*"

As the workshop concludes, eager students scramble to the front of the room vying to get a word in with Linda. Others linger, waiting for the swarm to alleviate so they can have their turn to sell themselves to this woman from Goldman Sachs.

In the spring of 2004, an estimated 1.2 million students graduated from American colleges with a bachelor's degree. They entered a difficult job market that, in some cases, could hardly reconcile the average of $116,000 in tuition they had paid at private colleges and universities to attain their diplomas (the average four-year tuition was close to $40,000 at public colleges and universities). The last few years had brought steep declines in entry-level job opportunities, and many students who aspired to great career heights had instead sought the sanctuary of graduate school, unpaid internships, or the solace of the first job opportunity that came to them for fear that they wouldn't find anything better. According to the National Association of Colleges and Employers (NACE), there was one glimmer of hope, however: Employers expected to hire 12.7 percent more college grads during the 2003–2004 academic year than they had in the previous year. It was the first projected hiring increase following four years of successive declines. Yet it was hard to be optimistic. There was now a huge glut of young, capable, degree-holding prospects, many of whom were competing for the same limited number of jobs that had opened up.

Business school graduates, in particular, found themselves entering a job market with little promise no matter where their diplomas came from. During the economic downturn that began in 2000, financial services firms were some of the hardest hit. Hundreds and, at times, thousands of layoffs were announced weekly. Yet students continued to pursue business degrees in the belief that such practical curriculums were the starting point for successful careers. In the 2003–2004 academic year, U.S. colleges graduated 250,000 to 300,000 students with business degrees. According to a 2004 salary survey by the NACE, undergraduate students who majored in economics or finance were taking in an average starting salary of $40,630 (not including bonuses).

At the Wharton School the job outlook was definitely brighter than elsewhere. Wharton had long held the distinction of being the most prestigious undergraduate business program in the country and a fertile ground for Wall Street recruiters seeking out new hires who they could rely on.

No matter what the economic climate, recruiters from the most elite investment banks, consulting firms and corporations make pilgrimages to Penn's campus each year knowing that they will undoubtedly find the talent that they need at the Wharton School. Wharton is not only the sole undergrad business program in the storied Ivy League, but according to *U.S. News & World Report*, Wall Street recruiters and Wharton itself, it also reigns supreme over all of the others. Its undergraduate program, which awards students bachelor of economics degrees, has since its founding in 1881 produced many of the nation's most influential investment bankers and titans of industry, including turnaround artist and Revlon Chairman Ronald Perelman; Jerome Fisher, the founder of Nine West Group; Brian Roberts, the Chairman and CEO of Comcast Corp.; and the CEOs of Estée Lauder and Tiffany & Co. Real estate moguls Donald Trump and William Mack also attended the school, as well as financial powerhouses such as Michael Tarnopol, the vice chairman of investment bank Bear, Stearns & Co., and Brian Finn, president of Credit Suisse First Boston. And this is merely to name a few of the business-building, deal-making and boardroom-ruling alumni who call Wharton their alma mater.

Such was the school's track record that at Wharton, it wasn't about whether a graduate could find a job, but rather how many job offers they could acquire—and of what quality. As one prospective 2004 graduate would note, "There's no such thing as unemployment at Wharton."

That notion seemed proven by the fact that many major investment houses such as Citigroup, Goldman Sachs, JPMorgan Chase and Morgan Stanley were still flocking to the campus looking for new blood. On *average*, students in Wharton's Class of 2004 managed to receive two job offers, mostly from investment banks. By the end of their first semester, more than sixty-five percent of the senior class had a job offer in hand. And this group was among some of the highest paid undergraduates in the country, making an average of $52,300–$10,000 more a year than the national average—with an average signing bonus of $6,800 and year-end bonus of $14,900. And those were just the *averages*. Some made closer to six figures in their first full year out of college, even in an economic decline.

To gain entrance into Wharton is a feat unto itself. It's an elite group of kids who are culled from applicants around the globe to comprise the school's next generation of students. Only fifteen to eighteen percent of applicants—roughly 700 students a year—are accepted into the Wharton undergraduate business program, and approximately 500 of those students matriculate. Wharton's Class of 2005, for example, has an average SAT score of 1436, a mere 164 points shy of a perfect score, putting the average Wharton student among the ninety-seventh percentile of college-bound high school seniors.

As these elite incoming freshmen arrive at Penn's tree-lined campus in West Philadelphia, they are met with a demanding curriculum geared toward arming them with the skills to succeed in the business world—and they embark on this training just days after arriving at the school. Wharton's courses are geared toward practical skills rather than a spectrum of theoretical ones, and the class schedules look more like an MBA's course load than an undergraduate's—except that students must endure these classes for four years instead of two. Although there are opportunities to take liberal arts classes, many of the more gung-ho Wharton students opt to take an extra finance class in lieu of "softer" subjects like sociology or philosophy.

While the tuition and fees that members of the Class of 2004 paid over their four years at the school is a hefty $120,000, the price young Whartonites have to pay for the honor of earning close to six figures their first year out of school is even steeper in terms of dedication and workload—and one that most early twentysomethings would be reluctant to dole out. To embark on this intense journey often means sacrificing the normal accoutrements of the college experience, whether it's enjoying an active social life filled with road trips and parties, participating in Greek life, or playing sports. Instead, many Whartonites opt to spend their free time in business-oriented clubs and organizations that expand upon their experiences in the classroom and bolster their résumés in the hope of impressing recruiters come their junior and senior years.

If a student weren't already competitive before they came to the school, then Wharton's infamous "curve"–on which almost every class is graded–and the pressure engendered when a group of overachievers gather will most likely make them so. For Wharton's student body is a competitive group that will raise the bar of competition for its members to nosebleed heights. Staying up until all hours of the night to complete a group project or struggling with a corporate valuation for a finance class is a common occurrence for a Wharton student. As they navigate this arduous curriculum with their peers, a type of groupthink begins to take hold, aligning their experiences and their perspectives. They soon learn that as long as they can keep a competitively high GPA (above a 3.4 at the very least) and sharpen their interviewing skills–which the school provides plenty of opportunities for them to do–then they are almost guaranteed to land a high-paying job in the financial services or consulting industries. Throughout their years at Wharton, their minds will be filled with the prospects that Wall Street can offer them, their classes will teach them what they need to know to succeed there and the recruiters that flock to the campus to wine and dine them will make them feel like they belong there.

For most Wharton students, their first real taste of this world comes when they embark on internships during the summer after their junior year. This is a time when a large percentage of Wharton's students make a mass exodus from Penn's campus in Philadelphia to the high-rises of Manhattan, where they will learn the ropes of the world's financial engine and work ungodly hours to impress the higher-ups at investment banks and consulting firms. During their internships, many Wharton students try to prove that they can handle the pressure of multiple deadlines and little to no sleep. All of this is done in the name of impressing the right people so that they will be on the short list when the firm they work for begins doling out job offers to their strongest candidates at the end of the summer.

But perhaps the most important and stressful time in a Whartonite's college career occurs during the recruiting period in the fall semester of their senior year. It is at this point that Wharton's students test their educations, their stamina, and their desire in a ten-week-long marathon of events, interviews and trials. The recruiting season serves as the culmination point for everything they have devoted themselves to working so tirelessly for throughout their years of pricey academic training. It's in these weeks that they will discover if it was all worth it. Where they land a job could solidify their place in the upper echelons of the Wharton hierarchy.

Over the course of these weeks, representatives from banks such as Goldman, Morgan Stanley and Citigroup, and consulting firms such as McKinsey, Accenture and Monitor, will put Wharton students through draconian interviews, during which they are bombarded with analytical questions that require complex mental arithmetic, forced to endure personality assaults, and required to parry trick queries–their answers to which, no matter what they are, will most likely be wrong. Even as they embark on myriad interviews, these students still have to complete the one-hundred-page projects that often take until 4:00 A.M. to finish, the midterm exams, and challenging classes that are the hallmark of a Wharton education.

It's this competitive drive and desire to be a part of the best, most elite firms that incites Wharton's students to push themselves to the brink during recruitment season. The price of failure is high. Every Whartonite knows how swiftly one misstep can bring a fall from grace. Answer one question wrong on net present value, or fail to hit it off with the key managing director or senior vice president of a bank, and it could mean a lost opportunity.

Burn one recruiter bad enough by being late for an interview or reneging on a job offer, and it could mean an early end to recruitment season. There is always another qualified candidate to take their place, and that candidate is most likely the person sitting next to them in class, or maybe a team member they just carried through the last group project.

Wharton's Class of 2004 took on the ten-week recruitment period as if it were the final sprint in a four-year-long marathon that had been more arduous than anything that they had ever endured in their young lives. They continued to run on inhuman amounts of sleep, running themselves to the point of exhaustion. Yet they still managed to keep their wits about them, as though they had tapped into some well of superhuman ability. For some of these overachievers, it's an adrenaline rush. It's as though it's a rite of passage that only a chosen few are capable of, or are willing to make the obvious social and physical sacrifices for, that makes them so proud.

Just as hundreds of Spaniards and thrill-seeking tourists fill the narrow, cobblestone streets of Pamplona each July to test their physical limits in the annual "Running of the Bulls," so do these aspiring future business leaders as they undertake a race that tests their stamina and their wits at every turn, knowing that any false move or stumble would mean the end of the run. But if they have mastered the knowledge, if they have the drive and determination, then perhaps they too can run with the bulls of Wall Street, and join the ranks of the financial and corporate elite who move markets, who reap fortunes and who shape history.

PART I

THE BULLRING

CHAPTER ONE

WELCOME TO THE
WHARTON SCHOOL

Every August they arrive in droves.

From Philadelphia International Airport, the New Jersey Turn-pike, I-76 and I-95, parents drive their children to the University of Pennsylvania in order to release them into the wilds of college life. As the family car navigates through the streets of University City in the western section of Philadelphia, its passengers are treated to a spectacle of students moving through campus sporting the bronzed glow and peeling noses of summers spent under the sun. Slung over their shoulders are duffle bags stuffed with crumpled T-shirts and jeans, their arms embracing boxes and milk crates carrying sundry belongings–CDs, toiletries, socks–as they anxiously flock into the massive collegiate gothic buildings that house the dorm rooms and frame the perimeter of the Quad. Like parasitic gatekeepers, gargoyles perch in various poses on the corners of the campus buildings, watching over the procession of this year's new crop. It is a hub of activity as the dorms seemingly swallow these family units whole and spit out new ones, absent a son or daughter and without the burden of their belongings.

As it is with the start of most school years, there is a sense of anticipation about things to come. It feels as if the air has changed. It's somehow fresher than the day before. Freed from the shackles of curfews and chores, it's a whole new beginning for the 2,400 freshmen joining Penn's ranks. There is a sense of anticipation about the friendships and future careers they will forge here. Their Penn diplomas will not only help them land jobs, but will travel with them throughout their lives, gracing the walls of their future homes and offices.

In these humid early days of college life, the 500 freshmen enrolled in Penn's Wharton School–the university's esteemed undergraduate business program–are just like any other fresh-faced seventeen- or eighteen-year-olds settling into their first day of college. They awkwardly break the ice with new roommates, scan the masses for potential friends and wander through campus frantically searching for their classrooms on maps. It is in this confused, dreamlike haze that they begin their foray into college life.

Come orientation, freshmen are divided into groups based on which of Penn's four schools they are enrolled in, whether it's the School of Arts and Sciences (known as "The College"), the School of Nursing, the School of Engineering and Applied Science or Wharton. Wharton's new students are now corralled together, looking just as lost as the engineering students who have been gathered together for their orientation. Yet, in a matter of days, their new world will come into sharper focus. The stark contrast between the experiences that lie before Wharton's new brood and the ones facing their peers enrolled in Penn's three other undergraduate schools will become startlingly evident.

These newly branded Whartonites soon begin to discover that during their time here, they will be defined not by what fraternity or sorority they join, but by the career choices that they make and the amount of effort they put forth to achieve that career. What they choose to tell their fellow students about their goals will become the foundation of their identities and friendships and will determine whether, in the rank and file of overachieving Whartonites, they are going to stand out.

In the late-summer swelter of August 2003, Wharton's Class of 2007 began taking their own measured steps into the world where some 77,000 Wharton alumni once trod before graduating to Wall Street or Corporate America's mahogany-paneled boardrooms. With no one else to cling to, the freshmen hang on every word uttered by their upperclassmen "Team Advisors" (TAs), who will guide them through orientation and provide a road map to their new life for the next four years.

Wearing blue Wharton T-shirts and shorts, the TAs herd freshmen from a luncheon to a two-hour advisory panel on course requirements and the services that the school offers. In the late afternoon, these packs of fresh Whartonites file into Huntsman Hall's Baker Forum for a welcome address by Wharton dean Patrick T. Harker, who is known on campus as "Professor Pat." The forum, a two-story rotunda with a sleek and modern wood-and-brick interior, is commonly used as a place for Wharton study groups to congregate during the academic year, but is enormous enough—4,000 square feet—to accommodate the entire freshman class today. As the room begins to fill, some students sit cross-legged on the floor waiting for the presentation to begin; others are excitedly making plans with new friends. In one cluster of students, two freshman guys compare notes on the drinking games they played in high school, while another member of their group sits on the floor, twisting her shoelace around one of her fingers as she surveys the crowd.

Lining the stairs before them is a clutch of Wharton faculty and administrators grinning down at the crowd. Within moments, Suzanne Kauffman DePuyt, Wharton's Managing Director in charge of student services, and Anita Henderson, the director of academic affairs and advising, step up to the podium and cleverly usurp the students' attention. Wearing the blue Wharton orientation T-shirts over their office attire, the two launch into their own rehearsed welcome.

"To be part of this community, you have to learn the language," they announce. Then, alternately, they go through Philadelphia's distinctive vernacular:

"We don't say downtown, we say *Center City*."

"We don't say Philadelphia Eagles, we say Philadelphia *Iggles*."

"You don't eat heroes, you eat *hoagies*."

"You don't go to the beach, you go to *the shore*."

And in unison "And you don't say hello. It's *YO!*" they exclaim in pep rally fashion.

The two women then ask the crowd to welcome Dean Harker, Philadelphia-style.

"Yo, Dean Harker!" the students yell.

"Yo, Class of 2007!" he replies. Then, as if the last routine had no impact on him at all, Dean Patrick Harker shifts to Southern-speak: "Welcome ya'll to the Wharton School."

Tall and fit, Harker defies the stodgy, bow-tied stereotype of a college dean. A handsome man with a chiseled face and a full head of brown hair, he looks more the part of a former college football player. He's not from the South, but rather from New Jersey—and he, too, was once a freshman at Penn, although in the College. Reminiscing about his first days at the school, Dean Harker talks about his freshman year roommate, who constantly snored, and his early feelings of nervousness, which later turned into anxiety.

"What have I gotten myself in to?" he recalls asking himself over and over again. "I was one of the smartest people in my (high school) class. Now I'm *surrounded* by smart people."

Harker, who also earned two master's degrees and a PhD from Penn, instinctively knew that these thoughts would also encroach upon the minds of the freshmen staring up at him. Most Wharton students are already deeply ingrained with a drive to achieve great things before they even set foot on the school's campus. They have tasted superstar status in high school, whether as class vale-dictorian, the kid labeled "Most Likely to Succeed" or some other high-flying honor. They are the ones who set the curve higher. And now, as members of Wharton's new freshman class, they are part of an entire class of overachievers like themselves.

As Wharton's freshmen begin to decipher their syllabi and christen their pricey textbooks with highlighter markers, they begin to learn another new vernacular that will stay with them long after their college careers. It's not Philadelphia's slang, but Wall Street's— a vocabulary filled with acronyms linked to some equation or theory that ultimately calculates, *Is there money in this or not?*

They will take a majority of their classes, spend many a late night and have some of their greatest collegiate achievements and failures in Huntsman Hall, a redbrick building looming eight stories high at Walnut and 38th Streets on the university's campus. The $139.9 million building was officially opened in 2002, complete with a ribbon-cutting ceremony honoring both the building and its namesake, Jon M. Huntsman, a Class of 1959 Wharton grad and founder of the multinational chemical company Huntsman Corp. The billionaire businessman put up more than $50 million to construct the new home for Wharton's business students. It was one of the most prodigious gifts ever given to the school by Wharton's extraordinarily generous and affluent alumni.

With the opening of Huntsman Hall, all of Wharton's undergraduate and graduate classes were brought under the same roof for the first time, a move that dismayed some Wharton MBA students who scoffed at the idea of sharing study areas with their younger (and sometimes more cocksure) brethren. Previously, most of the MBA classes were held in Vance Hall, and Wharton's undergraduate students called Steinberg Hall–Dietrich Hall their home. With its plain brick facade bordering Locust Walk, "Steiny-D" left much to the imagination, especially compared to the grandeur of Huntsman Hall, which has become the campus mecca for Wharton's Future Business Leaders of Tomorrow. Its towering cylindrical structure and the flocks of dark-suited students heading toward its entrances have garnered the building a plethora of tongue-in-cheek nicknames, the prevailing moniker being "The Tower of Greed" (although "The Death Star" is also a well-known favorite).

In Huntsman's modern, technologically advanced classrooms, Wharton students learn the underpinnings of Corporate America and Wall Street and how to succeed there. Escalators move them efficiently from class to class, and visiting CEOs are often entertained in its upper level, where window-lined conference rooms are furnished with black leather armchairs and stocked with refreshments. Students at the College take classes in buildings that date back to the nineteenth century and that sometimes have temperamental air-conditioning and wobbly desks, while the Wharton students have climate-controlled rooms with tiered, ergonomic seats (which swivel 360 degrees so students can work with one another more easily). At the front of the classroom, Wharton professors reign like the Wizard of Oz from their computerized terminal lecterns, controlling everything in the room from projector screens to the window shades.

Walking through a corner of campus that has undergone a facelift due to the successes of Wharton's alumni not only feeds the aspirations of Wharton students, who see where their academic training could take them, but also propagates the Wharton stereotype that Whartonites are single-mindedly competitive overachievers, and further widens the sharp divide between them and those enrolled in Penn's other, less-endowed programs. To students enrolled in the College, Huntsman is a stark reminder that the Wharton School's business program is Penn's "chosen child." And, in many ways, Wharton's students are taught to feel that way as well.

From their very first days of school, Wharton students are told that they are the best and the brightest. And if they weren't convinced of this before they arrived, they will soon adopt this belief and carry it with them like an invisible badge of honor. "Walking into Wharton and being told by the dean that we are the cream of the crop and we are at the world's best business school gave us a tremendous confidence," recalled Navin Valrani, a Class of 1993 Wharton alum who now heads several divisions of Dubai-based Al Shirawi Enterprises, one of the largest conglomerates in the Middle East. "You began to feel that you could achieve things far above the norm."

It is a school comprised of what one recent grad candidly describes as "a group of the most intense kids you will ever meet." Those students who aren't intense when they set foot onto campus freshman year quickly become so in order to keep up, he explains. Other alumni concede that Wharton's academic program carries with it demanding course requirements and punishing workloads that raise students' stress levels to a fever pitch and cause them to forgo many of the activities one expects typical college students to indulge in. Their peers in the College explain that Wharton students always seem too busy and wrapped up in their class work and prospective careers to relax and just hang out. All of these perceptions amount to a litany of stereotypes ascribed to Whartonites: type-A personalities, competitive, cutthroat, power-hungry, money-hungry—none of them exactly flattering.

Jon Gantman, a friendly and outgoing Wharton senior with sandy blond hair who grew up in the nearby suburb of Penn Valley, Pennsylvania, is from a family full of Penn alumni, including his mother and father. A member of the Class of 2004, Jon is the quintessential "legacy" student. (Roughly ten percent of each Penn class is comprised of legacy students. About one-third of the legacy students who apply to Penn gain admission to the school.) Soon after embarking on their college careers, Jon and his Wharton friends began making an extra effort to avoid being typecast or sounding snobbish to their peers in the College.

"Many of them will say, 'I go to Penn,' instead of 'I go to

Wharton,'" he explained. "Once I'm done with my Wharton classes, I'm a Penn student. Things become more based on the individuals and how they act. Unfortunately," he said in a disheartened tone, "it's the more outspoken Wharton students who create the stereotype."

"Wharton students don't like to be singled out as a Wharton student, especially freshman year," explained Beth Hagovsky, the director of Student Life at Wharton. "Socially, [all of Penn's students] hang out together. When they walk into classes, though, there is a divide."

Realizing that Wharton is often considered a separate, more elitist institution than its counterpart schools at Penn, the faculty has taken some strides to lessen the divide. A few years earlier, a small step was made in this direction when they changed the wording on the new freshman orientation welcome gift–a key chain on a blue nylon neck leash–to read "Penn/Wharton" instead of simply "Wharton." The Wharton "W," which was used for decades as a distinctive insignia for the school, has all but disappeared from campus as well. Instead, Wharton sweatshirts and other related paraphernalia are now emblazoned with the Penn shield.

For all of the pomp associated with Wharton, applying to the business school is deceivingly simple. It merely requires a prospective student to check the box on Penn's admission form that says "Wharton," an act that seems to underplay the weight of Wharton's demanding business curriculum and the dedication it requires of its students. Yet, gaining admission to Wharton is another feat altogether. Admissions officers admit a smaller percentage of applicants to Wharton–from fourteen to eighteen percent–than they do to Penn's three other schools, in some years by a fairly wide margin. For the past several years, Penn on the whole has tended to admit twenty percent of applicants. For the Class of 2007, Wharton received close to 4,000 applications, offered 700 prospects admission and matriculated 500 students. The average combined SAT score of those admitted to Wharton was 1440, fourteen points higher than Penn's overall average score. These scores put the average Penn and Wharton student in the ninety-seventh percentile of test takers, making them some of the best performers in the country.

For Shimika Wilder, an athletically built African-American senior whose quiet demeanor and eloquence make her seem older than her twenty-one years, the decision to check the box that said WHARTON was easy to make once she did some research. Raised in Upper Marlboro, Maryland, a small suburban town located twenty miles outside of Washington D.C., Shimika is the first person in her family to attend college. This pioneering role caused Shimika to set about her selection of colleges with even more than her usual trademark seriousness, because where she spent the next four years needed to suit both her interests and ambitions. She zealously did her research, buying a copy of *U.S. News & World Report*'s "America's Best Colleges" to serve as her guide.

Shimika was an avid athlete, running track and playing basketball, softball and volleyball at the Queen Anne School, the college preparatory high school she attended in Maryland. A self-described "Nike fanatic," Shimika dreamed of working for the flashy sporting goods retailer someday, perhaps in finance or marketing, and wrote about starting her own sporting goods store in her college application. "I thought business was the new wave of the future," she said. "I could go into any industry."

When Shimika discovered that Penn was in Division I athletics and that Wharton topped the *U.S. News'* list of undergraduate business schools, she grew fairly certain that it was the place for her. Penn also offered her more scholarship money than the state schools she had applied to. Moreover, Shimika liked the idea of getting a jump on the competition. Most other undergraduate business programs delay business course requirements, sometimes until as late as junior year. At New York University's Stern School of Business and University of Virginia's McIntire School of Commerce, business students don't start taking these classes until sophomore year. Berkeley's Haas School of Business doesn't even admit students into its business program until they are juniors. Wharton students, on the other hand, embark on their business studies from their first day of classes.

Out of the thirty-seven courses needed to attain a Wharton degree, only about a dozen must be nonbusiness-related. Yet, the weight placed on these courses is somewhat negated because Wharton students can choose to take three of their liberal arts classes on a much less stringent "pass/fail" basis. Whartonites have the option to enroll in close to ten more liberal arts pursuits if they choose. But oftentimes, the more business-minded types would rather forgo any classes that will distract them from their business studies.

"Wharton students didn't come here to learn about Plato and philosophy," expounded Shimika. "They're here to learn about the philosophy of money. They tend to discount the college classes. They aren't here to be intellectuals. It's about maximizing returns."

Wharton students specialize their business studies by choosing among one of seventeen "concentrations," such as accounting, finance, marketing or entrepreneurship, or they can design their own program. They can switch concentrations as late as their senior year. During her senior year, Shimika switched her concentration from finance to marketing with the hope of broadening her career options after graduation.

Academic advisors encourage students to cross-pollinate their studies among Penn's four different schools in order to foster exposure to multiple disciplines. Wharton's students have the option to declare minors from one of sixty different disciplines offered at one of Penn's other schools. The most overachieving Whartonites also have the opportunity to earn two degrees simultaneously by enrolling in one of three established joint-degree programs: the Huntsman Program in International Studies and Business (known as "Huntsman" on campus), the Jerome Fisher Program in Management & Technology (known as "M&T," it involves completing engineering degree requirements as well and is arguably the most demanding curriculum Penn has to offer), and Nursing & Health Care Management, a program between Wharton and the Nursing School that prepares students for careers in fields like hospital administration. If nothing else, these special programs, in which about twenty percent of Wharton students enroll, give students a chance to learn from different professors and work with students from Penn's other schools.

The students who embark on joint-degree programs find themselves even more stressed out than a typical Whartonite. Many of them opt to stay an extra year to lighten their course burdens a little.

"Engineering is actually more intense than Wharton. Sometimes it's a bit weird leaving a management class and going to 'Advanced Thermodynamics,'" recounted a fifth-year senior in the M&T program who is also enrolled in a sub-matriculation program that will award him a master's in biotechnology by the time he finally graduates. While his ten AP credits helped him avoid certain classes early on, the workload can still be overbearing at times. It's the payoff that makes it all worthwhile for some students. He hopes his three degrees will help him land a fast-track position at a consulting firm, preferably for the biotech or pharmaceutical industries.

"Doing M&T has molded how I've developed as a person," he said. "It catered to my schizophrenic needs of wanting to do this and that."

Growing up in Bombay, India, Shreevar Kheruka knew what Wharton was by the time he was twelve years old, but he didn't know about the University of Pennsylvania until well into his college search in high school. "The Wharton name would come up over and over," he recalled. "I didn't even know they were the same school."

Beyond the fact that Penn often gets confused with Penn State (the much larger state university based in central Pennsylvania), Wharton has developed such a strong reputation on its own that some people believe it to be a separate institution. It consistently appeals to scores of business-minded high school students hailing from such far-flung homelands as Mauritius, Argentina, China, Barbados and Portugal. International students representing forty different countries comprise fourteen percent of the Wharton Class of 2007's student body. In fact, Penn's campus as a whole is one of the most internationally diverse of the Ivy League schools, with students from ninety different countries making up ten percent or more of its 10,000 undergraduates.

Shreevar had also heard about other top American schools and seriously considered a handful of prestigious colleges, including Brown, Cornell, Berkeley, and Stanford. Yet Wharton, and the possibility of being able to earn a joint degree in business and engineering concurrently in the M&T program, reeled him in. M&T, he figured, would arm him with the perfect skills to help run his family's glass manufacturing business someday, and Shreevar eagerly sent in his application.

Following that anxious and nerve-racking ceremony of opening the envelope from Penn's admissions office, Shreevar felt both happy and disappointed. He had made it into Wharton, but he didn't make the cut for M&T. Always driven and rarely failing at anything he put his mind to, Shreevar decided to enroll in Wharton, determined to do everything he could to get into the M&T program by his sophomore year.

As his freshman year progressed though, Shreevar's ambitions quickly crumbled under the weight of his studies. He struggled through his first physics class—a prerequisite for the engineering part of the program required to get into M&T. Then, two weeks into the second physics class he needed to take, Shreevar walked out. Feeling defeated, he went straight to his academic advisor for help. He didn't want to take another physics class or earn a degree in engineering anymore. After a brainstorming session and a long discussion with his advisor, Shreevar dropped his M&T aspirations. Instead, he decided to pursue a minor in International Relations at the College, a skill set he figured he could use someday to expand his family's business further abroad and better deal with its international clients.

Each Wharton student graduates with a bachelor of science degree in economics. At the epicenter of the Wharton education is a checklist of ten required courses called "the core." During their freshman and sophomore years, Wharton students tackle this rigorous combination of courses in accounting, statistics, finance, management, marketing and the almost universally loathed Operations and Information Management (or OPIM).

It all begins with Management 100. Wharton's faculty devised the course when it set about revamping the undergraduate curriculum in the early 1990s. A combination of leadership training, public speaking, writing and teamwork skills, Management 100 is a program that has been lauded by the academic community and praised as an exemplary class by the American Association for Higher Education.

Wharton's freshmen meet their Management 100 Team Advisors and the other students in their class during the first days of new student orientation. It's a good way to ease them into their new surroundings, explained Jon Gantman, who now in his senior year oversees all of the Management 100 TAs. "Their TA is the one who takes them around during orientation. You go to all of your other classes and you don't know anyone. You come to Management 100 and you've met your TA, you've had lunch with them. And they ask you 'How's it going? Any problems with moving in?' "

Once classes commence, students are broken into smaller

recitation groups and are charged with the task of picking a local community-service project to work on throughout the semester. In addition to their regular full-class lectures, these subgroups meet once a week with their TA to design and implement their particular project and figure out how to raise the necessary money and get services donated. In essence, the fledgling business students are taught the ropes of management by being thrown directly into the fire of nonprofit work. While doing so, they are benefiting the Philadelphia community. One such project entailed helping inner-city seventh and eighth graders to explore their career goals. Another devised "Boo at the Zoo," a Halloween celebration at the Philadelphia Zoo for local area children. The freshmen in Jon's Management 100 group organized a "Diversity Day" event for the city's youth that was sponsored by local businesses, including a popular radio station that gave away gifts at the event.

Each student in Management 100 is required to write weekly papers evaluating themselves as a leader in their team and answering questions like *What kind of roles do you like to play?* or *What kind of negotiator are you?* All of the assignments relate back to what the students are being taught in their Management 100 class or what they are working on for their community-service project. It's a combination of writing assignments and speeches that culminates in a large group presentation at the end of the semester. By that time, students have come to know their group mates exceedingly well, so much so that it's hard to believe that just a matter of twelve weeks earlier they were complete strangers.

The course is considered by many Wharton students to be the most valuable classroom experience they have at the school, because in Management 100, friendships are made that will last throughout their years at Wharton. Some of them will rely on each other as study partners and choose to work with each other for group projects over the following three years.

If Management 100 is the collective group hug of business

classes during freshman year, then OPIM is considered the cold, harsh reality. It hits the freshmen when they buy the two thick textbooks on programming languages and databases that are required for the class. "There are so few kids who walk into that class and know what they are doing," said Jon. "If you don't keep up, you can get really lost."

OPIM is the epitome of practical education at Wharton. The class dutifully trains students on how to master different types of technology often used in a business setting. All of a sudden, terms like "deterministic modeling," "probability theory," "data mining" and "linear programming" are introduced into the students' lexicons. Formally called "Introduction to the Computer as an Analysis Tool," OPIM's curriculum is always changing to keep up with new technologies for programming and data management. Mainly, though, the class focuses on the most popular tool of the investment banking trade: Microsoft Excel spreadsheets and Microsoft Access databases. The students will use these skills to create economic models and analyze corporate financials for their classes, as well as to impress potential employers when it comes time to find a job. Students are also charged with the task of constructing their own Web page. Many Whartonites will later confess that they struggled through OPIM and remember very little about the programming languages that once were the fodder of their anxiety dreams during the second semester of their freshman year.

Anthony Sandrik enrolled in the Huntsman program and found that, by doing so, he had become part of a distinctive Wharton subculture that would somehow make the anxieties of freshman year even more overwhelming. Originally from Lebanon, Anthony's parents moved to the U.S. as teenagers after the civil war broke out in 1975. After college, they settled in Manhattan, where Anthony spent most of his childhood. While he was in high school, Anthony's father decided to retire from his demanding career in foreign exchange trading. His parents moved the family to Paris for a change of scenery and lifestyle. It was a dramatic change for Anthony, who admits that the Parisian teens he met were much more mature and sophisticated than his friends back in New York.

The experience bore in Anthony a curiosity about other cultures. Armed with a knowledge of five languages, including his parents' native Armenian, he wanted to pursue a life where borderlines rarely exist and to embark on a course of study that would offer him the chance to see even more of the world someday. But he also wanted a pragmatic degree. He had no interest in law or medicine. Pursuing business as opposed to a liberal arts education just made more sense to him. It seemed as if the Huntsman program was tailored to Anthony's dreams, and it was ultimately the reason he applied early decision to Penn over Yale.

When Anthony arrived on Penn's campus freshman year, he was placed in the Kings Court dorm on the same floor with all of the other Huntsman freshmen, many of who arrived from foreign lands or, like Anthony, were children of immigrants. Kings Court was across campus from the dorms of the Quad on Spruce Street where most of the freshman class lived, causing the Huntsman students to feel a bit alienated from their peers. It seemed to make sense to corral this group together, but as Anthony explained, too much of one thing isn't always a good idea.

"Freshman year was a disaster," he recalled. "All of the kids in my program taking the same classes and living on the same floor. People were going crazy: crying, yelling, especially during the OPIM midterm. They were all kids who had 4.0s in high school."

The tension is so great that it has spawned annual rituals on campus. During freshman year, young Whartonites perform a stress-relieving ritual that serves as a sort of rite of passage for the stressed-out and overburdened students. The night before freshmen take their Econ 1 midterms, they all gather in the Quad at midnight and perform the "Econ Scream," a collective roar that not only signifies one night of great tension and attempted release, but also serves as a precursor to many tense nights to come, as they endure even more strenuous course loads throughout their years at Wharton.

Sophomore year is considered by many at Wharton to be the most academically challenging time in their college careers. At this point, students' class schedules start sounding like a series of executive education seminars. They are now fully embedded in the pursuit of the Wharton core. It is during this time that the school requires three intensive courses: accounting, statistics and finance, or as some students like to dub them, "The Triple Threat." These are classes that are not only mentally taxing, but chock-full of group projects entailing case studies, presentations, and problem sets. Unlike the more intimate atmosphere of Management 100, the "Triple Threat" classes tend to be larger in size and full of long lectures, making the experience even more mind-numbing. "Sophomore year was awful," said Jon. "We all kind of suffered through it together. It's like pledging [a fraternity]."

This is also a time when the competition among Whartonites really begins to heat up. Almost every class at Wharton is graded on a curve, causing students to constantly compete with one another. On average, the curve allows for twenty to thirty percent of the class to get A's, thirty to forty percent B's, twenty to thirty percent C's and the remainder D's and F's. Some students view the curve as a good thing, where the majority of people get B's and it's next to impossible to fail. "If you go to classes and do the readings, you have already gotten a B," explained Jon matter-of-factly.

But at Wharton, where almost everyone was once a straight-A student in high school, the curve can be devastating. There are always a few stories of attempted grade sabotage floating around campus or at least a few pages ripped out of important texts. Some students keep to themselves when studying so as not to divulge some piece of knowledge that they might have that their classmates don't. There are also those who selectively "forget" to tell classmates about a study session, hoping to get a better edge.

The rivalry is particularly intense during midterms and finals. "When you're taking a test, you're nervously looking at the person sitting next to you and you're thinking, 'Is he going to be below me in the curve or am I going to be below him in the curve?'" said Nitin Rampat, a Wharton senior in the Class of 2004 who decided to stay at Penn for a fifth year to finish his joint degree in finance and bioengineering. One senior, who graduated with a 3.9 GPA in 2004, admits that she knew the GPAs of her fiercest competitors. "By senior year *everyone* knows each other's GPAs," she said, as if GPAs were as much a part of a person's identity as hometowns or birth dates.

As Anthony explained, many students even pretend they didn't study in order to throw off their peers. "What's really funny here is that people are overly modest," he explained. "Before exams, people will say they didn't even open a book. You don't want people to think you're smart or they will feel threatened by you and they will compete with you. But it's like, 'Yeah, come on, I know you have a 3.95 GPA, and you say you *never* study?'"

As much as they are put in direct competition with one another, Wharton students are also encouraged to work with each other. A common philosophy at Wharton is that it is essential to train students to work with other people before they venture off into the business world, where teamwork is imperative. Professors often break students into groups to work on corporate case studies or problem sets with one another. The experience ends up being a mixed blessing, however, especially at a school full of people who tend to be natural-born leaders with overbooked schedules that don't tend to accommodate flexibility.

"You have loud, obnoxious people who want to control everything. They won't incorporate other's ideas. And there's always going to be deadweight no matter what," explained Shimika, who said she discovered her worst flaws–her tendency to be intro-verted and a bit anal–while working on group projects.

At the end of a project, students are often asked to grade their teammates in peer evaluations. Every so often there is a student in a class who will "tank" another person, explained Anthony. "There are only five hundred kids in each Wharton class. So if someone found out you did that, your reputation goes sour," he said.

Group projects can also lead to cliquish behavior, sometimes leaving a few students to fend for themselves. Professors some-times tell the students to pick their own groups. Knowing that one weak member in a team can bring down the entire lot, the more strategic students of the group start surveying the crowd for strong teammates early in the semester, sometimes even before the syl-labus is handed out. At the beginning of classes, Shimika scans the crowd for the people who are the most enthusiastic participants and for those who have had previous coursework in the subject. She also looks for people who have different concentrations than her own so she can tap into their unique abilities. "It's crucial to get people who are not in your major. In New Product Develop-ment, for example, you want to have someone who is a finance major and someone who is good in stats," she explained.

Even being picky about your teammates doesn't prevent the pitfalls that occur when a group gets together. Shimika endured a couple of occasions where group projects became disastrous. On one such occasion, a team member got a concussion over the weekend before the project was due and failed to notify his group, which was meeting Sunday night for their presentation the next day. Shimika and her partner couldn't make up the work of their absentee teammate and had to exclude his section from the pre-sentation, which they feared would hurt their chances for a better-than-average grade.

Shimika also discovered that, in some cases, group projects can damage friendships. During her junior year, Shimika befriended an African-American woman who had sought to be a mentor to Shimika. They had decided to work together on a presentation about double minorities in the investment banking world. The project entailed conducting ten interviews with African-American women who worked at investment banks. As crunch time approached for the project, Shimika's partner's priorities swayed more heavily toward the sorority she was in. She rarely responded in a timely manner to Shimika's phone calls and e-mails, leaving Shimika to do most of the work on her own. Shimika conducted all ten of the interviews, only two of which her partner even participated in. Frustrated, Shimika spoke with her professor about her partner's lack of commitment. The day before the presentation was due, the two finally got together and worked feverishly from 3:00 P.M. to 3:00 A.M. to get it together. While the presentation went off without a hitch, it left Shimika with a bad taste in her mouth about her cohort. "You wouldn't know the drama that went on behind it," she said. "I guess it was good because when it happens in the working world, I can't cry about it. I just need to pick up the missing pieces."

Extracurricular activities are more often an extension of learning at Wharton than a distraction, as the focus on business even spills into life outside the classroom. "I haven't done any sports here at Penn because it takes away from your capacity to do other extracurriculars," said Shimika. Instead, the former sports fanatic spent her free time holding posts such as vice president of budget and finance for the Black Wharton Undergraduate Association, national conference co-chair of the University Honor Council, and vice president of committees for the Alpha Kappa Psi Professional Business Fraternity. She knew the titles would look impressive on her résumé and, perhaps eventually, serve as an advantage over her peers when it came time to find an internship or a job.

Most other Wharton students know that as well, and many of

them join one of the forty business-related organizations that have sprung up on campus, in order to look that much more impressive to recruiters than their peers. At Wharton, clubs and organizations with names such as the Wharton Hedgers and Traders, the Wharton India Economic Forum, the Wharton Analyst Group (called WAG), and the Wharton Warren Buffett Club spring up annually.

Beth Hagovsky, who helps Wharton students set up these clubs, said many more of them perish after a couple of years. "Some of the students really think that by starting this, it could be the next great Wharton club," she said. "Some of these kids are just so overextended, though." Free time is a much-needed luxury for many Wharton students, and Beth tries valiantly to get Wharton students to let go of their self-induced competitiveness and hang out in a more relaxed atmosphere. One such effort was a cookie-decorating station that was set up in Huntsman in order to create a better sense of community among Wharton students. "At least for five minutes they are looking at each other as goofy cookie decorators instead of thinking 'Oh, you busted the curve for me,'" she said.

As many Wharton students realize after a few years at the school, Wharton's practical education will take them far in their future careers. But some wonder if the long hours they spent on group projects and studying to beat the curve has somehow lessened what should be the time of their lives. Ultimately, they remind themselves of the goal at hand and continue on.

"Sometimes I find myself defending Wharton," said one senior who admitted that he, too, could have spent a lot more time forging friendships instead of trying to beat the curve. "The preprofessionals are like most Wharton students. They are here to find a job and that colors all of their experiences."

CHAPTER TWO

GOLDMAN OR BUST

As a high school senior, Regi Vengalil dreamed of becoming a "Master of the Universe." Living in the suburbs of Seattle, the first-generation Indian American envisioned himself four years down the road a newly minted college graduate with a prestigious business degree in one hand and an even more prestigious job offer in the other. Postgraduation he planned to work on Wall Street and become part of a world that holds the golden promise of six-figure year-end bonuses and Park Avenue penthouses. To succeed in this high-stakes environment of billion-dollar deals, seventeen-year-old Regi knew that he had to go to the best business school in the world.

It was no great surprise that in the spring of 2000, Regi chose to attend Wharton over the other business-oriented programs he was accepted into at the University of Chicago and New York University (which had offered him a generous scholarship). To him, the choice came down to prestige. It wasn't just that Wharton was the only undergrad business program in the Ivy League; it also reigned supreme over all of the others. Regi thought that if he didn't accept Wharton's invitation to attend the school, he would always wonder whether he could have been successful competing against "the *best* students in the *best* business school in the world."

Even more important, though, was what a school like Wharton could offer him postgraduation. Wharton lures recruiters from the most elite investment banks and consulting firms looking to bestow signing bonuses and the potential of lifetime financial security to young aspiring moneymakers like Regi. The recruiting process would provide Regi with access to the best jobs and the right connections to help his career get started. If a person hopes to ascend someday to the godlike status of a managing director at a major investment bank, or perhaps the CEO of a Fortune 500 company, getting a degree from Wharton is the place to start.

Many of Wharton's classes, whether purposely or not, focus on preparing students for what is considered the career of choice: investment banking. Any incoming student who once thought that banks were the places they go to open savings accounts or use an ATM machine would soon embrace a whole new definition of the term "banking." Such commercial banks are quickly forgotten next to the lure of Wall Street's investment banks, the engine of the world's financial system (although today, as Glass-Steagall antitrust banking laws become a thing of the past, once purely commercial banks like Citigroup—formerly Citibank—are increasingly providing investment banking services to their clients). Even during their first days of college, students at Wharton are inundated with information about signing bonuses, starting salaries and the hierarchies of investment banks. Their conversations with one another, whether it's between classes or at a party, are punctuated by discussions of which internships at which investment banks hold the most weight on a résumé with recruiters. With all of this chatter, the mania about the field quickly becomes infectious.

"The idea of investment banking, not necessarily what investment banking is, but rather the idea of it, was sexy," recalled Regi in an e-mail. "It created delusions of grandeur—of being a multimillionaire in your twenties—in even the most mild-mannered students,"

Now as a senior, he admits that he was once as consumed as his peers by the notion of becoming a banker.

On no other group at Wharton does this mentality take a tighter hold than the two-thirds of the class who declare concentrations in finance. Finance classes are considered the hardest and most prestigious of the courses offered at Wharton, and are viewed by students as a prerequisite to landing a high-paying job at a top investment bank. Other concentrations are considered less influential on one's résumé and easier to endure, and therefore place those students lower in the Whartonites' imaginary caste system. Come junior year, this becomes more apparent as Wharton students start declaring their concentrations and taking upper-level courses in their chosen fields.

"Wharton classes are more real-world, realistic-type stuff, especially in finance. There's a concept of 'this actually goes on,'" explained Shreevar Kheruka. "Management classes are more fluffy, and the College classes are more laid-back."

Landing a high-profile internship by junior year is also considered a necessity for someone who wants to enter the banking or consulting world postgraduation. Recalls a graduate of Wharton's Class of 1996: "Someone told me once: 'During your freshman year summer you're scooping ice cream. During your sophomore year summer you're making someone else's coffee. During your junior year summer you'd *better* be doing something *real*.'"

Wharton students learn that summer breaks, with the exception of the one after freshman year, aren't for beach time or barbacking jobs at the local pub. It should be strictly business. For a student hell-bent on Wall Street deal-making, the quest is to land a position as a summer analyst at an investment bank. Many students end up at one of the large global banks such as Morgan Stanley, Goldman Sachs, Merrill Lynch or Citigroup. These banks—called "bulge brackets" because they are large investment houses that are often lead underwriters for large stock deals and therefore wield a lot of money and power on Wall Street—have the budgets to hire, train and pay scores of interns. Powerhouse

Morgan Stanley, for example, has more than 50,000 employees based in twenty-eight countries.

While an internship by no means guarantees a job offer, for many students it's viewed as the best way to bolster their resumes and get in front of the decision makers. To forgo a high-profile internship after junior year could take them out of the running for interviews and potential job offers during the fall recruiting rush in their senior year. Most Whartonites start recruiting for summer internships early in the spring semester of junior year. The marathon of interviews that Wharton students embark on during this time serves as a nerve-racking trial run that often causes them to commit the common faux pas that novice interviewees often make (such as accidentally sending a cover letter to a Credit Suisse recruiter that says they'd "love to work at Lehman Brothers"). But the process also helps steel their nerves and prepare them for the inquisitions they will endure in their full-time job interviews in their senior year.

After enduring the "Triple Threat" classes of sophomore year, many Whartonites take a breather from pulling all-nighters in Huntsman Hall and the stiff competition of projects and exams and travel to far-flung locales. Each fall, close to twenty-five percent of Wharton's juniors decide to take their studies abroad, embarking on one of fourteen approved programs in places such as Buenos Aires, Hong Kong, Paris and Sydney. As a junior, Regi attended the Universidad Pontificia de Comillas (ICADE) in Madrid. To knock out some of his liberal arts requirements, Regi took an art history class called "The History of the Prado," along with a Spanish class. Regi's Spanish was so-so when he arrived in Madrid and improved during his stay there, although he admits that his ego kept him from being the best foreign-language pupil.

"My friends did better (speaking Spanish) than I did," he said. "Other students would start speaking and they didn't care if they were wrong. They did so much better than me."

Regi also took a business class at ICADE, but it proved to be a joke compared to Wharton's classes. "In terms of business prep, the curriculum at ICADE was worthless," complained Regi. "The way the professor described the course, she said it was an introduction to finance, accounting and marketing. It was the minimal amount of information—like what we cover in the first two weeks of finance here."

In January, juniors—especially those who went abroad first semester—barely have time to unpack their belongings and new holiday booty after winter break before they are met with a calendar of on-campus recruiter presentations and "résumé drop" dates for the investment banks and the handful of other companies searching for interns during the spring semester. To make sure they are ready for the rush, Wharton's Career Services staff had begun prodding them months ahead of time to get their résumés completed and polished by the time they returned for classes in January. After two and half years of intense academic training, there is little time to reflect on career options before the internship recruitment frenzy begins. It is an onslaught that many Wharton students embark on out of sheer momentum.

Regi returned from his winter break fully prepared to participate in the rush. Getting an internship at an investment bank was the next step in the plan that he had laid out as his most promising path to Wall Street. But in April 2003, his plans changed dramatically. Regi, who was an avid runner, played soccer and had never smoked a cigarette, was hit with the second spontaneous lung collapse that he had endured in less than a year and a half.

"I was a two-sport athlete in high school," he said. "And now all of a sudden I'm undergoing blood tests and have three chest tubes."

When his left lung collapsed during winter break his sophomore year, Regi endured some complications that kept him from returning to school until a week after the second semester started. Just a few days into classes Regi caught pneumonia and was laid up for weeks. "It was the scariest moment of my life," Regi recalled. "It was one of those indescribable moments. I truly understand the fickle nature of life."

The doctors told Regi that, should another lung collapse occur, he would require surgery. Regi took it easy for the rest of the semester and tried not to work too hard over the summer so that he would be well rested and healthy for his trip to Spain in the first semester of his junior year.

"When I got back [from Spain] I was like, 'All right, time to get into investment banking," recounted Regi. But just as internship recruiting had gotten well underway, Regi's right lung collapsed. Yet again, Regi was in the hospital and his fate was uncertain. Making matters worse was the fact that it was the weekend of Spring Fling, the annual April festival on the weekend preceding the end of spring-semester classes and the rowdiest party weekend at Penn. It was three days' worth of carnivals, rock concerts, frat parties, and general debauchery all done in the name of blowing off steam before finals. Regi thought most of his friends would scarcely have time to hang out with him at the hospital with so much going on. Still, many of them came to visit, even if it meant missing a couple of hours of drunken revelry. Students from Regi's cross-cultural awareness class (his favorite) came to visit as well. Lying in the hospital at Penn and realizing the magnitude of what had happened to him and the lack of control he had over it, Regi started rethinking his long-held career plans. Suddenly, 80- to 120-hour workweeks at an investment bank didn't sound so sexy anymore.

"I got a much different mind-set," declared Regi. "It helps you figure out what's important in life. And that was being okay and spending time with the people I care about."

Regi began asking his Wharton peers which investment banks they were applying to for internships. Inevitably, they would tell him that they had applied to as many as possible. For some that meant every single bank that had a posting on the Career Services

Web site. When Regi asked why they had blanketed the banks with their résumés, their replies almost always fell along the lines of "because it sounds interesting." That wasn't a good enough reason for Regi, who began asking some questions of himself.

"It seemed like a fair majority of people were doing it because everyone else was doing it," he explained. "That's what we do here, and all of a sudden I just didn't see it happening for me."

Regi had his surgery on a Thursday and was back in class on Tuesday. He knew that if he missed more than a week of classes he would be too far behind to catch up before finals. "My professor told me, 'I had a molar removed and I took more time off than you,'" he said with a proud smile. After taking some time to catch up on coursework and reflect on the situation, Regi thought that perhaps he wanted to do something more fulfilling with his summer—and quite possibly his life—than banking.

Close to half of the students seeking internships for the summer of 2003 found them through On-Campus Recruiting Services. Two-thirds of Regi's class would end up working in the financial services industry that summer, a majority of them as analysts at investment banks. Very few consulting firms hunt for interns during the internship-recruiting period, and even fewer had come to the school in recent years as the recession decimated their ranks and hiring budgets. In fact, only about eight percent of Wharton's juniors held internships at consultancies such as Bain & Co. or Mercer. Similarly, there weren't very many résumé-building opportunities at corporations. With a limited number of internship options available outside of investment banking, students were forced to compete for fewer spots, leaving the majority of Wharton's third-year pupils eagerly eyeing the investment banks that were looking to stock their offices and bullpens with potential prodigies.

Throughout the internship-recruitment season, Wharton's aspiring Wall Street wunderkinds are even further bombarded with rhetoric about the ultimate brass ring that every finance major at Wharton should be striving for: to become an investment banker. If they can stick with it and impress the right people, then investment banking, they are told, can be the doorway to executive posts or at least an early retirement. During this time, students begin mentally calculating signing bonuses and ranking the investment houses they hope to work for in order of prestige and pay. And they quickly discover that the only thing more prestigious than becoming an investment banker is becoming an investment banker at the most elite of deal-making houses—Goldman Sachs.

The investment banks are chatted about during student orientation and expounded upon in the dining halls and common rooms of Penn's dormitories throughout a student's four years at Wharton. Students who had never envisioned themselves as investment bankers before soon weigh the idea in their heads and become convinced that being an investment banker, especially at Goldman, is proof that they were a bona fide success at the nation's only Ivy League undergraduate business program. From that point on, almost everything in their consciousness revolves around making themselves look as attractive as possible to recruiters from top investment houses come recruiting season.

Gaining entrée into the high-stakes world of billion-dollar deals at Goldman soon becomes an opportunity coveted by the most ambitious of young Whartonites. To these students, Goldman equals prestige. It's a firm known for hiring only the best, and it uses this talent to reap the utmost rewards of capitalism in almost every deal it touches. Goldman advises on some of the world's largest mergers and acquisitions, underwrites the most popular IPOs and stock offerings, and boasts some of the best analysts and traders in the business. But Goldman's magnetism is more than just its deals. Since its founding in 1869, Goldman has cultivated a reputation for doing everything with a touch of class.

Even analysts have assistants to answer their calls and even those assistants receive year-end bonuses.

Some students spend hours getting versed in Goldmanspeak, learning the company's 135-year history and memorizing a laundry list of the firm's major deals. They even mold themselves to fit in with Goldman's renowned culture by memorizing the fourteen Goldman "Business Principles," a company treatise on the way Goldman employees are expected to think and act. This is perhaps one of the best exercises for these students to embark on because, as it is widely rumored, to not fit in at Goldman can make it miserable to work there.

Those select students who land internships at Goldman are both revered and reviled by their classmates. During the summer internship season of 2003, at least thirteen students from the class of 2004 would enter the halls of Goldman's New York offices. For some Whartonites, the Goldman culture turns out to be a natural fit. Just as there is a certain hubris among Wharton students, there is an equal, though perhaps more veiled, elitism at Goldman Sachs. It's the sly confidence of a company with such a strong reputation and status as one of the top performers on Wall Street that it feels little need to advertise or display its logo and keeps most of its inner dealings close to the vest.

Because of its excellence and renown, Goldman has been a leader in advising mergers and acquisitions even in the worst of times—including the most recent recession. In 2002, when the economic downturn made for few news-breaking deals, Goldman advised drug giant Pharmacia in its $60 billion acquisition by Pfizer that July. It was the biggest deal of the year, accounting for fifteen percent of all M&A activity on Wall Street and further bolstering Goldman's nine-year reign as the top-ranked M&A advisor. Goldman also consistently ranks as one of the leading underwriters of IPOs and secondary offerings. In December 2001, while the markets were still reeling from the September 11 terrorist attacks, Goldman led a $3 billion IPO for insurer Prudential Financial. The firm had also led the sixth-largest domestic IPO of all time in the spring of 1999–its own, making it the last of the bulge-bracket banks to go public.

At a place where billion-dollar deals are the norm, one would think that Goldman would give rise to a slew of superstar bankers, as the investment banking profession is prone to do. Yet Goldman steadfastly maintains its "Goldman first" philosophy, making it clear to top-notch employees that egos don't have a place at its 85 Broad Street offices. But those ego-suppressed gentlemen (and women) bankers are rewarded handsomely, with senior members of the firm pulling in $5 million to $10 million in bonuses each year.

All of the dollar signs flying around Goldman create a gleam in a Whartonite's eye, even though it would take them decades at the firm to achieve such salary heights. Actually, students landing a coveted spot in Goldman's Financial Analyst program can initially expect to make about the same amount that they would at any other major investment house on Wall Street as a first-year analyst, which in the last couple of years has been about $55,000 a year plus a $5,000 to $10,000 signing bonus (referred to as a "relocation bonus" at some banks), and anywhere from a $5,000 to $30,000 year-end bonus. During the high tide of the economic boom of the late 1990s, jobs were plentiful and Wharton grads were landing signing and year-end bonuses almost one and a half times these amounts. The decreased starting salaries and shrinking bonuses that came with the economic downturn in 2000 haven't deterred students from the career choice though. The opportunity to make big money is still there, and so is the Goldman Sachs reputation that fuels the craze hitting Wharton's campus each recruiting season.

Shimika Wilder had an impressive GPA and a big head start on her Wharton peers heading into the junior-year internship-recruiting season. At a career fair she attended her sophomore year, Shimika discovered that both Goldman and Citigroup awarded a ten-week internship to minority students that paid $5,000 for the summer. To get the scholarship, she needed to impress them with her academic record, interviewing skills and an essay. A self-proclaimed type-A personality, Shimika knew her writing skills weren't her strong point and took her essay to Penn's writing mentors at the Kelly Writing House. She made sure she didn't leave until the essay had become a brilliant account of the three years that she spent working for the local Pizza Boli's while she was in high school.

"I started out as a phone girl and left as a manager. It's a skill set that I learned that I thought would be good for investment banking," explained Shimika.

The essay, she said, got her to the first round of interviews; her academic record and composure took care of the rest. Shimika received offers from both firms and without a moment's hesitation, she chose Goldman. "It's the most coveted. It's the best of the best in investment banking," she said proudly. "It embodies the excellence and the drive to be the best."

Shimika was also accepted into Sponsors for Educational Opportunity (SEO), a New York–based nonprofit that provides minority students with internship opportunities at ten of the most widely respected investment banks. SEO only accepts 200 students into its investment banking intern program, out of a pool of roughly 2,000 applicants. Even though Shimika had already locked up her internship at Goldman and didn't need SEO's services to land a summer job, she knew that the connections she could make through the group could help her out later down the road.

During her internship sophomore year, Shimika was placed in Goldman's media and entertainment group, where she worked sixteen- to eighteen-hour days. She had yet to take many of the upper-level finance classes that Wharton offered, so she was delegated the more qualitative work, preparing company profiles, compiling news reports, gathering financial information that would later go into client presentations and occasionally building a simple financial model, more or less for practice.

As part of her membership in SEO, Shimika was required to go to a series of speeches and dinners hosted by various investment banks throughout the summer. Most of these events quickly devolve into schmooze fests where recruiters and young interns embark on mutual courtship dances with one another. To Shimika, it meant precious face time with the recruiters at other banks where she might want to work someday. The banks that SEO members work for are supposed to allow these interns to attend the events sponsored by the other member banks graciously. But the rivalry to hang on to promising young talent sometimes gets in the way.

"There would be backlash at work when I told them that I was going to another bank's seminar," recalled Shimika. "They'd say 'I thought you loved us. Why are you going to a Morgan Stanley event? Aren't we more important than SEO?' "

For the first three weeks of her internship, Shimika had an SEO event scheduled almost every night. She had to leave the office by 5:00 P.M., dragging out her already taxing day even longer, and sparking resentment among some of her fellow interns who didn't realize that, after all of the SEO-sponsored events for which she was permitted to leave early, Shimika was returning to the office to catch up on the three to four hours of work that she had missed. The schedule soon became grueling.

"You're in New York City, the best city in the world, and then you realize that this is an industry where you don't come home at night," she explained.

For all of the glory of landing the holy grail of investment banking jobs, there is a form of masochism that soon reveals itself in these students' pursuit of power and riches. The analyst training programs that they embark on at the investment banking houses are sometimes satirically referred to as "white-collar slavery," requiring young analysts and associates to work 80- to 120-hour weeks. With only 168 hours in a week, that leaves an average of ten hours a day to feed and clean themselves, catch a few hours of sleep, and commute back and forth to the office. When they begin their stints, analysts receive an apparent perk: a company-paid cell phone, and sometimes even a pager or BlackBerry. But they soon find out that these "perks" are to insure that they are equipped to be at the beck and call of their superiors no matter what the hour, weekend day, holiday or family occasion.

The investment-banker lifestyle is one that a rare few early twentysomethings would embrace, with weekends full of model-building projects rather than model-gazing parties. It's a profession that requires a similar single-minded devotion to dedicating one's life to the priesthood–except that this is about mammon, not spirituality. Lasting two to three years, most analyst training programs are punishing and intense months of reviewing deal reports, spreadsheet scrutinizing, photocopying and last-minute scrambling, during which young analysts are constantly reminded that they are at the bottom of the ladder in the bank's hierarchy. On each project, there is a "deal team," usually comprised of the analyst, an associate, a vice president, and a managing director (called MDs in the industry), all of whom can make demands of the analyst.

With all of these people to answer to, analysts find themselves faced with a constant barrage of requests and deadlines. They can spend hours tweaking an Excel spreadsheet financial model or getting a chart to look just right in order to suit the exacting (or just capricious) demands of a VP or an MD. At times, they also serve as glorified assistants who can be sent on multiple trips per day to the copy center or for the occasional pickup of coffee or lunch for their colleagues.

Analysts are also the employees responsible for much of an investment bank's behind-the-scenes research, creating spreadsheets and using PowerPoint to put together "pitch books," which are used to sell a client on the financial benefits of certain transactions (such as an acquisition or a divestiture) or a new way of financing (such as a stock offering or a debt issue). Even though some industry sources say pitch books rarely lead to new business, inordinate amounts of an analyst's time are spent determining a company's valuation and what its performance is compared to its peers in the industry in order to create the reports (which are then printed on some of the finest quality paper stock at expensive printing boutiques).

"It's funny. You're mistreated when you get there, and then five years down the road you're the one mistreating people," said one Wharton grad, who quickly tired of the investment banking lifestyle postgraduation. Many aspiring investment bankers burn out before they attain the status of associate, VP or even MD that they dreamed of at Wharton. The pyramid of workers at a bank leaves room for few at the top levels, and many burned-out analysts end up leaving the investment-banking world after a couple of years, usually to pursue an MBA or another career altogether.

For some Wharton students, to be able to prove that they can stick it out and climb through the ranks at a bank is the epitome of success. Should they grab that brass ring and persevere past those who weren't "good enough" or those who folded under the pressure, then, they believe, they have attained the ultimate prize. Alumni looking back on their experiences at Wharton wonder whether it was the school or the highly overachieving student body that led to these crazed packs of juniors and seniors hungrily searching for their place in the investment-banking world.

"I don't think it's the school's fault. It's just sort of the culture of the place," ventured Class of 2000 Wharton alum Christopher Albergo. "A lot of Wharton students think that when you're done with school, if you didn't get an investment-banking job, or at least a consulting job, it was because you couldn't.... You'll get a job. But is it the *right* job?"

It was the heart of spring semester junior year, and Shreevar Kheruka was having a medical crisis. After returning from a trip home to India over winter break, Shreevar came down with a terrible bout of malaria that left him hospitalized for five days and laid up for close to four weeks. Soon thereafter, Shreevar tore the anterior cruciate ligament (ACL) in his knee while skiing in Park City, Utah, over spring break. By the time he recovered, he had missed ninety percent of the summer internship résumé drops through On-Campus Recruiting Services (OCRS)–a division of the Career Services department devoted to attracting recruiters to Penn's campus and helping students land internships and jobs.

In an act of desperation, Shreevar gathered together the names and contact information of the recruiters from all the investment banks and financial services firms he could find on the Career Services Web site. He wrote personal e-mails pleading his case to recruiters at close to sixty firms. Only five firms got back to him, two of which expressed their condolences that he had been sick, but explained that they were unfortunately already fully staffed for the summer. Capital One, Goldman Sachs and one smaller bank took enough pity on Shreevar to offer him a shot at an interview. Even in the very final stretches of recruiting season, Shreevar had managed to impress the folks from Goldman so much that they offered him a post on their fixed income, currencies and commodities trading desk for the summer. Trading wasn't exactly the most prestigious investment-banking position, but he didn't hesitate to take them up on their offer. Shreevar knew that recruiters act fast, especially at Wharton. By April of their junior year, more than three-quarters of Wharton's Class of 2004 that sought internships had attained one. Even with everything that he'd been through, Shreevar scored an internship at a top-tier bank, and he considered himself one of the luckiest of the bunch.

PART II

THE YOUNG BULLS

CHAPTER THREE

THE TEN-WEEK INTERVIEW

Sixty-five flights above the masses moving conveyor-belt style on the mid-summer sidewalks outside of Rockefeller Center in midtown Manhattan, patrons of the Rainbow Room were dining in air-conditioned majesty as the restaurant's gold-and-silver draped windows sparkled with miniature prisms reflecting off a massive crystal chandelier. The Rainbow Room's guests sipped $14 cocktails and ate $150 prix-fixe meals while a twelve-piece big-band orchestra urged them to try the dance floor once they were done. The beats were strong, swift, and complicated, just as Benny Goodman would have liked.

One floor beneath the Rainbow Room's dinner tables filled with revelers drinking fine wines are the offices of Lazard Frères, the highly regarded "boutique" investment bank. Boutique banks are referred to as such because they specialize in offering specific advisory services, and Lazard was renowned for its legendary advice on mergers and acquisitions. On the Friday night of July Fourth weekend in 2003, Jessica Kennedy, a determined intern for the bank, feverishly worked in a cubicle located just below the Rainbow Room's den of godlike trappings. It was closing in on midnight and Jessica, a twenty-year-old Wharton student who had recently finished her junior year, was one of the last people remaining in the office. Almost everyone, even the other summer analysts, had managed to escape in order to enjoy part of the holiday weekend. She had been working for hours on end when she realized that she had better refuel if she was going to make it through the night. Her particular palate had a strong craving for Chilean sea bass and steamed vegetables from Mangia, a restaurant down the street (on Lazard's tab, of course). But the place was closed for the holiday, foiling Jessica's plan and forcing her to use the "seamless Web," an online food-ordering service, to order a turkey burger. It soon arrived sans bun and charred around the edges, punctuating an already long, lonely night. Her one social outlet was the occasional e-mail she received from friends who, like her, were also stuck working at their respective banks that weekend.

Jessica ate at her desk and quickly went back to work on a pitch she was asked to put together for a prospective client. She planned to work as late as necessary to insure that every angle was covered and that everything was in order before she turned it in. Not long after midnight, the quiet of the office finally compelled Jessica to leave. She wasn't completely done with her work, but she was ready to go home. It was a rare occurrence for Jessica, who had become known around the office for being a workhorse who seldom knew when to quit. Jessica would manage to get some sleep that night before returning to her cubicle, ready to put in a thirteen-hour day on a Saturday that most people were spending with friends or family.

A petite blonde from Austin, Jessica's Texas cheerleader good looks often led her colleagues and her peers to underestimate her competitive drive and her passion for everything that she put her mind to, especially investment banking. She had a close-to-perfect 3.9 GPA in the Joseph Wharton Scholars honors program and had been interning at Lazard as a summer analyst for five weeks now. Before she even started her internship, Jessica realized her beauty, long flaxen hair, and her role as captain of her high school's national championship cheerleading squad could prove to be a detriment in a profession in which only fifteen to twenty percent of bankers are women—and a far smaller percentage hold positions at the top. Jessica soon grew to disdain people who stereotyped her. She once went to lunch with a male associate at a bank who promptly ordered her a Diet Coke when they sat down to eat.

"I don't drink Diet Coke," said Jessica, with a tone of indignation as she recalled the situation. "He was very focused on my cheerleader background and my sorority." The incident only made Jessica hit the ground running and work harder when she embarked on her internship weeks later. "I didn't want anyone else to assume that stuff about me," Jessica declared. "I would rather be viewed as overly ambitious than as a Diet Coke–drinking sorority girl."

Jessica was born with a drive and discipline that few other people her age possess. Her parents were nineteen years old when she was born; her father passed away when she was seven. Jessica greatly respects her mother, who raised Jessica and her younger sister by herself before remarrying when the girls were in their late teens. Her mother always accommodated Jessica's strong sense of independence at an early age. "She always treated me like a little adult," Jessica explained. "She was always really supportive and never tried to direct my decisions. I never even had a bedtime because I didn't need one. I'd be up in my room and yell down, 'Mom, I'm tired! Come tuck me in!' "

Even in her teenage years, Jessica seemed to avoid the exploratory stages that her girlfriends had gone through. Jessica had no interest in partying or getting drunk. To her that was a waste of time. Instead, she was determined not only to be the first person in her family to go to college, but the first person in her family to go to an *Ivy League* school.

Jessica was one of only three Wharton students working at Lazard for the ten-week internship during the summer of 2003.

She had gone through dozens of interviews for summer internships during the second semester of her junior year. It was a grueling process that pitted her against some of her closest friends and classmates, who were all vying for the handful of jobs the banks were offering. "I only dropped my résumé for investment-banking internships because that fits my personality. The hours fit my personality," Jessica explained. "I was interviewing five times a day for weeks."

Jessica's hell-bent desire to get her foot in the door with a bank seeped from her pores. With her track record at school and her obvious willingness to work marathon hours, she was an especially hot commodity among recruiters. The minute she opened her mouth, they could tell that she lived and breathed investment banking, and many banks soon asked her to join them for the summer. But Jessica had already fallen in love with Lazard, a firm that was founded by three brothers in 1848 in New Orleans and, a year after that, relocated to San Francisco in time to make vast riches off of the Gold Rush. The good fortune allowed Lazard to start banking operations and later open offices in Paris, London and New York, where it established itself as one of the most prestigious advisory boutiques. Even though Jessica's other offers were enticing—especially an offer from Goldman Sachs—she was too far gone to consider any other place. "I thought maybe these are the kinds of people I want to be with. I got the sense that Lazard was a banker's bank with an elite number of individuals, and I wanted to be part of that culture," she said.

One month into her internship, Jessica made her mark. At a cocktail party being held for Lazard's new intern class, Jessica bumped into Gary Parr, the recently hired deputy chairman of Lazard. Parr was a big hitter who had brought in multibillion-dollar deals for Morgan Stanley's financial institutions group before being recruited by Lazard's Bruce Wasserstein, who had gone on a costly hiring spree of dozens of high-profile bankers to beef up Lazard's mergers and acquisitions business. (Wasserstein was formerly the chairman and CEO of Wasserstein Perella, a prominent investment bank that he founded in the late 1980s. He joined Lazard after his firm was acquired for $1.37 billion by Dresdner Kleinwort in 2000). Jessica confidently struck up a conversation with Parr, and the next day she e-mailed him to tell him that it was a pleasure to meet him. "I was sticking my neck out," admitted Jessica. Indeed, most summer analysts wouldn't have been so bold as to reach out to someone so high in Lazard's ranks.

Parr soon requested that they meet. A few days later Jessica was sitting in Parr's office and listening to him talk about the industry. It was then that she realized that she had found her role model. Parr embodied the type of banker that Jessica dreamed of becoming. By the end of the conversation, he had lent her a book called *Financier: The Biography of André Meyer*, Cary Reich's four-hundred-page tome on one of the most influential investment bankers of the twentieth century, the man credited for sparking and executing more mergers and acquisitions than anyone else in the industry's history. The book, Parr told her, reminded him of why he wanted to be an investment banker.

Jessica only had the weekend to read the thick book. To her dismay, she ended up spending the entire weekend in the office and couldn't get through it. She returned the book knowing that eventually she would buy herself a copy. If Gary Parr recommended *Financier*, then Jessica undoubtedly felt she should read it.

The only time Jessica left 30 Rockefeller Center during her internship that summer was either to pay a quick visit to the gym, grab a cup of coffee or get into a car that would take her to her sublet apartment downtown during the wee hours of the night. On several occasions she left the fluorescent lights of Lazard's offices only to be greeted by the soft illumination of a sunrise brightening up the inky blue night skies of Manhattan. It was at these moments that Jessica would explore the city through the windows of a Cadillac or Lincoln Town Car as she returned to her apartment where she slept an average four or five hours a night. During especially trying days, she would get only two or three hours of sleep, take a shower, put on a fresh suit and head back to Lazard for another day of calculating corporate valuations, maintaining logs of the communications between senior bankers and clients, making charts and graphs for a pitch book, or anything else an associate, vice president or director at the bank needed her to do.

There were times when the work pushed Jessica's physical limits to the brink, especially when the all-nighters started becoming common occurrences. After one such sleepless night, which was preceded by a string of nights with only one or two hours of sleep, Jessica hit a wall. By 3:00 in the afternoon on a Thursday, she was shaking and on the verge of tears at her desk. Completely depleted, she couldn't for the life of her remember the easiest things. Even logging onto her computer seemed complicated. "Emotionally I was okay. But there was a huge difference between my attitude and how I was physically," admitted Jessica, who recalls how helpless and embarrassed she felt as her body broke down on her.

She allowed herself a minor meltdown in the bathroom and then returned to her desk. A voice-mail message from the vice president overseeing a project she was working on gave her enough fortitude to pull through. Merely a "thank you" to her and two of her colleagues on a job well done and an update on where they stood on the deal, the message quickly reinvigorated Jessica, who sought out the praise of her superiors like rare gems. That week, Jessica would log close to 140 hours at the office.

Scattered throughout Manhattan that summer, dozens of other Wharton students with internships at investment banks were similarly sacrificing sleep and friendships in the hope of getting noticed by a managing director or vice president and being fondly remembered at the end of the summer when interns are considered for full-time job offers. (To have to reinterview at the end of the summer for a full-time job usually means a young intern either wasn't good enough or didn't make enough of an impression with the people at the bank who could go to bat for them). Because summer analysts must compete with their fellow interns for offers, standing out at an investment bank means working on as many projects as possible and never leaving the office before a higher-up. It also means being available seven days a week. Many students don't take more than a couple of days off during the ten-week stint (Jessica took a half day off only once). Weekends almost always entailed late hours at the office or at least being on call should an associate need them to whip up a PowerPoint presentation or conduct some research for a client who, while reading his Sunday newspaper, had the sudden urge to see how hard it would be to initiate a hostile takeover of a smaller competitor.

During her internship at Lazard, Jessica was a generalist who worked across Lazard's various specialty groups. She helped wherever the next fire needed to be put out. The lack of specialization allowed her to work on a variety of deals, but it also meant that she was fair game for anyone looking for an eager summer analyst to do his or her grunt work. In overzealous Whartonite fashion, Jessica spent the summer unflinchingly trying to prove that she was more than capable of handling the tasks the investment bank doled out to her. The work brought out what she calls her "inner perfectionist." Putting tabs on documents and highlighting important information in financial reports came to her as readily as breathing. She became more demanding of herself and her work as she put together pitch books and presentations and spent hours upon hours navigating Excel spreadsheets. "The only time I wasn't feeling well or unhappy was when I didn't have enough work," she professed. "Every day I wanted it to be hard so I could show them I was doing it."

In fact, Jessica's work ethic caused her to alienate herself from the thirteen other members of her summer analyst class. She got along well with the full-time occupants of her analyst "pod," but with her peers who worked in other divisions, it was another story. Some saw her as a brownnoser, always at the ready in front of the people who mattered. Others were envious of her drive, yet put off by her overzealous dedication to the work. Jessica knew that if she hadn't logged so many hours or taken on so many projects that, perhaps, she would have forged stronger friendships, but she felt she was at Lazard to do the work and impress the powers that be. Making friends was lower on Jessica's list of priorities.

"It resulted in a gulf between me and my analyst class," admitted Jessica. "They would ask questions about me of the other people in the class who attended Wharton. They'd ask, 'What is Jessica like at Wharton?' They had no idea because I was just putting my head down and working."

A friend of hers who was a VP at a bulge-bracket bank made her feel better about the whole thing. "He told me: 'Any banker that is any good goes through this.' It helped a lot."

The summer analyst programs often begin in June soon after a slew of Wharton students—mainly juniors—relocate to New York, where they unpack recently purchased suits and pinstriped shirts in sublet apartments and vacated NYU dorm rooms. They arrive with a quiet confidence that they will know by the end of their ten-week run whether or not they will be a star investment banker— or even an investment banker at all. In their first days on the job they meet the analyst class that they will go through the training and the trenches with in the upcoming weeks. The lot typically includes a couple of familiar Wharton faces, as well as a plethora of juniors from other blue-blood Ivy Leaguers such as Princeton and Harvard, or similarly high-ranked schools such as M.I.T.,

Duke or Stanford. It's in these first days of training with students from other schools that Wharton students realize just how helpful their vigorous business education will be at the banks.

At Goldman Sachs' 85 Broad Street offices, Shimika Wilder was basking in the fruits of her labors at Wharton. Her first week as a returning intern was proving to be a breeze now that she had taken some upper-level finance classes. Earlier in the week, her analyst class–close to forty interns in all–had been gathered in a room going over the ins and outs of financial modeling, pitch books and other tasks that they would be expected to do over the summer. As Shimika looked around the room, she had noticed that the Wharton students were eerily quiet. In fact, they seemed downright bored. They had been through these equations and spreadsheet lessons dozens of times in their classes and they were eager to apply their skills on some real deals. But first they had to wait for the rest of their analyst class to catch up.

"Wharton sets a higher standard," proclaimed Shimika. "The people from Harvard have a great economics program, but they don't have the coursework for modeling and accounting and things like we do. Those students had a tougher time during the training. We were just further along on the learning curve. Wharton students didn't have to ask as many questions."

Other things, though, didn't come as easily to Shimika that summer. She thought that by her junior-year summer internship at Goldman, the tough hours and rigorous work schedule would be old hat. But nothing quite prepares a person for the type of exhaustion that is earned from days on end without a good night's sleep, as Shimika quickly remembered from her first summer with Goldman.

"It's not a work-life balance," she said. "I cried a lot during my internship. In my first week, I worked 120 hours. I came home, got in the shower and just cried. I wondered 'Should I quit?' I was sacrificing my life. You have no friends, family, vacation. I thought that I wouldn't even have time to spend the money I was making. It's a huge tradeoff."

In her second summer with Goldman, Shimika was placed with some of the same people she had worked with the summer before in the expanded technology, media and telecommunications group, where she concentrated on IT (information technology) services firms, dot-com companies, and sports organizations, all industries that Shimika thought were "sexy." With a few more finance classes under her belt this time, Shimika was handed more difficult tasks. During an average day at Goldman that summer, Shimika easily spent six hours editing pitch books, several hours on Excel working out financial models and conducting research, and a couple of hours in meetings or on conference calls. She reviewed financial stats, created capital structures and conducted analysis, all duties performed by the full-time analysts, a post she now aspired to after she graduated from Wharton.

It was during this summer that Shimika had a chance to really get her hands dirty and create her first pitch book on her own. The work she did that summer was empowering, but the inefficiencies of the banking hierarchy and the amount of work and time it required sometimes offset that reward. She grew frustrated with bankers who would roll into work at 10:00 in the morning only to leave for a meeting followed by a two-hour lunch. If she submitted work to them the night before, they wouldn't get back to her until 6:00 the following evening. And the added work they'd request would then keep her in the office until 2:00 in the morning. Her frustration was compounded by the fact that a summer analyst could be assigned to work on several deadlines for various projects at the same time. Many summer analysts quickly experience this frustrating cycle of hurry up and wait, and the hours and stress levels can soon become overtaxing.

Most deals have one member from each level of the bank's hierarchies on the team: managing director, vice president, associate and analyst. The director or managing director (called the "MD") is at the top of the banking pyramid. They are the ones who seek out and land the client and make sure they're happy. MDs travel a lot, making "sales calls" to the upper-level management at the companies that their bank is courting for business. That way, the MD hopes, the CFO or CEO will call them first when it comes time to do a deal.

The vice president also works closely with the client and serves as a liaison between the MD and the associate, who is in charge of the grunt work. Formerly associates themselves, VPs have more free time as well as greater compensation. VPs also travel to client sites, often at the last minute to cover for an overbooked MD or to land a deal on their own. Among other tasks, they oversee the production of pitch books and delegate this work to those below them in the bank's hierarchy.

Associates have usually joined the bank straight out of some prestigious MBA program. Like analysts, they work long hours and can easily put in 80 to 110 hours a week at the office. Associates do the math that lets a company know whether a possible merger or acquisition will ultimately be worth the money or whether a stock offering is worthwhile. Much of this is done using comparable company analysis or "comps," which associates use to figure out how much a company is worth based on the values of their publicly traded peers in the industry. They also pass along less rewarding assignments and research to the analysts they are working with to create pitch books. They then make sure that the work is done properly before a VP or MD sees it.

All of this bureaucracy results in long hours of waiting for the analysts, who are anxiously poised for approvals and the new demands issued from those above.

Eager to make a good impression, summer analysts will try to take on every project that comes their way, often resulting in monumental workloads and myriad tight deadlines. Their full-time colleagues quickly weed out analysts who can't keep up. Once this happens, these unfortunate summer analysts soon find themselves with fewer responsibilities and projects than their peers, a sure sign that they won't be invited back for a full-time job at the end of the summer. But as a result, those who shine are rewarded with even more work, causing them to pull superhuman feats of mental stamina on little or no sleep.

After working 100 to 110 hours a week during the first eight weeks of his internship at Goldman Sachs (and eighty to ninety hours during the last two weeks), one student had seen enough to make a decision about his next career step. "I saw the very best and the very worst of investment-banking life," he said. "You have a high level of responsibility, you get introduced to interesting people and you're assigned intensive and analytical work. I don't think there are too many work environments that let a twenty-year-old kid do such important things. Yet, I confirmed every horror story I had ever heard about the lifestyle. In ten weeks, working seven days a week, I had one day off. And on that day, I felt guilty for not being in the office."

The twenty-one year old then pointed out the gray hairs that had begun sprouting among his dark locks.

While they are all referred to as "summer analysts," the duties of summer interns at Wall Street's financial institutions can be decidedly different depending on the divisions of the bank that they work for. There are three main areas where a student can land: corporate finance, sales and trading and research.

The jobs that people generally consider "investment banking" are the ones in corporate finance, which is the arm of the bank that deals with clients, underwrites IPOs and security offerings, handles corporate restructurings, and advises on mergers and acquisitions. Investment bankers in corporate finance typically put in more hours than anyone else, endure a multitude of grunt work in their first couple of years, are often the ones wearing the most expensive suits–because they are responsible for making the face-to-face presentations to corporate clients–and taking home the biggest bonuses, because their clients drive the overall business of the bank.

Sales and trading internships are generally the second most popular banking choice among students. In many ways, the division is like corporate finance's rascally little brother. While the hours are shorter, they are more intense. Famously immortalized in Michael Lewis's *Liar's Poker*, the trader lives in a gritty and frenetic world of risks, constantly waging bets in a variety of markets: stocks, bonds, derivatives, options, foreign exchange and commodities. Traders must have strong analytical skills and be able to think fast on their feet. Their clients are the "buy side" financial institutions such as Fidelity Investments, which manage baskets of investments of retirement or mutual funds for their investors, as well as provide the money managers for smaller funds or hedge funds. (Because the banks are the ones selling the stocks, bonds, and securities to these institutions, they are referred to as the "sell side").

Research department analysts are more or less the bookworms of the group. They spend their time investigating and evaluating which investment opportunities are worthwhile (or not worthwhile) for the bank's clients or its sales and trading desks to pursue by issuing "buy," "hold" and "sell" recommendations. They spend their days doing research and writing reports on everything from large-scale economic forecasts and interest rates, to minutiae such as valuations of software firms or how the launch of a new product will affect a company's bottom line. They can work late into the night at times, but their responsibilities rarely eat up their weekends.

For the summer of 2003, two-thirds of Wharton's juniors landed internships in the financial services industry and forty percent were analysts of some sort at an investment bank. Goldman

Sachs, Morgan Stanley and the increasingly high-profile UBS Warburg came out on top for handpicking the largest number of summer protégés from Wharton. Salaries for a summer analyst position ranged from $800 to $4,800 a month. Even those on the high end of that range won't hesitate to point out that given all of the hours they worked over the summer, they were actually getting paid less than minimum wage. ("I could have worked at McDonald's, gotten the same hourly wage and a lot more sleep," one student complained after conducting a cost-benefit analysis of his summer pay.)

During the summer between his junior and senior year, Jon Gantman figured that he managed to save $5,000 by avoiding paying Manhattan rents. He also believed he saved his sanity.

Early on during the recruiting rush his junior year, Jon realized that the eighteen-hour days required of investment bank interns weren't for him. "You can get so bogged down in the summer internship herd mentality at Wharton," Jon said. "They push us to concentrate in finance and go into investment banking."

Jon even went so far as to drop his finance concentration for a concentration in management. He was tired of the thoughtless number crunching that his finance classes entailed. Management classes, on the other hand, taught him how to be a strong leader and how to resolve conflicts and create strategies within a team. Being a Management 100 TA tapped into Jon's experience as a counselor at a camp in central Pennsylvania, where he spent many previous summers as a leader, mentor and confidante to his summertime charges.

While the internship recruitment season raged, Jon often found himself wishing that he could return to the camp and work there over the summer. But he knew that taking an internship was imperative for his job hunt come senior year. Jon received several offers from companies and banks to join them for the summer. To the astonishment of many of his Wharton peers, he turned down a prestigious internship working in Goldman Sachs' credit risk advisory division.

"My friends were awesome about me turning Goldman down," explained Jon. "The real Whartonites, though, were like, '*What* are you doing?'"

Instead, Jon had opted to head twenty-three miles northeast of Manhattan to Purchase, New York, to PepsiCo's headquarters, where he spent the summer doing strategic planning for Pepsi's Sierra Mist brand. During the day, Jon researched the markets where the soft drink was selling the most and tried to determine the drivers for success in those markets, whether it was pricing, distribution or ad spending. Jon liked the experience and the perks that came with the internship, including a bright-green Mountain Dew–branded Xbox gaming system and autographed pictures with pop stars (and Pepsi promoters) Beyoncé Knowles and Jessica Simpson.

The downside of the job? The addiction. "I'd get headaches from the caffeine withdrawal," said Jon, now a bona fide Pepsi fanatic.

During the evenings, Jon and his roommate, Mark (also a Wharton student), would play softball with their colleagues or hang out and drink beer, as Jon would wax on about the business he hoped to start someday. Jon held fast to his entrepreneurial aspirations—both of his parents have had successful careers that they had forged on their own.

Jon's mother, Susan, is a lawyer whose résumé included work at a private law firm, as a county prosecutor and as an advocate for children from abusive homes. She helped get Pennsylvania's Child Protective Services Act passed, and in the fall of 2003 she was running for Superior Court judge for the state of Pennsylvania. Jon's father, Lewis, was formerly a local real estate developer who worked on the King of Prussia Mall, one of the world's largest shopping complexes. Each was a pillar of the community, and Jon admired their perseverance and dedication to the careers they loved so much. Seeing what both of his parents had done with their lives, Jon couldn't imagine being someone's lackey. To him, it was yet another reason not to pursue a career in investment banking.

On Goldman Sachs' trading floor, Shreevar Kheruka was feeling well rested, but stressed out. He had finally gotten used to rising before the sun and being at his desk by 6:00 A.M., but the pace was too fast and furious for the first four hours of his waking day. From 6:00 A.M. until 10:00 A.M. the Goldman trading floor was a whirlwind. When he arrived in the morning, Shreevar would frantically track, monitor and summarize the transactions that had occurred overnight in the markets around the globe for one of Goldman's partners. As Tokyo's exchange closed, he'd print out a report on their trades, and then it was on to the midday report for London. After an hour and a half of chasing and recording these trades, Shreevar would price exotic options with a broker over the Reuters machine, one of the six computer terminals he faced at his cubicle each day. Exotic options are somewhat complicated variations of regular or "plain vanilla" options that have different payoff triggers or serve as an option on an option. In text messages, the broker would tell one of the exotic-option specialists sitting near Shreevar which options their clients wanted to buy, and then Shreevar would track down the prices that they needed.

Come 10:00 A.M., another round of options was expiring, and Shreevar would quickly create a report on which ones the firm should try to exercise by comparing the market price with the option's strike price. He would then get back on the Reuters machine, this time messaging brokers who represented clients who held the options that Shreevar had deemed tradeworthy. All the while, he fielded calls from brokers, which on some days seemed to be nonstop.

By 11:00 A.M., Shreevar needed a breather. Usually at this time, his ninety-person intern class would be shuttled to one of several events scheduled throughout the summer. They would attend luncheons with the firm's managing directors, who would tell them war stories and give them advice. But sometimes they would just wander the trading area, picking the brains of the traders in different divisions. Shreevar would later digest his lunch while reading the global news roundup that Goldman Sachs compiled and e-mailed to everyone on the floor each day. They were the lengthiest e-mails Shreevar had ever received. He rarely ever finished reading the entire thing before 3:00 in the afternoon, when everything turned upside down again.

At this point Wall Street trading was coming to a standstill, and he needed to begin running the end-of-day reports. Laid out before Shreevar was a painstaking twelve-step process designed to summarize the trades of the day and update the firm's books. It was also a way to ensure that the traders kept all of the promises that they made to the brokers who relied on them for a certain number of options at a particular price. Shreevar would work the phones, furiously calling brokers to learn what the closing prices were on different currencies. It was up to him to see that everything was in order. The late afternoons, much like the mornings, moved at a lightning pace. Before he knew it, it would be 6:00 P.M. and time to go home, meet his friends at a bar or prepare for yet another intern event.

The "meet and greets" organized in the evenings gave summer analysts a chance to see the more human side of traders, who typically had no time for niceties. The group of young bulls would assemble for food and drinks and listen to their elders explain the work their particular group performed. In the days of the dot-com boom, these meetings would take place at a fancy downtown bar or restaurant, but now they were relegated to Goldman's cafeteria, which somehow made them seem less important to Shreevar. Occasionally, he and his colleagues did make it to the drinking establishments in and around Wall Street, especially on Friday evenings. It was there that Shreevar learned an important lesson about trading.

"One thing you don't learn by being a trader is how to deal with people. Their job makes them aggressive and the people they meet on the street don't understand where they are coming from," he explained, taking on a slightly disdainful tone as he confesses that he too had started to get frustrated with people who didn't make decisions fast enough. "I'm much calmer now, but it hasn't totally subsided," he would say two months after his internship ended.

Jessica also became worried about the way her work at Lazard might be affecting her personality. One morning, there was no time for sleep and Jessica, who was working toward putting in an inhuman 140 hours for the week, returned home to change her clothes and put her hair back in a ponytail so that she could turn around and go back to the office looking somewhat refreshed and a lot less wrinkled. When she got back to her desk, she discovered that in the less than two hours that she had been gone, the graphics department had been anxiously trying to locate her and had left her a few somewhat vexed messages. It was at this point that her exhaustion set in, and so did the frustration. She wanted to yell at someone, and it worried her that maybe it would be harder than she thought to hang on to her normally friendly demeanor while working at an investment bank.

"When I got out [of work], it wasn't *okay* to treat people that way. I had to check myself," admitted Jessica. "You have to keep a sense of humor. I keep telling my friends that investment banking isn't going to make me a nasty person."

On the last day of Jessica's internship, she sat alone in one of

Lazard's conference rooms eating sushi and reflecting on her ten-week run at the bank. Jessica understood that the tension-packed days filled with deadlines at the bank caused her colleagues to be short with one another. While she didn't like the fact that people weren't nice to each other all of the time, she was impressed with the quality of the work she was doing and her exposure to some of the bank's highest-ranking members. It was then that she realized she was happy at Lazard and that she was indeed cut of the cloth needed to become an investment banker.

Other students would learn the opposite. Many of them couldn't wait to get out of the bullpens of the banks and back to school.

"Some students intern at investment banks and then completely forgo it, saying 'There is *no way in hell* I am going to get into this,'" recalled Anthony Sandrik, who spent his summer assisting traders at a hedge fund in New York. "When you start to brag about the number of hours you work per week, you've got a problem. It doesn't make you any more of a cool person."

Anthony had forgone internship recruiting his junior year. He spent his second semester junior year in Madrid, bypassing all of the investment banks' information sessions. His father helped Anthony out by putting him in touch with someone he knew at a hedge fund in New York. Even though there were times that Anthony attended to such menial tasks as picking up his boss's cell phone at the Verizon store, he didn't mind the picayune details. It was all worth it to him because he had the opportunity to do everything his more seasoned colleagues did—except trade. He conducted research on investments, called banks and summarized news for the traders. "I did everything from getting them lunch to helping them do research," explained Anthony. "The way I look at it, if they went and got their own cup of coffee they could lose ten thousand dollars."

Anthony and his colleagues would come in around 7:00 or 8:00 A.M., giving them an hour or two before trading began to catch up on what had happened the previous night in overseas markets. They left a couple of hours after trading ended for the day, usually around 5:00 P.M. The hours in between were a blur and Anthony was never bored. "Trading is more compact hours and more intense," he said. "In investment banking you wait around a lot. You submit a report and you wait for someone to revise it. It's a really long process."

One summer analyst at Goldman who grew frustrated with the waiting created an Excel spreadsheet that counted down the seconds until the end of his internship in August. He disseminated his electronic invention among his analyst class who, on their more frustrating days, frequently checked the countdown to freedom. Those who realized banking wasn't for them seemed happy for their internship experience, though. Now they knew not to waste their time senior year chasing after the banks. Others, like Shimika, who planned on taking a full-time job at a bank, saw it differently.

"This is a ten-week interview process, a ten-week sprint," she said. "You can't wait until that day when your (computer) log-in no longer works."

Noting how tired she was by the end of the summer, she added, "But you have to maintain the image of success at all times and keep on sprinting."

CHAPTER FOUR

BATTLE OF THE BULGE BRACKETS

In the first weeks of September, scores of recruiters from Wall Street's investment banks arrive on trains from New York's Penn Station into Philadelphia's 30th Street Station bound for the University of Pennsylvania. Upon arrival, they cut a trail past the traffic that is edging and honking its way onto the exit ramp to I-76—referred to locally as the Schuylkill Expressway—the main artery to Philadelphia's western suburbs. Alongside the highway to the east lie the muddied waters of the Schuylkill River, a 128-mile watercourse that once hosted eighteenth-century revolutionaries, then later gave itself up to the coal mills and lumberyards of the Industrial Age, the abandoned remnants of which still litter the river's banks.

As the recruiters make their way down 34th Street, they leave Philadelphia's urban trappings behind and enter the leafy confines of Penn's campus. Standing on the pristine sidewalks are clusters of students deep in conversation, who gesture and smile. Shops and cafés line the streets, and the brick structures of academia ring the interior courtyards of Locust Walk. Beyond University City to the north and west is the city's less desirable western quadrant—a place where abandoned buildings and poverty, while not as rampant as a decade ago, are still common plagues. Here on campus, though, there is a sense of community that is more reminiscent of a village than a city. It's as if an invisible force field encircles Penn's kingdom. For once one enters the belly of the place, it becomes increasingly difficult to imagine any part of the harder side of life existing anywhere near Penn's manicured landscape, let alone just a few blocks away.

Wall Street recruiters make these annual pilgrimages to Penn's campus because they know that the odds are high that they will find the talent they need. "Wharton is like a finishing school for investment banking," said a banker from a large bulge-bracket bank. "You just don't have to train them that much going in." These reps from the investment banks of Wall Street and some of the world's largest corporations arrive at Penn's campus armed with presentation folders, glossy color pamphlets and even computer disks with short promotional videos and PowerPoint presentations that they will hand out to students at the information sessions they host that evening. All the while, the recruiters are preparing to preach the gospel of the investment banks that they represent, evangelizing to Wharton's students the many reasons why the students belong at their bank–even if they really don't.

It's early in the semester when these corporate soldiers arrive. In the short time that the recruiters are visiting the campus, they will try to cast a wide net, hoping to appeal to as many students as possible in order to insure that they don't miss out on a prize Wharton prospect. Many of Wharton's students have recently returned from summer stints at the firms these recruiters most rigorously compete with for both financial dealings and young talent. The rivalry is heated as they embark on this race to win the students' attentions early on and lure them away from the "exploding" offers–job offers that expire after a certain date so recruiters can look for someone else to fill the slot–that they may have received from the banks they had interned for over the summer. If a recruiter finds out that one of their competitors is going to be on campus before them, they may even try to reschedule their information session with Penn's Career Services office for an earlier date. Because they all try to schedule their information sessions as early as possible in the semester, the first few weeks can be hectic for Wharton's seniors. Students can spend every night of the week at these events, sometimes dropping in on three presentations in one evening.

Most of the recruiter information sessions occur in campus buildings—Huntsman Hall, the auditorium in Logan Hall off of Perelman Quad, or the Inn at Penn, a high-end hotel on the shop-laden strip on Walnut Street. In their freshly pressed suits, crowds of eager young recruits gather outside these venues anxiously awaiting the bank's presentation. The display makes it seem as if the Young Republicans had arrived in full force to Penn's campus. This year, the top three bulge-bracket banks among Wharton students (in order of prestige) are Goldman Sachs, Morgan Stanley and Citigroup. Many students believe that working at one of the bulge-bracket banks—instead of a lesser-known firm, or a smaller boutique bank—for a couple of years after graduation will be their ticket into some of the nation's top MBA programs. The bulge brackets have big reputations and big budgets for hiring young recruits, and they attract hundreds of students to their presentations.

"There were people hanging off the balconies to get in," laughed Anthony Sandrik about one such event. "These presentations are pointless, because we already know everything about the firm."

As the students file into the auditoriums, meeting rooms and banquet halls where the information sessions are held, they are greeted by one or two of the bank's employees, who are usually analysts or associates who have been asked to put on human resources hats for the night and answer any and all questions about working at their particular bank. Some banks even appoint Wharton "captains," who are recruiters–usually recent Wharton alums–dedicated solely to the pursuit and capture of Wharton students during recruiting season. After attending a handful of information sessions, Wharton students discover that the presentations are exceedingly predictable. The hour usually opens with a greeting from one of the mid- to upper-level employees of the bank, typically a vice president or a managing director who graduated from Wharton. They warm up the room with a joke about banking, recruiting or business school, or they tell some anecdote that seems to be poking fun at the bank they work at but, in truth, is actually a complimentary tale.

At Goldman Sachs' information session, one student recalled how the presenter told the audience a story about a partner who was notorious for being quiet and consistently coolheaded (a rarity in the investment banking profession). One day, the partner could be heard screaming at the top of his lungs in his office. Everyone could hear it. While this type of behavior can be a fairly common occurrence in the tension-filled office, it was unusual that this particular partner was screaming. Everyone stopped what he or she was doing, recalled the presenter. Hearing this, the students listening to the story began to wonder: *Did the partner finally have that breakdown he was working toward all of these years?* Or *I wonder who screwed up? And what was it that they did?*

The story was starting to get a little more interesting, making the audience feel like they were being made privy to some secret scandal–and a scandal at *Goldman Sachs* of all places. Now fully enrapt by the presenter, the audience stared unblinkingly at him and eagerly waited for the delivery of the denouement to the tale. But the conclusion disappointed. As it turns out, the partner was screaming at a vice president who had been rude to his secretary. There were no really juicy tidbits of gossip about Goldman for these students to cling to and share with their friends as they had hoped. With the tale, the presenter managed to reassert a long-held Goldman mantra that the firm is renowned for: that everyone at Goldman Sachs is treated as an equal. It was enough to bolster the impressions of the already gung-ho Goldman worshipers in the room. Some of those who weren't exactly superstars at Wharton hoped that Goldman's recruiters would remember that mantra and treat them as equals, too, when they reviewed their résumés and chose candidates for first-round interviews.

Following the presenter's "sales pitch," investment bank recruiters usually proceed with some sort of audiovisual presentation, generally a video starring employees of the firm, all of whom are smiling and selling the merits of their workplace and their impact on the world. In hopes of quashing the Waspy banker stereotype and appealing to certain minorities that are sorely lacking in some of their ranks (especially African-Americans and women), the banks also strive to display a diversity of ethnicities among their labor forces. The videos are montages of clips that include interviews with people from different divisions of the firm, saying how much they absolutely love working there. Most Wharton students are waiting for this formal part of the presentation to end so they can corner a recruiter and regale them with how great (and hireable) they are. They are hoping to prove to the recruiters that if they hire them, they will give a grand performance that could be used in the bank's video for next year's young recruits to watch.

As the final credits roll, most presenters open the floor up for a question-and-answer session. At larger bank presentations, about half a dozen or more employees of the bank will position themselves around the room and answer the queries of the anxious students who flock to them. As the group of students increasingly encroaches on the recruiter's personal space, claustrophobia sets in. Yet the recruiter continues to smile; her face sobers up only to look more interested when a student is in the process of posing a question. It's a fleeting type of celebrity that these bankers enjoy, and that power will remain with them throughout the recruiting process.

Wharton's students are also putting their well-earned skills to work. They know quite well the means by which they can get noticed by a recruiter. "We know what to ask and what not to ask," said Anthony Sandrik. "That's why you come to Wharton. At no other school do you get taught these things."

When the students encircle a recruiter, there is almost always one aggressor who plunges his hand into the middle of the circle to shake the recruiter's hand first. The tactic usually works as the recruiter turns his or her attention toward the boldest of the students. Anthony even learned that standing to the left of the recruiter is the best place to position oneself. "If you stand on his right side, then his handshake will be short with you. If you stand on the left, then he has to step into you while shaking your hand," he explained. Students also know that speaking with an analyst instead of a senior vice president or managing director isn't going to get them far. So they seek out the power players at their firms of choice in order to get in at the top.

As the students jockey for position, many of them grow impatient with brown-nosing classmates who have strategically positioned themselves in front of the recruiter and are asking inane questions just to get floor time: "Can you tell me what you think are the five qualities that make a great analyst?" Questions like this one are softballs; they are questions that every Wharton student knows the answer to because they have studied them inside and out whether in class, with Career Services personnel or at their internships. The "five-qualities-that-make-a-good-analyst" question is almost unavoidable at banking interviews. A fair majority of students already have their responses at the ready: "hardworking," "great at multitasking," "team player," "excellent quantitative skills," "works well under pressure" and so on. For the recruiters, it's probably the hundredth time that he or she has heard the question, whether it's being posed by a young hopeful recruit at an information session or uttered from their very own mouths during an interview. With well-rehearsed patience, though, the rep from the bank responds, prattling off a list that sounds much like the student's own. "The analysts aren't going to give some honest answer. They're just going to give the official answer," complained Shreevar Kheruka after attending myriad information sessions.

Meanwhile, as an exchange like this continues, one or two of the students watching the eager (and inquisitive) student monopolize the recruiter's attention start getting anxious. Their muscles tense up, they are ready to pounce once they have the chance. They know if they aren't one of the first students to gain the recruiter's attention and strike up a conversation, then sitting through this whole information session has been a waste of their already limited time. If they get to the recruiter too late, they will end up getting squeezed out as the ambitious pack of students tightens its hold around them. "If you go to the same company information sessions as your friend, you become enemies at it because you're both trying to get the recruiter's attention," said Shimika Wilder, who had her fill of these sessions while recruiting for internships. Luckily she was able to forgo them senior year because she had already met many of the key recruiters from the top banks over the summer through her participation in SEO.

Some students get so fed up with being crammed out of the ingratiating packs hounding the recruiters that they skip the events altogether, asking friends to sign them in at the beginning of the session. When the bank's recruiters review their résumé or interview them later in the semester, they may check to see that the student was in attendance, an added bonus point for them in the contest to win the job. Even if the recruiter asks them questions about the session, the student can easily ad-lib a response because almost all of these events play out in exactly the same way.

"These information sessions do a great job of marketing the

firm, but ultimately it's B.S.," said Shreevar. "You get excited about them, and then you have to do a reality check."

Many banks and consulting firms host cocktail parties after their information sessions. The swarming masses of well-groomed Whartonites move slowly and awkwardly down the sidewalks of Penn's campus toward these receptions, hoping that the cocktail hour will give them yet another chance for face time with a recruiter. At the bar or restaurant, these students nervously balance hors d'oeuvres on small paper plates and wine glasses in their left hand, leaving their right hand free and ready for a handshake should they encounter a senior-level person from the firm. Then all they have to do is distract him from the chatty student who has had his ear for the last twenty minutes.

"At the cocktail parties it's a free-for-all," said Jon Gantman. "I hate those parties. There are all of these people talking about themselves the whole time." Jon quickly became discouraged by the herd mentality that investment banking engendered among his peers at Wharton. He was searching for something above and beyond the status quo. "I want a 'dare-to-be-great' situation," he said, quoting one of his favorite movies, *Van Wilder*. It's a comedy about a student who, in his seventh year of college, realizes he's afraid to graduate. "I'm waiting for that to come along, and that's not going to be something five hundred kids are going to see a presentation about."

As recruiters continue to invade campus, the banter among Wharton's seniors becomes overwhelmingly career-focused. Their social calendars are now filled with cocktail hours and dinner parties with banks, consulting firms and companies, as opposed to fraternity mixers or nights out at Smokey Joe's (lovingly known as Smoke's) or the White Dog Cafe. Even during a rare evening out with friends, the conversation always seems to veer toward the inevitable topic of finding a job. "Whenever we go out to bars and stuff we are a lot like middle-aged guys. All we talk about are careers and interviewing," scoffed Anthony, who admits that he couldn't help but indulge himself. "At Florida State or UCLA, they go out and talk about girls or sports or *something*."

As the recruiting season takes a tighter hold on these Wharton students and their schedules become increasingly overburdened, their appearance becomes more professional and their demeanor more intense. During autumn's days and nights, Wharton seniors are often spotted on campus in a combination of pinstriped shirts and dark blue or gray suits as they head from classes to interviews in and around campus. To non-Whartonites, the recruiting season only serves to compound and enhance the Wharton stereotypes on campus and further alienate Wharton's young prospects from the rest of their peers.

Luckily for the Class of 2004, this recruiting season was looking a lot more hopeful than the previous year. Wharton had recently been named the top undergraduate business program in the country by *U.S. News & World Report*, again solidifying its reign as number one for the fourth consecutive year. Barbara Hewitt, the associate director of Career Services for Wharton undergrads, described the mood as "cautiously optimistic." National unemployment figures were finally recovering from the highs of the post–tech boom recession, and recruiters from investment banks were telling her that they were expecting to increase the number of students they hired for full-time positions this year by forty to fifty percent over the prior year.

Barb, a mild-mannered woman from Collegeville, Pennsylvania, didn't think she could stand to see yet another group of heartbroken students stranded post-graduation. The last couple of years had been especially hard, and recent Wharton graduates had experienced some unprecedented downfalls. Mass layoffs on Wall Street, corporate scandals affecting banks and brokerage houses and the uncertainty of the U.S. economy due to the war in Iraq had all wreaked havoc on Wall Street and kept the job market from rebounding to anything close to resembling the promise it held back in the late 1990s.

The dismal state of affairs was noticeable on Penn's campus. In 1999, the year before the market crumbled, 408 firms came to recruit, scheduling a remarkable 14,761 interviews with students, according to a Career Services survey. In 2003, the number of companies on campus had dropped twenty-one percent to 319 and the number of interviews to 11,383 later surveys showed. In addition, the average number of job offers Wharton students landed fell from three to two. But the most startling statistic, especially to Career Services, which strives to place as many students as possible in jobs before graduation, was the fact that 8.5 percent of the Wharton class of 2003 was still looking for jobs at the end of the academic year. For those who graduated in 2000, only a paltry 3.8 percent–about twenty students–were jobless.

During the recent downturn, consulting firms had been the most noticeably absent of all of the companies that traditionally hired scores of Wharton students. Over the last two years, their presence on campus became minimal during recruiting season, and Barb estimated that the number of jobs they offered was cut by close to seventy-five percent. In the fall of 2001, some seniors had even locked up job offers with consulting firms only to have them rescinded or their start dates significantly delayed a month or two before graduation. By then, it was too late for them to take advantage of the other opportunities that Penn's annual recruiting rushes offered and many of them were left jobless for months after graduation. One Wharton grad ended up taking a sales job at The Gap to make money. Folding pastel-colored sweaters was a far cry from where she had expected her $120,000–plus Wharton education to take her.

Now seniors from the Class of 2004, who had witnessed the personal carnage of those students before them, were nervous about depending on the consulting firms for jobs and even more reliant on the opportunities offered at the investment banks. The consulting companies arrive on campus well after the investment banks have had the first crack at Wharton's seniors. And many students try to play it safe by sending out dozens of résumés to the banks, no matter how little their interest is in joining them. Even those who really only wanted to work in consulting drop résumés for investment-banking posts, hoping to secure a job offer early in the semester so they can breathe a little easier.

The recent launch of a new online résumé-dropping system called PennLink had helped the students route their résumés in bulk in a matter of minutes to the various firms scheduled to do on-campus interviews in the weeks ahead. Prior to the widespread use of the Internet, On-Campus Recruiting Services (OCRS)—provided Wharton students with cubby-hole "dropboxes" in Steiny-D where they would stand in line for up to an hour and physically drop their résumés and cover letters that they painstakingly worded, formatted and printed out on cotton bond paper. Then, in a week or two, they would receive notification of whether or not they had been selected for a first-round interview. The system was effective, but imperfect. With the Web-based system, the whole process became a lot more streamlined and a lot less time-consuming.

Seniors rely heavily on PennLink, which lists firms that are hiring, the dates recruiters will be on campus for information sessions, job descriptions and what kind of material the student needs to submit in order to apply for the job. Students use PennLink to drop their résumés for both summer internships and full-time posts. They can store up to ten versions of their résumé, several recommendations, and unofficial transcripts in the database so they can readily shoot the information to potential employers with an e-mailed cover letter. Résumés are sent to recruiters with a click of the send button. Some students will drop over one hundred résumés during the first weeks of recruiting, sometimes making multiple attempts at one bank. In a matter of days after dropping their résumés, students find out if they made it to the first round, usually through an e-mail from Career Services or the recruiters themselves.

The only students allowed to exploit the On-Campus Recruiting Service's Web site for full-time positions are seniors or graduate students scheduled to graduate during the current academic year. During the recruitment season, students religiously check PennLink's "Daily Recruiting Deadlines" section, which lists the dates by which they must drop their résumé. Once they push the send button, their résumé goes into the ether and lands in the hands of the recruiter. Now the student must wait for an e-mail that says whether or not they have been preselected for an interview.

For students who believe that their résumé "fell through the cracks," or who forgot to drop their résumé on time, Wharton has set up a system to give them an added shot at getting face time with their firms of choice. At the beginning of the school year, Wharton allots its students 1,000 points each to use as bidding chips for interviews. Whoever bids the most points to interview with a firm wins one of a handful of open interview slots that the school has reserved with the company in advance. During the fall recruiting season for the Class of 2000, several students who had hoped to get their foot in the door at Goldman bid all 1,000 of their points to meet with the firm's recruiters, possibly risking the chance to use the points to get in front of a more accessible investment bank such as Lehman Brothers. Top consulting behemoth McKinsey was also bombarded with students wagering their points.

As his fall semester classes began in September 2003, Regi Vengalil was embarking on his final year at Wharton, but his mind was on the future. During a mid-afternoon break at the Au Bon

Pain's café outside of Huntsman Hall, Regi was contemplating which recruiters he was going to visit that day at CareerLink, the university-wide career fair that Penn was conducting four blocks away at the Sheraton Hotel. The café's metal tables were filling up with his Wharton classmates lugging textbook-laden messenger bags and backpacks, most of them emerging from a business lecture or seminar. Even though it was still early in the semester, the chatter among the students at the café indicated that the pressure was already on—the talk was not just about challenging syllabi and project deadlines, but also about finding a job worthy of their prestigious degrees.

Regi is tall and lean with spidery fingers and the inky black hair and dark complexion that he inherited from his parents, both of whom are Indian immigrants. Dressed in what is seemingly the Whartonite uniform for this time of year—a powder-blue button-down shirt tucked into khakis—Regi looks much like his peers. The business-casual look is commonplace among Wharton students, who never know when they will bump into a recruiter that they want to impress while wandering around campus.

In lieu of a time-consuming and pressure-filled internship at an investment bank that would tax his body as it healed, Regi had worked for Seed Ventures, a nonprofit that helps disadvantaged high school students gain job skills. Seed Ventures helped set up individual savings accounts for students. For every dollar a student earned toward college and put in their account, Commerce Bank—one of Seed Ventures' partners—would match it. The experience made Regi more determined to use his business degree to make a difference. "I really liked what we were doing. I want to combine the analytical rigor of the commercial banking sector with helping people," he explained. "You know, something that is challenging intellectually, but socially good."

Regi doesn't make decisions lightly. He chooses his words carefully, debates over most things and tends to seek out the most moral and ethical stance. While he was studying in Madrid junior year, Regi wrote a paper about bullfighting for his Spanish class and took an unpopular anti-bullfighting stance. Regi didn't support the idea of bullfighting as a sport, but he did make a point of saying that cultural traditions were important—just not to the extent of treating animals inhumanely. "If it's supposed to be a sport, then it should be treated as a sport," he argued. "There should be a possibility that the bull will live."

After his semester abroad, Regi met his family in southern India for winter break. The homeland of his parents was one of the most breathtakingly beautiful places Regi had ever seen. The region was known as "God's own country." But the splendor of the landscape was upsettingly offset by the abject poverty of the people who lived there. The trip made Regi thankful for what his parents had achieved in their lives and what they had provided for him and his older sister. Regi's father had left India in the 1970s to work as a medical technologist in Libya under Muammar al-Qaddafi, where he worked for three years and made enough money to help put his brothers through school. Regi's mother was a nurse at the time. The U.S. was undergoing a shortage of nurses and made an international plea for help. Regi's mother answered the call and immigrated to the U.S., where she and her husband (who immigrated a couple of years later) started a family. Seeing the risks his parents had taken and the place where they came from had a profound impact on Regi and intensified his desire to make a difference in the world.

Regi was considering graduate school, but he wanted to work for a few years first. He thought long and hard about joining the Peace Corps. He had already filled out the application and written the two required essays. Now he was just waiting for his older sister, a medical student at nearby Drexel University, to proofread them before sending them off. The next step would be to meet the

Peace Corps representatives who were going to be at the career fair that day.

Many Wharton seniors try to steer clear of the CareerLink. They have been there before and know the drill. But for anxious Wharton sophomores and juniors looking for internship opportunities, and seniors fearing that they have yet to make a connection with a recruiter at their firm of choice, CareerLink is yet another opportunity to ingratiate themselves with recruiters. For seniors who do decide to attend, it will be a quick hit to one or two key firms and then back out into the September sunshine. "They are so funny," said Shimika with a smile. "Everyone is there with their power suits and their Wharton folders. Many of them are sophomores and juniors."

CareerLink is more generalized in its offerings, hosting ninety-five companies and organizations ranging from food giant General Mills to nonprofits like Teach For America. Yet the mix is noticeably imbalanced by the large percentage of companies hailing from the financial-services industry. Scouts from Goldman Sachs are there, and so are those from Morgan Stanley, Lehman Brothers, JPMorgan Chase and a slew of other investment houses. Students—even sophomores—come armed with their résumés in hopes of making an impression that will lead them onto the path of landing a full-time job.

The corporate participants at CareerLink man card tables stacked with handouts, pamphlets and freebies, each stationed next to one another like stalls at the county fair. Kraft Foods gives out Balance Gold energy bars and General Mills has a variety of snack foods free for the taking. Some of the reps sit behind the tables passing out brochures, pens or key chains that market their firm while delivering their sales pitch to the students crowding around them. Other recruiters from less popular employment destinations stand at the ready, trying to actively engage students passing by with the hope that they can get them to stop for a second before heading off to a more popular destination. The three recruiters for the accounting firm PricewaterhouseCoopers looked noticeably bored as they endured the remaining hour of the fair with no students in sight. Meanwhile, the seven representatives stationed at the table for investment bank UBS Warburg were hurriedly trying to answer the questions that the throng of students at their table launched at them, so they could get to the next row of students waiting to speak with them.

Within hours, the floors of the rooms at the Sheraton are littered with business cards that have fallen out of the myriad folders of information that students are saddled with. Some companies even offer bags–emblazoned with their company logo, of course– to help students haul off all of the material. As the ranks among the students thin, so does the energy level displayed by the corporate reps. It's been a long day, and most of them have been on their feet the whole time.

In the late afternoon, Regi made his way to CareerLink to speak with the folks from the Peace Corps. After chatting with the recruiters for a while, Regi asked them if the lung collapses he had endured would hinder his chances of being accepted. The response he received left him discouraged.

"She was pretty honest with me," he said. "She said, 'It will put a stall on you and put a red flag on your application. You just need to prove you want to go.'"

It was a blow that made Regi rethink some of his recruiting plans. He wandered around the career fair for a little while longer, just to see what else was out there.

CHAPTER FIVE

THE WHARTON WAY

The University of Pennsylvania was spun from the dreams of a Renaissance man. Benjamin Franklin was not only a founding father of the United States, but also a newspaper publisher, a philosopher who spawned a plethora of popular catchphrases, a diplomat and an inventor who devised bifocals, the lightning rod, and the urinary catheter. He was a self-educated man dedicated to the pursuit of higher education. Yet even Ben Franklin, with his huge appetite for knowledge, knew that a person's mind could only cover so much intellectual territory in a limited amount of time—he believed it was important to arm young people with practical skills that would prove beneficial to their futures. In an effort to make these beliefs a reality, Franklin published a plan in 1749 called *Proposals Relating to the Education of Youth in Pensilvania*, which sought to provide the city's youth with a practical education that was "most useful and most ornamental." The proposal suggested reforms to the existing Charity School of Philadelphia, founded in 1740, outlining the foundations of what later became the University of Pennsylvania and are, in many ways, still upheld at the university today.

The Academy and College of Philadelphia (the new name for the school after Franklin's proposal was enacted) held its first classes in 1751. Graduating six years later were seven students who would become Penn's first group of alumni. Students at the school were taught a curriculum unlike the religiously focused trainings of the four other American colleges of the time: Harvard, William and Mary, Yale and Princeton, and also differed greatly from those in contemporary Europe, where upper-level learning was reserved purely for the elite. Across the Atlantic Ocean, classes focused more on the fancies of courtiers and monastic teachings than on the skills of merchants. At Penn, students studied foreign languages, the classics and sciences, while also learning the skills necessary to innovate and build businesses and improve the community. It was the first liberal arts program of its kind, and it would influence higher learning throughout the fledgling nation. In the decades that followed, Penn expanded its offerings, establishing individual schools dedicated to specific vocations in order to provide thorough training in those fields. One of the first such endeavors was the country's first medical school, which opened in 1765, followed by the opening of the first university teaching hospital, later to be called the Hospital of the University of Pennsylvania (known by its acronym, HUP), which opened in 1874.

It was in the second century of Penn's revolutionary academic atmosphere that mining mogul Joseph Wharton, the son of a wealthy Philadelphia Quaker family, who had made his own riches in nickel, cobalt, steel and zinc, decided that the university would be a perfect place to launch the nation's first collegiate-level business school. Joseph Wharton had cultivated his metal business, which served as the foundation for the Bethlehem Steel Corporation, during the early part of the Second Industrial Revolution. It was a time when landmark inventions such as Alexander Graham Bell's telephone and Thomas Edison's phonograph were revolutionizing the business world. During this period the economy relied heavily on the railroads and mass-produced steel. Having to constantly fend off international steel competition—especially from

Britain—Wharton grew well versed in economic protectionism, preaching its merits to his fellow American businessmen. Wharton believed that nations gained riches through the division of labor, in which the talents of several workers are combined to create a product that one person alone couldn't possibly have created. But he believed that the division of labor should remain within geographic borders so one nation's workers could build up their country's wealth without interference from foreign competition.

Seeking to create an institution that would extol the virtues of his protectionist beliefs, Wharton (who didn't attend college because of an illness in his youth) wrote a letter to the University of Pennsylvania's administration, beseeching them to create a business school that would prepare America's young men to become business leaders. One of his primary requests was that students take three courses: business law, finance and accounting. In 1881, Wharton endowed $100,000 (the equivalent of about $2 million today) to Penn for the school that he hoped would produce "pillars of the community."

Founded more or less as an experiment, the Wharton School of Finance and Economy—as it was first known—required the writing of the first business-school textbooks and the hiring of the first business-school professors. A former attorney named Albert Bolles was the first to take on the challenge. In the spring of 1883, Bolles, who a few years earlier had left his legal career to become the editor of *Bankers Magazine*, began teaching Wharton's students the subjects of finance and commercial banking with a conservative bent that upheld Joseph Wharton's academic goals and personal beliefs.

In 1884, Wharton graduated its first class. There were five graduates, two of whom would go on to become influential figures in global politics: Robert Adams, Jr., who became a U.S. Minister to Brazil, and Japanese native Shiro Shiba, who later became a right-wing member of the Japanese Diet.

Just a matter of years after Wharton first opened its doors, the depression of the 1890s sent the country and its thriving economy into a tailspin. The cost of cultivating the zealous growth of the Second Industrial Revolution had begun to outweigh the demand for the multitude of products produced from it. Companies embarked on vicious price wars in the hope of moving more products. Inevitably these measures caused their bottom lines to suffer, and many firms soon began to bleed cash. Farmers who were experiencing rising costs to produce and ship their crops were facing increasing difficulty obtaining credit as prices for their crops fell. Tensions in the workforce increased as unions formed and laborers began to protest their hours and wages. By the end of 1893 financial panic hit when the value of the dollar, which was determined by the gold standard, plummeted because gold reserves had fallen to drastic lows due to prodigal government spending that had eaten up the surplus.

Amid the rubble of the depression stood John Pierpont Morgan, a banker who changed the face of investment banking and corporate America in ways that would last far beyond his own lifetime. J.P. Morgan believed that the price competition that helped spur the depression must be curbed in order to create growth. Starting with the railroads, Morgan's investment house, J.P. Morgan & Co., arranged mass consolidations among bankrupt rail operators and then moved onto other industries. By the time he was done, he had created or financed the syndicates that would develop into AT&T, General Electric and U.S. Steel, the last of which became the nation's first billion-dollar corporation.

As once-small, owner-operated outfits morphed into large conglomerates, it created the need for a new corporate structure that entailed breaking these large companies into divisions. Corporations now had departments that specialized in areas such as marketing or accounting, and managers were needed to supervise the books, keep track of resources and oversee production (as well as lead the growing labor force that was hired to produce the companies' increasing diversity of products).

The Wharton School, under the school's first director, Edmund James, responded to the evolving nature of business at the time by adding to its roster of course offerings such disciplines as insurance, transportation, industrial management and product marketing. In several cases, Wharton was teaching these subjects at the same time they were being pioneered in the business world. In fact, Wharton was the first school to teach marketing (then known as "merchandising"), and its professors became leaders in consumer research, first delving into the psyche of consumers and then later analyzing various marketing challenges.

Leading the charge toward specialized education was professor Emory Johnson, who would later serve as Wharton's dean from 1919 to 1933. An expert on the transportation industry (he helped develop the Transportation Act of 1920, which put an end to government control of the industry and charged carriers with the task of regulating themselves), Johnson taught Wharton's students the ins and outs of the railroad industry and other transportation-related issues. Just as he was a specialist in the transportation industry, Johnson urged professors and students to specialize in their respective lines of study. In an effort to institute such focus, he was the first to break Wharton's faculty into academic departments by subject. Johnson also spearheaded efforts to provide academic-advising and career-advising services to students. These services not only helped students to determine and plot out individualized curricula for the area of study that they chose, but also helped them turn their specialty into a career after graduation. These initiatives served as the foundations of Wharton's extensive Academic Advisory and Career Services departments of today.

Just two decades after its founding, the "experiment" that was Wharton had become a thriving reality. Enrollment grew to the point that the school desperately needed its own home on campus. In 1904, the Wharton School moved into Logan Hall, where its classes would be held until the 1950s. Dozens of other undergraduate business programs followed Wharton's example in the years to come, including the University of California at Berkeley's College of Commerce (later to become the Haas School of Business), and New York University's College of Commerce, Accounts and Finance (later called the Stern School of Business), as well as graduate programs such as Dartmouth's Tuck School of Business and the Harvard Business School. In 1921, Wharton expanded its business teachings beyond the collegiate level by introducing its own MBA program, which soon grew into one of the most prestigious graduate business programs in the country.

The same year that the graduate school enrolled its first students, Wharton professor Joseph Willits and research professor Ann Bezanson, who held a PhD from Harvard in economic history, opened a research center "to study the economic and social problems of business." Called the Industrial Research Unit (IRU), it was the first research center to be opened at a business school, and it began a long-standing tradition at Wharton of relying heavily on research to help mold its curriculum. The researchers at the IRU examined wage structures and sought to improve industrial working conditions, analyzing the cost of the training and employment of minorities, as well as the economic impact of labor strikes. Years later, research would focus on the intricacies of labor relations and the economics of unemployment. Willits established such an expertise in the field that he was later called upon by President Herbert Hoover to serve on the U.S. Emergency Committee for Employment. (Decades after its founding, the IRU was renamed the Center for Human Resources, reflecting the changing work environment that had become based more on intellectual capital than industrial labor).

Following World War I, undergraduate enrollment at Penn surged, breaking the ten-thousand-student mark for the first time. The ensuing prosperity of the 1920s brought about new business innovations and high-flying stock prices in a bullish stock market. It was a time of unprecedented growth, with companies such as Ford Motor at the forefront, pioneering such workplace dictums as the five-day, forty-hour workweek. Somewhat ironically, the most popular discipline of study at Wharton at the time was insurance—a line of study that would prove to be quite in demand.

On one dismal Tuesday in October 1929, the financial world came to an abrupt halt as the stock market collapsed. Within three months, stocks had lost $26 billion in value. "Black Tuesday" was the precursor to the worst depression in the nation's history. A run on the banks two years later would only deepen the impact of the Great Depression and send the country into an economic tailspin. By 1933, 11,000 banks had failed or were folded into other banks to stay afloat. More than a quarter of the U.S. working population was out of work.

The dismal economic environment and public distrust of the banking industry spurred the creation of the Glass-Steagall Act (the act was actually comprised of certain sections of President Franklin D. Roosevelt's Emergency Banking Act), which would greatly alter the future of investment and commercial banking. Glass-Steagall called for commercial banks to split from investment banks and forbade the commercial banks to deal in or derive more than ten percent of their revenue from securities, in order to prevent the abuses experts believed had led to the financial panic of 1929 to 1933. No longer could a bank use its assets—including depositors' money—to back risky financial transactions such as IPOs. As a result, firms like J.P. Morgan would split into separate outfits. (J.P. Morgan became the commercial bank and Morgan Stanley became the securities firm). In 1956, Congress further extended the power of the Glass-Steagall Act by prohibiting banks from underwriting insurance.

As Wharton marked its fiftieth anniversary in 1931, the U.S. economy was now two years into the worst downturn in its history, and many businesses and individuals were trying to pick up the pieces. Thomas Sovereign Gates, a lawyer and investment banker who had become the first president of the University of Pennsylvania a year earlier, would successfully lead the school through the ravages of the Depression and set about restructuring both the university's academic and athletic programs and creating provisions for student health. Gates became one of the first major fund-raisers for the school, drumming up $5 million in donations from Penn alumni under his Bicentennial Plan. During Gates' tenure, the College of Liberal Arts for Women and the School of Social Work were founded, and the legendary George Munger was hired as the school's football coach.

In 1940, FDR and former president Hoover graced Penn's campus to deliver speeches as part of the university's bicentennial celebration. The country was steadily recovering from the effects of the Great Depression, and the alphabet soup of initiatives from FDR's controversial New Deal legislation was remaking the economy, including programs such as unemployment relief (the WPA) and the establishment of the Securities and Exchange Commission (the SEC). Consulting on programs like FDR's National Recovery Administration (the NRA) were Wharton professors such as George W. Taylor, a noted academician in the field of labor and industrial relations who would serve under five presidents, and who was credited with helping to settle more than 2,000 labor strikes.

The outbreak of World War II would similarly remake the

Wharton School. The number of faculty members at Wharton fell from 165 to 39 as many professors and administrators were mobilized to help organize the country's resources for the production of wartime necessities such as guns, ammunition and airplanes. In 1943, faculty members at Penn were busy working on sixty government research projects. A couple of years into the war, the G.I. Bill was passed, prompting hundreds of veterans to matriculate in the school after their tour of duty and subsequently swelling the school's enrollment, as well as its finances.

Adding to the school's attraction to prospective students was its participation in the Ivy Group Agreement. In 1945, a group of eight highly respected universities comprised of Brown, Columbia, Cornell, Dartmouth, Harvard, Penn, Princeton and Yale gathered to establish a set of guidelines–athletic and academic–for their intercollegiate football programs. In 1956, these Ancient Eight would officially become the Ivy League, and eventually become some of the most selective (and some of the most expensive) colleges in the country.

This new national profile increased interest in Penn and further boosted Wharton, where enrollment continued to climb. By 1948, Wharton dean C. Canby Balderston had managed to raise $2.3 million to construct a new home for the school. Named Dietrich Hall after D. Wellington Dietrich, the uncle of two Wharton alumni and benefactors, the brick-and-stone building opened in 1952. Built along Locust Street, Dietrich Hall established the thoroughfare as a major artery of campus. (The four-block stretch of Locust Street that ran through campus would later be closed to automobile traffic, becoming Locust Walk in 1964.)

The extra room provided by Wharton's new building proved necessary. Two years after Dietrich Hall opened its doors, women were allowed to enroll in Wharton's undergraduate program. In 1954, fifteen pioneering women sat in Wharton's classrooms.

Today, close to 200 women matriculate into Wharton each year, comprising approximately forty percent of each incoming class.

It was during the bull market of the 1950s and 1960s that corporations zealously flocked to Wharton looking to recruit young talent. Diversified companies, or conglomerates, arose en masse after World War II. These corporations were in need of managers with a variety of well-honed business skills to oversee their various enterprises. A career as a businessman came into fashion, and many Wharton students envisioned themselves as "company men," prepared to spend their lives moving up the ranks at one company until retirement. In 1968, Wharton renamed its Industry Department the Management Department to reflect the growing need for well-trained managers in Corporate America. The school expanded its managerial research to include disciplines from Penn's other schools, and it also opened technologically advanced management research centers.

Wharton's Finance Department also changed dramatically at the time. Professor Irwin Friend had helped popularize the program in the early 1960s when he conducted a comprehensive study that challenged the conventional wisdom that mutual funds, which are comprised of stocks or bonds based on a particular investment theory, performed better than individual stocks. He presented his findings to the Securities and Exchange Commission and changed the face of the mutual-fund industry. His work led to the growth of index funds, which are designed to provide investors with the same returns of a particular stock index, such as the S&P 500 or the Russell 2000.

In 1969, Wharton opened the Rodney L. White Center for Financial Research to further its study of financial markets. Designed by a group of investment bankers who sat on Wharton's Finance Department Advisory Committee, the center's researchers initially focused on the study of the capital asset pricing model for determining a stock's value. The model weighed the risk of holding an asset against the total return of the investment in order to determine its value, and the bankers saw vast benefits in using such a model to guide investing strategies. In the years to come, Wharton's professors would develop other financial reforms that greatly affected business on Wall Street. They conducted studies that ascertained the value of money managers and the affect of getting rid of fixed commission rates on stocks, an issue that would come to the forefront in the 1970s.

Research was becoming more specialized and practical at Wharton, to the point where more theoretical teachings were left to Penn's other schools. By 1975, Wharton turned over the teaching of the social sciences to the Liberal Arts College (since renamed the College of Arts and Sciences), freeing its resources to develop an even more in-depth business curriculum. Students were still encouraged to round out their education with courses from the College, but their curriculum at Wharton was becoming increasingly professional.

The years of protests that began amid the Vietnam War and the Civil Rights movement in the 1960s bled into a decade of unrest for the U.S. economy and Wall Street that would foment changes at Wharton. In 1971, President Richard Nixon unveiled his New Economic Policy, which called for the institution of wage and price controls in the hope of staving off inflation and unemployment. Nixon's plan also called for the abandonment of the gold standard in response to the growing realization that the Federal Reserve had created more dollars than could be supported by the country's gold reserves. The move not only hurt the value of the U.S. dollar, but also currencies around the world whose values were based on the dollar. Neither of these moves fully cured the lethal combination of inflation and rising interest rates that had led to a sustained period of "stagflation"–a term coined by economists at the time. Compounding the nation's economic woes were sharp rises in oil prices instituted by OPEC in 1973–1974 (and later in 1978–1979). By 1974, U.S. inflation had risen to a peak of eleven percent, and investors responded accordingly. Close to a quarter of investors had pulled out of the stock market by 1975. Economists and other officials scrambled to find a solution to the country's economic woes.

For Wall Street, the answer seemed to lie in the bond market and in new investment products that could help hedge against the risks of the stagnant economy, such as money-market mutual funds. Money-market funds, for example, allowed investors to put their money in low-risk government securities, certificates of deposit and commercial paper for companies that reap dividends based on short-term interest rates. This sparked an explosion in other new financial instruments such as futures, swaps, and hedge funds, and completely changed the face of the investment landscape. The bond market, which had traditionally hosted conservative investors and retirees, was now a marketplace filled with all types of investors desperate to improve their finances. Companies that were having a hard time raising money through the traditional path of issuing equity began floating bond issues. Accordingly, the bond market took off in the late 1970s and into the early 1980s.

At Wharton, the 1970s marked a period of expansion on several fronts. The school added more specialized study centers such as the Wharton Entrepreneurial Center, which opened in 1973. Also added were Wharton's MBA Executive Education Program, as well as dual-degree programs that combined studies at Wharton with those from Penn's other schools. Not only did these initiatives expand Wharton's student base, but they also increased the opportunities its students could pursue postgraduation.

The first of the dual-degree programs to be introduced at

Wharton had its start in 1967, when Wharton and Penn's medical schools opened the Leonard Davis Institute of Health Economics. Three years later, MBA students could enroll in a joint-degree program in health care management that awarded graduates both MBA and MD degrees. (It wouldn't be until the late 1990s that a dual-degree health care management program between Wharton and Penn's School of Nursing was offered to undergraduate students at the school).

By the late 1970s, technology was increasingly changing the face of financial dealings on Wall Street and in Corporate America. The NASDAQ market, which dealt in smaller securities, was formalized when it was linked to computers in the early 1970s, starting a revolution in electronic trading. In 1979, IBM, the bellwether of the technology industry, floated a $1 billion issue that was the largest in American history. In response to the changing marketplace, Wharton and the School of Engineering joined together to launch the Management and Technology dual-degree program, blending skills in engineering and applied sciences with management skills to create leaders in the growing technology sector and elsewhere. In the 1990s, M&T was renamed after Jerome Fisher, the founder of shoe retailer The Nine West Group and a graduate of Wharton's Class of 1953. Fisher endowed $5.5 million to the program, which now admits fifty-five undergraduates annually.

The M&T program was a natural fit with the university's advances in computer science and other technology. Penn had been a leader in the technological revolution since Penn's Moore School of Electrical Engineering, in collaboration with the U.S. Army, had brought to life the world's first general-purpose electronic computer in 1946. The Electronic Numerical Integrator and Computer, known as ENIAC, was a hefty precursor to today's computers, incorporating more than 17,000 vacuum tubes, weighing more than thirty tons and costing nearly $500,000 to build. By the late 1950s, the Wharton School was increasingly using Penn's computing might in its own research, particularly for data analysis and processing, and eventually for economic modeling. By the 1970s, Wharton became a leader in the use of heuristics, a method of problem solving that uses trial and error to solve a range of complicated problems. (Heuristics is now widely used to root out and identify computer viruses.)

As Wharton continued to augment its program offerings, it attracted even more students. The MBA program had expanded rapidly after the opening of Vance Hall in 1972, which physically separated the graduate and undergraduate programs and allowed the school to accommodate hundreds more graduate students. In 1981–Wharton's one hundredth birthday–the school had begun renovations on Dietrich Hall. They built an annex in front of the building, naming it Steinberg Hall after Saul Steinberg, a Wharton alumnus and former CEO of insurer Reliance Group Holdings, who had made his riches leasing computers to IBM in the 1960s. (When Reliance went bankrupt in 2001, Steinberg's fortunes were greatly diminished.)

Renovations on Steinberg Hall–Dietrich Hall, or "Steiny-D," were completed in 1983, the same year that Wharton's dean, Russell E. Palmer, introduced the "Plan for Preeminence," a five-year project designed to further bolster Wharton's faculty and improve the quality of admissions applicants across Wharton's undergraduate, graduate, PhD and executive education programs. During this time, Wharton continued to integrate its teachings with Penn's other disciplines and launched a program in international management for MBA students that combined the study of economics with those of languages, international culture and politics. Leonard and Ronald Lauder funded the Lauder Institute of Management and International Studies in honor of their father, Joseph, who founded the Estée Lauder cosmetics company with his wife, Estée. As part of the program's curriculum, students spend at least two months abroad. (A decade later in 1994, a similar program called the Huntsman Program in International Studies and Business was initiated for undergraduates). Wharton erected a 30,000-square-foot building called Lauder-Fischer Hall in 1990 to house the international studies program as well as the Wharton Real Estate Department, which had been founded in 1983. (In 1998, real estate titan Samuel Zell–who isn't a Wharton alum–would give the department a $10 million permanent endowment, and the center was renamed the Samuel Zell and Robert Lurie Real Estate Center).

Outside the confines of Penn, the booming markets of the 1980s heralded a period of mass consolidation among prominent corporations that many described as "merger mania." Hospitals, publishing houses, banks, airlines ... it seemed as though no industry could escape the wave of consolidation that occurred during the decade. Many of these mergers and acquisitions were financed through leveraged buyouts, in which a company acquires another company with borrowed funds such as bonds, and uses their assets as collateral for those loans in the hope that future cash flows will pay them off. Many of the bonds used for the transactions in the 1980s were risky, high-yield junk bonds. Bankers would barely touch junk bonds in the past, given the fact that they were at a high risk for default. But in the late 1970s, these bonds became a prevalent (and inventive) way to raise capital. The move to adopt them as a financial tool was spearheaded by a Wharton MBA from the class of 1969 named Michael Milken and the firm that he worked for, Drexel Burnham Lambert.

Even though there was a flurry of activity on Wall Street and in the corporate boardrooms, working at an investment bank had been something few Wharton students embraced in the early 1980s. Instead, pursuing a concentration in accounting was all the rage. The Big Eight accounting firms were seen as the kings of the financial services industry, and business students everywhere were clamoring to get their foot in the door at an Arthur Young or an Ernst & Whinney. They also looked to the big conglomerates that were in need of number crunchers, such as General Electric. As the mass consolidation hit Corporate America and continued into the early 1990s, the accounting firms, with fewer clients to audit, followed suit. The Big Eight has since become the Big Four. As the 1980s wore on, these firms were still considered beneficial to have on one's résumé, but the number of jobs that they could offer young recruits fresh out of Wharton had dwindled, as had their prestige, at least in comparison to banking and brokerage opportunities.

But the charms of Wall Street would wane significantly on October 19, 1987, when the Dow Jones Industrial Average fell 508 points on a day now known as "Black Monday." The Index lost twenty-three percent, almost twice the percentage lost in the crash of 1929. Adding to the banking world's shrinking reputation was the downfall of the "junk bond king" and his court. In 1990, Michael Milken pled guilty to securities fraud and related charges and was sentenced to ten years in prison (the term was later reduced to two years' jail time and three years' probation).

"There was a picture of Milken in Steiny-D. It was actually removed," recalls Navin Valrani, a Class of 1993 grad who remembers that, for a time, the "Decade of Greed" had left a bad taste in people's mouths about bankers and the industry they worked in. "A lot of people [at Wharton] were doing accounting and management. They were looking for something more secure."

In 1994, Judith Rodin became president and CEO of Penn, and soon initiated a series of revitalization plans that would shape the university and Wharton as it entered the twenty-first century. Formerly the provost of Yale University, Rodin's new role at Penn made her the first female president of an Ivy League institution. (A 1966 graduate of Penn's College of Women, Rodin was also the first Penn alum to be elected president of the school.) During her administration, Rodin unveiled a series of programs designed to improve the long-strained relations between the university and its West Philadelphia neighbors; renovate and expand the school's buildings, programs, and services; create jobs; and improve the university's finances. As a result, crime rates dropped dramatically and hundreds of new jobs were created in the University City area. For students living on campus, the College House System at Penn was revamped to include more faculty-in-residence, and the eleven newly renovated College Houses offered expanded ameni- ties such as game rooms and darkrooms.

As the campus environs improved, so did Penn's reputation. From the time Rodin took over, Penn's position in the *U.S. News & World Report* rankings of major research universities climbed from sixteenth to fourth place by 2002 (it has been in the top five ever since). Annual fund-raising had almost quadrupled to more than $400 million a year and, with the aid of better investment management, the school's endowment had more than tripled to $3.5 billion by 2003. More money meant better facilities and the ability to attract better faculty and, with a ranking that was only surpassed by names like Harvard, Princeton and Yale, Penn was able to be more selective about the students it admitted. Since 1993, the number of applicants has risen thirty-seven percent to more than 18,000. The school cut in half the percentage of appli- cants admitted and increasingly became the first-choice university for many top students. Average SAT scores also have risen from around 1340 in 1993 to 1412 in 2003.

Following suit, Wharton also began receiving a record number of applicants and became increasingly selective throughout the 1990s. The size of Wharton's faculty has grown from 174 in 1990 to more than 260 members today, making it one of the largest business-school faculties in the world. Endowments have also reached an all-time high as alumni grow more generous. And while Penn was ranked as the fourth- or fifth-best university in the country, Wharton was consistently in first place for its undergraduate business program. Much of this success and growth was due to the enterprising efforts of Wharton dean Thomas P. Gerrity, who, like Rodin, led a restructuring effort throughout the 1990s.

The former CEO and cofounder of an information systems and management consultancy called Index Group (the company was later bought by Computer Sciences Corp. in 1988), Gerrity's management expertise, as well as his technological background, helped him transform Wharton's programs during a decade of great change and innovation. Named to the post in the early 1990s, Gerrity set about revamping the undergraduate and MBA programs at the school, with a focus on business ethics and management. As a reflection of the growing globalization of business, as well as the growing influence of technology on the business world, he added online learning programs and launched Wharton executive education programs around the world.

Gerrity spent the early part of his tenure preparing Wharton students to enter this newly defined world by providing them with classes that would arm them with the tools to successfully navigate it, building upon an initiative that was spearheaded by his predecessor, Russell E. Palmer, who served as dean until 1990. In 1988, Palmer initiated a survey 300 CEOs about the changing needs of Corporate America and the skills that were essential for students to learn before entering the working world. The survey not only helped the school determine what areas it was lacking in, but also started a tradition of turning to executives to discover the changing needs of the corporate world.

When Gerrity became dean, he took the changes that Palmer had made at the school one step further and fully revamped Wharton's curriculum for the first time since the 1960s. Gerrity hired a firm to survey students about their level of satisfaction with various aspects of the school, including what types of classes they wanted to see added to the curriculum and ways to improve teaching. (To this day, students work closely with the faculty and administration to continually reinvent the school's curriculum and improve its environs.) The surveys resulted in a program that approached business education as an integrated series of skills that build upon one another. It was then that the beginnings of Wharton's "core" curriculum came into being. Gerrity, who believed that business school students should master management skills as much as they master high finance, endorsed the creation of new classes such as Management 100. To keep up with the changing technological needs of businesses, OPIM was created, training students in Excel, Visual Basic programming languages and other types of database management tools heavily relied upon at investment banks, consultancies and corporations. More hands-on field assignments were added, and professors were increasingly held to task by their students. Overseeing the changes in the curriculum at the undergraduate level was Janice R. Bellace, the vice dean of Wharton's undergraduate division from 1990 to 1994. Bellace, who is currently both a legal studies professor and management professor at Wharton, not only advocated the training of leadership skills, but also wanted to prepare Wharton's undergrads for the global economy by implementing a mandatory foreign language requirement and helping to establish—and later run—the Huntsman Program for International Studies and Business.

When the economy started picking up in the mid to late 1990s, concentrations in finance and entrepreneurial management, with all of their promise of power and the American dream, quickly became intoxicating to many Wharton students. Investment banks were prospering, raking in billions of dollars in fees for huge mergers and acquisitions. Technology and telecom stocks were going through the roof, and the investment banks were at the ready to underwrite their initial public offerings, many of which saw their stocks soar one hundred percent or higher the day they started trading. Some of these companies had garnered $1 billion market caps even though they hadn't yet turned a profit. By the late 1990s, upper-level bankers were taking home multimillion-dollar bonuses at the end of the year. The industry had become sexier than ever.

Adding to the banks' already euphoric times was a move by Federal Reserve chairman Alan Greenspan that changed the provisions of the Glass-Steagall Act, effectively more than doubling the percentage of revenue that could stem from securities at a commercial bank to twenty-five percent. The increase sparked mass amalgamation and expansion among banks that would greatly accelerate in a few years when, in 1999, Congress determined that the Glass-Steagall protections were no longer necessary. In its place came the Gramm-Leach-Bliley Act, which threw out the Glass-Steagall restrictions limiting relationships between commercial and investment banks and opened the way for banks to provide a host of services.

As a result, a bout of multibillion-dollar mergers between the banks ensued. In 1997, Morgan Stanley bought retail brokerage house Dean Witter, along with its Discover credit card business, for $10 billion. (In April 2005, Morgan Stanley announced plans to spin off Discover Financial Services.) Financial giant Citigroup was borne out of the $48 billion merger between Citibank and Travelers Group, which owned investment-banking outfit Salomon Smith Barney. Switzerland's banking behemoth UBS AG bought the 121-year-old investment bank PaineWebber for $12 billion, creating one of the world's largest private-banking companies. Another Swiss bank, Credit Suisse First Boston, bought U.S. investment house Donaldson, Lufkin & Jenrette for more than $12 billion in November 2000. And Chase Manhattan swallowed up the esteemed white-shoe investment bank of JP Morgan for $33 billion a few weeks later.

During this time, the bar for starting one's own company, especially in the technology sector, had been lowered significantly as eager venture capitalists funded start-ups at a record rate, hoping to stumble upon the next Amazon or eBay. Some Wharton students founded their own companies–and secured financing–straight out of college. Many others opted to work for companies that were only months old and held the promise of making them rich with stock options.

For young entrepreneurs-to-be, Wharton introduced "The Wharton Business Plan Competition," which four years later, in 2002, garnered 180 submissions and attracted 200 venture capitalists looking for the next big thing. In 1999, Wharton added Internet entrepreneurship to its course listings, one of twenty entrepreneurship courses that the school offers each year.

Under Gerrity's watch, technological initiatives at the school also flourished. A group of Wharton MBAs created the first business school intranet called SPIKE, which allowed for access to the Internet, messaging and online student services, and would later add collaborative learning tools. The school's Computing Information Technology Department also unveiled WRDS (Wharton Research Data Services), an online system that provided Wharton students and faculty with financial information and research. So impressive was the array of information that WRDS accessed that fifty other business schools soon licensed the technology. In 1999, the school launched another information-chocked Web site called Knowledge@Wharton, which compiles in-depth financial news and research by Wharton faculty and students. (The site has more than 340,000 subscribers.)

Beyond the revamped and revolutionary curriculum at Wharton, perhaps the most visible of Gerrity's accomplishments was the amount of money he helped raise for the school during his tenure. By 2001, Wharton had garnered a total of $445.8 million in a seven-year fund-raising effort called "The Campaign for Sustained

Leadership," far surpassing an initial goal of raising $350 million for new facilities, academic programs, financial aid and faculty research. It was the largest fund-raising campaign in the business school's history, which not only helped pay for the $139.9 million Huntsman Hall, but also for six research centers and the creation of twenty-six endowed professorships, twenty-nine endowed MBA scholarships and 145 undergraduate scholarships.

Over the course of Wharton's 155-year history, the school's faculty has been lauded for its innovative approaches to economics and business education. Russian immigrant Simon Kuznets, a Wharton professor from 1931 to 1954, spent many of his years in the U.S. studying economic growth at the National Bureau of Economic Research. At Wharton, he taught economics and continued to research reliable methods for determining the gross national product by combining numerical data with innovative ideas about economic growth and social change. In 1971, Kuznets was awarded the Nobel Memorial Prize in Economics for his lifelong research.

Nine years later in 1980, Wharton professor Lawrence Klein was awarded the Nobel for his work in the field of econometrics, which combines mathematics with economic theories to forecast trends in things such as consumer spending, exports, and monetary supplies. In 1977, finance professor Jean Andrus Crockett became the first female to chair a Wharton department and later became the first woman to chair the Federal Reserve Board of Philadelphia.

Economist Jeremy Siegel, a finance professor at Wharton since 1976, is renowned for his ability to prognosticate stock trends. In 1994, *BusinessWeek* named him the best business school professor in the world. His bestselling book *Stocks for the Long Run* has become an investing bible to many. Such is Siegel's reputation that he commands up to $20,000 for keynote speaking engagements.

Knowing that they have access to one of Wall Street's great minds, Wharton students flock to Siegel's class, which today is a multimedia spectacle complete with Bloomberg terminals and stock tickers. It's rumored that some students who aren't enrolled in his class sneak into his lectures to hear what investments he will discuss that day and then run out of the room to act on his advice. "He's amazingly popular. Everyone sees him on CNBC and any cable news network that covers the stock market," said one student who tried but couldn't gain admission into Siegel's class. "For the first two weeks there are probably fifteen or twenty [extra] people trying to get in the class."

Siegel is only one of Wharton's many esteemed faculty members. The school hosts an influential lot of academicians who have advised on major government economic initiatives, sat on the boards of some of the world's largest corporations, given expert testimony in groundbreaking court trials, and shared their knowledge across the globe. They are also the most published group of professors at any business school.

But perhaps Wharton's greatest claim to fame is its ability to consistently churn out some of the most prominent business leaders in the country from its 77,000 alumni, 41,500 of which were in Wharton's undergraduate program. The school was the stomping ground for such business magnates as real estate mogul Donald Trump, who built his fortunes in Manhattan properties such as the Trump Tower and Atlantic City casinos such as the Trump Taj Mahal. One of the most recognizable billionaires in the world, Trump recently became the coproducer and star of his own hit reality television show, *The Apprentice*. (Trump's oldest son, Don, graduated from Wharton and his daughter Ivanka is a member of Wharton's Class of 2004). Other prominent Wharton alumni include Wall Street heavyweights Michael Tarnopol, the vice chairman of Bear Stearns & Co., and Brian Finn, the president of Credit Suisse First Boston. Investment guru Peter Lynch earned an MBA at Wharton and went on to manage Fidelity Investments' Magellan Fund from 1977 to 1990. In that time, his fund had a 2,700 percent return, making him an all-star investor by anyone's standard. Brian Roberts was a graduate of Wharton's Class of 1981 who went to work for the small cable business that his father, Ralph (also a Wharton graduate) had founded. Now the business—Comcast Corp.—is the nation's largest cable company, employing more than 55,000 people. Once he began to run the show in 1990, Roberts became known for taking the cable industry by storm, convincing Microsoft's Bill Gates to invest $1 billion in his company, and buying up AT&T's struggling cable TV assets.

The power and influence of Wharton's alumni are woven into the fabric of the school and are evident just by reading a campus map. Penn's 269-acre campus is dotted with buildings named after those who, more often than not, had some affiliation with Wharton, whether it was the graduate school or the undergraduate program. The epicenter of campus for most students, Perelman Quad, is named after 1964 Wharton grad Ronald Perelman (who also received an MBA there in 1966), a self-made billionaire and a corporate raider who took control of cosmetics maker Revlon, among other companies. The generosity of alumni made rich off the opportunities that Wharton helped afford them is also evident in new buildings such as the David Pottruck Health and Fitness Center, the bulk of which was paid for by Pottruck himself, a graduate of the College who went on to receive an MBA from Wharton in 1972. Twenty-five years after he was awarded his diploma, Pottruck attained the enviable and lucrative post of President and CEO of Charles Schwab, a financial services outfit known for revolutionizing online trading in the 1990s (he has since resigned from the post). Pottruck's massive fitness complex, which is open to all of Penn's students, rivals most of Manhattan's elite private health clubs. The center boasts a rock-climbing wall, a pro shop, a juice bar and an indoor swimming pool so large that it fills the noses of those walking across the street with the smell of chlorine.

The current chapter of Wharton's history is being written under new leadership and in an era of financial uncertainty and weakened confidence in both Corporate America and Wall Street. The tech bubble burst in 2000, causing hundreds of thousands of people to lose their jobs, especially in the technology and financial services industries (both of which have traditionally hired scores of Penn students). The impact of the spiraling stock market was compounded by a slew of corporate scandals and the September 11 terrorist attacks. Penn lost sixteen of its alumni in those attacks, ten of whom had graduated from Wharton. Recruiting on campus waned through 2002, and some companies abandoned on-campus recruiting altogether. As bonuses became skimpier, students became increasingly nervous about being able to find their place in the business world postgraduation.

Leading Wharton through these times is Dean Patrick Harker, who, in 1984, became the youngest faculty member to receive an endowed professorship in the history of the Wharton School. Harker was appointed dean of the business school in 2000 when he was forty-one years old and, as dean, he has focused his attentions on the integration of technology and learning, further expanding upon the software simulations used in Wharton's classes, as well as e-learning initiatives. He has also sought to expand Wharton's reach beyond the boundaries of Philadelphia.

In 2001, Wharton opened its first satellite campus outside of Philadelphia, offering an MBA program for executives in downtown San Francisco. The center's executive education programs expanded on the school's long history of teaching mid-career executives the ins and outs of a changing business environment and economy. Wharton now offers more than 200 executive education programs, enrolling close to 10,000 executives each year. Harker has also forged an alliance with France's prestigious business school, INSEAD. The two schools have joined forces to share resources, conducting joint research and faculty exchanges. They also allow graduate and PhD students to take classes at both Wharton's Philadelphia and San Francisco campuses, as well as at INSEAD's campuses in France and Singapore.

As for the university, plans for expansion are being laid out by the school's new president, Dr. Amy Gutmann, a former provost and political science professor from Princeton. Like past leaders of Penn and Wharton before them, Gutmann and Harker are leading a new generation of students and faculty through the boom-and-bust cycles of Wall Street and beyond. As in the past, new leaders of business and finance are emerging from the ranks of Wharton's recent alumni—perhaps some of these new stars will rise from the Class of 2004.

PART III

THE RUNNING
OF THE BULLS

CHAPTER SIX

HEDGING IN AUTUMN

During the late summer months, hundreds of birds flock to Penn's campus from unknown parts to take up temporary residence in its tree-lined landscape as they begin their migration south. A virtual arboretum, the main east-west thoroughfares of Penn's campus were named by Philadelphia's founder, William Penn, for the trees indigenous to the area: chestnut, walnut, spruce and locust. At the heart of Penn's campus is the brickwork avenue called Locust Walk, a four-block stretch of Locust Street that has been closed to traffic since the 1960s. Here, the foliage juxtaposes with the stone-and-brick facades of Penn's buildings and underscores the feeling that one is treading upon an Ivy League campus. As autumn takes hold and brings a tinge of chill to the air, Penn looks even more regal, as the campus becomes hued with tints of burnt orange, amber and gold.

The changing of the seasons was something that took Grace Yoon a few years to get used to. Originally from Los Angeles, Grace grew up in Southern California's endless sunshine. After living in West Philadelphia for three years, Grace had more or less accepted Philadelphia's changing seasons, even autumn's slow decline into the grayness of winter. For Grace, the most difficult differences to overcome while establishing her new life were cultural. There was a different pace here, a different mind-set.

"Everyone on the East Coast is so driven," said Grace, a petite Korean-American with raven-colored layers of hair framing her round face. "My first impression walking down Locust Walk was that everyone was looking straight ahead and walking fast. I walk briskly, but they were *passing* me."

It was an alienating feeling for a freshman just starting out at school and acclimating to a new lifestyle, a new geography and new friends. Most of the friends she had grown up with chose to stay close to home and attend school in California. When Grace started taking classes at Wharton, she sometimes wondered if she had made the right choice. She had been turned off by some of her Wharton classmates and their bold, competitive spirits. In contrast, Grace has an unassuming nature and benevolence about her that defies Wharton stereotypes. She speaks softly and smiles often. Even when she is stressed out or in a bad mood, she doesn't raise her voice.

But like her fellow Wharton peers, what Grace does have is the prototypical Wharton type-A personality. She cared deeply about her grades and had long harbored a drive to succeed in almost everything she set out to do. In high school, Grace had been class president of her 760-person class for three out of four years (she chose not to run in her sophomore year). It was a major accomplishment, because her high school bused in kids from the inner city, making it a melting pot of ethnicities, social backgrounds and cliques that, for the most part, had voted for her.

By her senior year at Wharton, Grace would join her classmates on another front: She was consumed by thoughts of where the next few years and her career would take her. She had already tried on several hats and was anxious and a bit confused about what to do. Grace had spent her freshman-year summer as an intern at a movie production company, where the CFO taught her the ropes of the financial end of show business. In her sophomore year, Grace interned for a Morgan Stanley brokerage firm back home in L.A., spending the summer making cold calls and doing cost-basis analyses. And this past summer she gained marketing savvy at cosmetics maker L'Oréal, where the freebies and employee discounts on makeup and other products were an added bonus. Working in the brand-management department for L'Oréal's Garnier hair-coloring division, Grace spent the summer sitting in on strategy meetings and conducting research on the company's hair-color promotions, which she later presented to the Garnier team and Maybelline's human resources staff at the end of the summer. It had been a great experience, just as those in the previous summers were, but none of these posts were screaming out as lifetime careers to Grace.

At Wharton, there were kids in her classes who, as early as freshman year, knew exactly what they wanted to be doing postgraduation—and exactly who they wanted to work for. As the years passed, it seemed that more and more of her fellow students grew increasingly certain about where their futures would lead them. It was a constant reminder to Grace of her indecision.

"It seemed like everyone else had the investment-banking mentality," said Grace. "My professors were great, telling me there's a lot of opportunities out there. But the mentality persisted and the competition got more heated."

Grace was starting to take on some of that mentality, too—she knew she had to start focusing her career search soon. She didn't have much time to settle back into her apartment on campus and unpack her belongings from her summer internship before the recruiting season would be in full swing. Grace wasted no time sending her résumé to the Career Services office for some helpful hints and met with them to get some interviewing pointers. "They are helpful when you come to them," explained Grace. "But it's really for those people who are overachievers and who know what they want to work on."

In the early weeks of September, Grace embarked on a marathon of company information sessions held by investment banks, sometimes attending three a day. She thought the recruiters were nice and the sessions were informative, and she grew increasingly confident that she should play it safe and follow the same path as her peers, who were vigorously dropping their résumés with the Goldmans, Lehmans and Morgan Stanleys of the banking world. But for Grace, working at an investment bank wasn't really the most appealing option. She didn't like the idea of sacrificing her social life and regularly logging 80- to 100-hour workweeks. On the other hand, doing so would be a surefire way to get into top MBA programs such as Harvard's and Stanford's a few years down the road (she thought that she might consider Wharton again, too, mainly because of its "brand name").

As if to convince herself more than anyone else, Grace could rattle off a plethora of prototypical reasons to justify working at a bank–the skills one learns, the networking opportunities– justifications often used by Wharton students. But Grace ultimately admitted that banking wasn't something she felt passionate about. She wasn't sure exactly what it was she felt passionate about, really. Pursuing the well-heeled route of working for an investment bank seemed like the best option, or so she had been told. As if to further justify it and excuse the fact that she would be sacrificing the first part of her twenties if she chose to work at a bank, Grace proclaimed in a somewhat matter-of-fact tone: "Well, I can always do what I *want* to do later on in life."

By early October, as the initial rush of company information sessions at Penn began to wind down, students who had written and rewritten their résumés were sending them off to potential employers en masse. Grace had dropped her résumé with several investment banks, including Citigroup and Credit Suisse First Boston. She decided not to drop for the most competitive firms, but did limit herself to those that had good reputations–and, more importantly, those where she thought she stood a chance. Citigroup was competitive, but they were vast and hired a lot of analysts. So there was a good chance she could at least get invited to an interview. Just in case those didn't pan out, Grace sent résumés to American Express for a marketing position, as well as to PepsiCo–two of the largest corporate recruiters on campus.

Grace was also eagerly eyeing the consulting firms, but they weren't scheduled to do information sessions and accept résumés until after most of the first-round interviews for the investment banks had been doled out. Consulting was the second most popular career choice among Whartonites. About fifteen to twenty percent of Wharton students end up in the consulting industry, bringing in starting salaries ranging from $40,000 to $56,000, not including an average signing bonus of $5,000 to $10,000.

Young business analysts (or BAs, as they are called at many consultancies), work a lot of hours, but nowhere near the number that investment bankers do. And while BAs are in charge of analyzing statistical data from a corporate survey or some other research conducted by one of their teammates, they don't spend all of their time in front of a computer. The downside of the profession, though, is the travel that consulting requires. Often, BAs are part of a team assigned to a client on a project basis, and they must remain close to a client's site. Sometimes that means being away from home for as many as five days a week for months at a time. Each team works together on their client's particular issue in order to implement a solution or a new business plan. BAs are a large part of that process, and therefore teamwork, problem-solving skills, analytical prowess and spreadsheet literacy are qualities coveted by consulting recruiters.

At some firms, BAs do a lot of the research and analysis and barely interact with the client, whereas at other firms BAs meet with the clients (as a member of their team) early on. Most BAs will do everything from menial tasks such as making copies, to creating surveys or polls, to interviewing clients in order to ascertain the problems the company is having. Because they are assigned to different client projects every two to six months, consultants gain exposure to a variety of industries, broadening their experience and helping them establish a network of corporate contacts should they ever want to move to the other side of the table.

Grace had two consulting firms in mind: Bain & Co. and McKinsey. If Wharton students view Goldman Sachs as the holy grail of the investment-banking world, then McKinsey is the holy grail of the consulting world. Founded in 1926, the firm is a bellwether in the industry, catering to two-thirds of the companies in the Fortune 1000. A job with McKinsey can open a great many doors as well—seventy CEOs of major corporations in the Fortune 500 reportedly got their start at the firm.

Undergraduates who pass McKinsey's rigorous and complicated maze of interviews and tests are hired as business analysts. They serve as generalists at first, learning the ropes from consultants across a variety of industries or functions. As they gain more experience, they begin to specialize. Should they ever have a question, there are plenty of people to turn to. Mentoring at McKinsey is imperative; one would be hard-pressed to find an analyst without at least one mentor at McKinsey, if not several. Analysts tend to stay in their post for about two years before deciding whether to vie for a promotion to associate or enroll in graduate school. McKinsey manages to keep its ranks filled with intellectuals and multiple-degreed employees by sometimes providing school loans to those who want to attend an MBA program or law school. As at other consulting firms, should they return to the firm postgraduation and work there for a specific number of years, the loans are forgiven. Should they go elsewhere, their loans must be repaid on a pro-rata basis determined by the length of time they spent at the firm. This was a key perk that made McKinsey alluring to any Wharton student considering a career in consulting. To Grace, it seemed like everyone was applying to McKinsey—even those who didn't want to go into consulting. She considered getting a job there a long shot.

Even with all of the indecision and anxiety Grace had felt going into recruiting season, she was confident that she would get a job offer from L'Oréal. The offer wasn't formal yet, but it was pretty much understood that the folks she worked with at L'Oréal would reserve a place for her should she want it.

L'Oréal was "a good safety option," she would explain with a shrug. It made the arduous recruiting process she faced in the months ahead more manageable in Grace's eyes. She knew that no matter what happened, she would have at least one offer.

Shreevar Kheruka was facing an internal dilemma of his own heading into recruiting season. Following his internship as a summer analyst on the Fixed Income, Currencies and Commodities trading desk at Goldman Sachs, he had flown home to Bombay to visit his family in the weeks before classes started. While in India, he spoke with his grandfather and father about the glass-manufacturing business the family had run for decades. His family had sent Shreevar to school in the U.S. hoping he would return home after graduation armed with the skills to help run the company. But now Shreevar wanted to stay and get a couple of years of work experience in the U.S. before returning home. While he missed his family terribly, he enjoyed living in the States. At Penn, Shreevar had joined the Phi Sigma Kappa fraternity, where he made some of his closest college friends. He had even lived with the brothers in the frat house his junior year. (After suffering through his bout of malaria during the second semester of his junior year, his parents had insisted he spend his senior year living in a place with a real kitchen.)

Now back at Wharton, Shreevar was surrounded by friends who were consumed by the recruiting process and the fate of their futures. They talked about moving to New York City and sharing apartments with each other. Shreevar was torn.

"I have a lot of emotional pressure," he said. "I go home two or three times a year and my family is very close-knit." The guilt was compounded by the fact that his three sisters have married and moved away from home. Shreevar's seventy-four-year-old grandfather was still a very active part of the family business, clocking in nine to ten hours a day at the office, but he wanted to start thinking about retirement. "My granddad said to me recently, 'I don't have more than four years of working at this level anymore. I want to relax and I want to teach you as much as possible before that,'" recounted Shreevar.

When Shreevar did the math, he realized that staying in the U.S. for a few years after graduation might not fit into his grandfather's plan.

Some of Shreevar's friends at Wharton were dropping over a hundred résumés. Many of them hadn't gotten the internships that they had hoped for the previous summer and were worried it was going to happen again. "They're overcompensating," critiqued Shreevar. He was in a different boat, though. Whatever job he accepted would have to be worthy of disappointing his family. So Shreevar decided to drop résumés solely for companies that he'd really want to work for (although some of them advertised for "U.S. citizens only," Shreevar applied to them anyway). He knew he didn't want to be an investment banker. He didn't even apply for a post at Goldman Sachs, where he had interned.

"Putting in the long hours is fine if you're learning something, but spreadsheets and modeling? Doing that for two years isn't for me. I want to learn how companies work," he declared.

Goldman had invited him to their information session in early September. Getting invited to these events is usually a sign that a firm may want a particular student back in their ranks, but Shree-var still abstained from submitting his résumé. "Having the Gold-man Sachs name on my résumé [from his internship] and the contacts I made will be unbelievable," he said. "I don't think I'm giving up much at all."

More appealing to Shreevar was a career in consulting, venture capital or private equity. Consulting would give Shreevar exposure to a variety of industries. Plus, he would be working with a client for months, enough time to really learn about the business. He had similar notions about venture capital and private equity, both areas that focused on financing and building companies. By the end of September, Shreevar had dropped his résumé with a dozen companies.

If he got a job offer that he couldn't refuse, then he would just have to break the news to his family.

Jon Gantman was secretly holding out hope that the small busi-ness that he had dreamed up and was pursuing with four of his friends might get funding in the eleventh hour of his senior year and he wouldn't have to work for anyone. They had created a prospectus for a service that would deliver college necessities such as sheets and clock radios to students—items often forgotten when college kids move back into their dorms—and called the venture the "One Stop College Shop." While some would write off the endeavor as a pie-in-the-sky dream held by a bunch of twenty-one-year-old guys, Jon would quickly dispel any such notion by displaying a high level of passion and commitment to the enter-prise. With the help of an entrepreneurship class at Wharton, he and his friends had written business plans, created marketing ma-terials, and contacted suppliers. Jon was also seeking other ways to become an entrepreneur. He and a group of ten other guys—all Wharton students—were trying to organize regular meetings so they could brainstorm ideas for another possible business.

"I don't see us as your typical Wharton kids. We're not necessarily a Wharton crew," he said of the group. "Basically we're looking for anything that keeps us from doing a real job next year. If any ideas that we come across sound good, then we'll jump on it."

Even if the One Stop College Shop didn't take off or the new group didn't come up with an idea, Jon vowed that he wouldn't give up on his dreams of becoming an entrepreneur. "You're only one idea away from doing something great," he proclaimed. It was a mantra that Jon relied on heavily.

As the résumé-dropping season began, though, Jon still planned to play it safe, submitting his résumé to fifty-five companies through PennLink. Thinking it would be a good way to keep his mind open to new things, Jon applied to forty companies that he had never heard of before. They were companies that didn't require a cover letter, so Jon quickly shot his résumé off to them just to see if he could get invited to a first-round interview. The remaining fifteen companies were places at which Jon could possibly envision himself working someday. Unlike most of his Wharton friends, who were barraging the investment banks with their résumés, Jon was only dropping his at two—Lehman Brothers and Citigroup. He wasn't even sure if he would accept an interview with either of them if he were invited.

"Investment banking is a narrow skill set," he explained. "It's crunching numbers and modeling. You don't get what is behind the numbers you're analyzing. The bottom line is that what you're doing is just working with numbers. You can't see how they fit into the bigger picture. I personally feel that those numbers are worthless, especially with investment banking."

As Jon explained, his goal was simple: to find something he was passionate about. And he was disturbed that many of his Wharton peers didn't view the job-hunting process the same way he did.

Jessica Kennedy was dealing with a crisis. She had borrowed an internal Goldman Sachs handbook on valuations from a friend in order to get a leg up with the firm should she have an interview with them. The book was like a bible of investment banking that was considered priceless among Wharton students, especially to those who wanted to work for Goldman someday. Any extra insight into the company and how it operated could perhaps give her an added edge during the interview process. Jessica's plan had been to review the important pages and then return the book to her friend. Before leaving Steiny-D, Jessica quickly checked her e-mail at one of the Internet stations, leaving her belongings on the floor and placing the thick book on top of the computer monitor. Realizing she had very little time to make a meeting, Jessica hurriedly logged off and grabbed her bag, leaving Steiny-D and the book behind. After walking a few blocks, Jessica realized what she had done, and darted back to the computer she had used. It had only been a matter of minutes, but the book was already gone.

"They stole it! Can you believe that someone would steal this book from another person?" she asked, exasperated.

Jessica felt terrible. Not only did she miss out on the opportunity for the inside scoop on Goldman, but her friend who had trusted her with the book would, too. It was a bad start to the recruiting season, but luckily Jessica was one of the Wharton students who didn't really need an added edge. Her academic record and experience at Lazard would be proof enough. Jessica was also the exception to the rule when it came to students who pursue investment banking purely for the sake of following the herd or the pursuit of riches. She really *enjoyed* investment banking.

Jessica is the epitome of the overachieving Whartonite. She was a finance concentration, a member of the Joseph Wharton Scholars honors program, held the prestigious post of vice president of corporate relations for Wharton Women and was well on her way to graduating summa cum laude, an honor only the top five percent of the class receives. Most importantly, though, Jessica loves Wharton. "Wharton fits me perfectly. I will be involved with this school forever," she exclaimed. "I'm very career-focused," she said, sipping on the grande nonfat latte she loves to drink at Starbucks. "Even more than most Wharton students, if you can believe it."

Ironically, Jessica began her studies at Penn in the premed program, with the hope of becoming a surgeon. But she was soon deterred by the lack of control that medical professionals had with insurance companies and, at times, their patients. While researching the career path in high school, she heard about surgeons declaring bankruptcy and nurse managers having to kick patients out of the ICU because their insurance wouldn't cover their bills.

"I didn't want to go to school and be completely powerless," explained Jessica. During her first year in the premed program, Jessica aced her classes, earning a perfect 4.0 both semesters. Yet, she couldn't help but be lured in by the intensity of the business students enrolled in Wharton and transferred into the program her sophomore year. "I wanted to push myself and make it matter. I didn't want to be restrained by the restrictions in place," she said.

Jessica did have some reservations about the switch at first. She was well aware of the prejudices that students at Penn's other schools held about Whartonites. Basically, they thought that Wharton students believed they were better than everyone else. "I also thought: 'Am I going to sacrifice a college experience? Did I want to be in Wharton where it was allegedly a lot of hard work and cutthroat and competitive?'" she recalled. "But in the end, it was perfect. I got here and it was smaller [than the College] and people were so diverse, but we were so similar in personality."

Jessica's soon adopted a new career goal: to become a vice president of an investment bank by the age of twenty-seven (or perhaps twenty-eight). "I think we need a woman who loves investment banking. I want to be the first woman to run mergers and acquisitions at some large bank," she proclaimed. "A lot of people will say that I'm being unrealistic. I'm not just looking for the next step. I do it because that is what's driving me."

During her junior year, Jessica had considered applying for Wharton's sub-matriculation program, which awards a few exceptional Wharton students who opt to stay an extra year with both a bachelor's and an MBA degree. But Jessica was in a hurry to get her hands dirty at a bank, and she already felt that the years she spent at Wharton were business education enough. Plus, she wouldn't have her stellar grades to show off on her résumé if she enrolled in the sub-matric program. (Wharton, like other top MBA programs including Harvard and Stanford, has a policy of grade non-disclosure with recruiters). It was one more reason to start her career as soon as possible. "I didn't want to work as hard as I did to go to a mediocre investment bank," she explained.

From her time at Lazard, Jessica knew well the personal sacrifices that investment banking entailed, especially in the first few years as an analyst. She could have taken it easier over the summer, but she was determined to make a good impression. "I took a half day off this summer," she said proudly. "I mean, you need this opportunity to prove that you can do it. I'm not going to cut out early to meet friends for a drink. I'm just not going to do that."

Through not-so-subtle hints from her summer colleagues, Jessica knew that she was soon going to get a job offer from Lazard. She had really liked the intimacy of a smaller boutique bank that Lazard engendered—her analyst class over the summer had been about a quarter of the size of analyst classes at the big bulge-bracket banks. But she also wanted to make sure that Lazard was the best of all possible options, and there were other top-notch banks that Jessica wanted to explore. Jessica submitted her résumé to a handful of them: top bulge-bracket firms such as Goldman and Morgan Stanley, and other boutiques like Gleacher Partners.

The smaller investment houses such as Gleacher Partners, Roth-schild and The Blackstone Group hired only the best Wharton students, and they tended to pay analysts more handsomely than the larger banks. Jessica was also taking a shot at private-equity positions for JPMorgan Partners and Blackstone. Entry-level posts in private equity are almost always awarded to people who have attained the level of associate after two or more years as an ana-lyst at an investment bank first; a rare few talented undergrads are bestowed the honor.

By mid-September, Lazard extended a formal offer to Jessica.

"It's one thing to hope for the best; it's another to have an offer letter with numbers," she would write in an e-mail. All of a sud-den all of the other prestigious firms didn't seem as appealing. With Lazard's offer in hand, Jessica knew fairly well that her deci-sion was already made. "No firm has everything, but Lazard is a place that has close to everything," Jessica said.

While other Wharton students were going through mental pros-and-cons lists about the companies they were submitting their résumés to, Shimika Wilder had the peace of mind that most other Wharton students wouldn't feel until well into the recruit-ing process. After spending two summers interning at Goldman Sachs, she had earned herself a full-time job offer at the bank.

"I bypassed the whole recruiting process," she said with a tone of relief. "I didn't go on any on-campus interviews."

It was a Monday in early September when Shimika received the news. By Thursday, her summer internship manager was call-ing her to ask if she had made a decision yet. Shimika knew that recruiters for Goldman were pressed to get a fast response. Many of the other banks had extended "exploding offers" to their sum-mer interns, and Goldman wanted a shot at interviewing these students before they accepted an offer from another bank. That meant the bank had to act swiftly, and to do so would require knowing how many full-time posts it would actually have available to offer.

It didn't take Shimika long to accept, but she did wonder whether she had limited her options by solely pursuing banking throughout her college career. There were the tradeoffs that investment banking entailed. The cost of living in New York was one of them, and the one-hundred-hour workweeks that she would be spending in the office were an even bigger one. But Shimika soon came up with a litany of reasons why she should stick with banking, one of which was the power it would bestow upon her.

"Investment banking is unparalleled in terms of the amount of responsibility you get a such a young age," she said. "Plus there's an adrenaline rush. I want to pick up the *Wall Street Journal* one day and see a deal that I did."

Ultimately, her decision was based on what working at a bank like Goldman Sachs could do for her résumé. Shimika knew that she didn't want to be a banker for life—the work-life imbalance that investment banking entails wasn't something she wanted to endure for too long. She had dreams of going into sports and entertainment law someday, perhaps becoming a sports agent like the one Tom Cruise played in the movie *Jerry Maguire*. Working at Goldman Sachs for a few years would not only carry a lot of weight with potential employers down the road, but it would be a surefire way to get into a prestigious law school as well.

"I want to pay off my loans, and banking will jumpstart my career. I can go anywhere afterward," explained Shimika. "So it's really not *why*, but *why not*."

After accepting Goldman's offer, Shimika had the luxury of turning her attentions to her schoolwork and possibly start studying for the LSATs, the entrance exam to law school that she knew she wouldn't have enough time for once she started working at Goldman.

Anthony Sandrik was taking it easy, too. But it wasn't because he had landed a job offer. Anthony just knew what he wanted. He liked the fast-paced environment of the sales and trading floors, which were filled with younger guys who Anthony knew would be a lot of fun to work with. He also liked the idea of formulating trading strategies based on current events and market-moving news, whether it was business, politics or even the weather. The hours traders work were another plus: they don't have to work on the weekends.

"With trading you come to the office at 8:00, you work your ass off and then you're done at 4:00," he said with a shrug. The work would be intense, but having more predictable hours and free time than investment bankers was a big selling point for him. "I don't know what kind of person is attracted to investment banking," Anthony said. "You're sacrificing your entire social life for it. For some people they do it for two years and then they move onto something else. It prepares them for other careers. But it's just not something I want to do."

The only problem with the sales and trading post that Anthony coveted was that not many banks were advertising slots on their trading floors during the recruiting season. In some ways, it made recruiting easier for him because he had so few options, but Anthony grew concerned that he might be limiting himself too much. Everyone else seemed to be hedging their bets by dropping dozens of résumés, but Anthony stuck to his guns, submitting résumés to only a handful of companies, all of which were in sales and trading posts. So far, the traditionally hectic recruiting season was proving to be a breeze.

While Regi Vengalil was still interested in joining the Peace Corps, he decided to look elsewhere for a fulfilling postgraduation plan. On his own initiative, Regi sent his résumé to the World Bank and was considering doing the same with the International Monetary Fund, neither of which recruited undergrads on campus. Regi was torn about applying to the IMF, though. He wasn't a big fan of their fiscal austerity programs with developing nations, which he said sometimes caused worse swings in countries undergoing economic crises. He felt the World Bank was doing a greater good with its development programs, which emphasized local investment and sustainable growth. He weighed the two in his head and debated them with his friends.

"One of my friends characterized it as the Martin Luther King versus the Thurgood Marshall approach," he said, implying that one could work outside the system to change it like King, or do so from the inside like Marshall. "There's definitely virtue in both styles. That was my compromise with the IMF. I could be an agent of change."

Even with his optimism, Regi realized that he was a far cry from the people who are usually hired by places like the IMF. They usually have graduate degrees, in particular PhDs.

The other, more realistic option that appealed to Regi was working in a public-finance division at one of the investment banks. Public-finance jobs are far from glamorous–their clients are not Fortune 500 firms trying to take each other over but instead cities and municipalities that need to obtain financing for major public works projects such as building toll roads, stadiums, schools or hospitals. They are deals that rarely make front-page headlines. Only five of the banks had public-finance posts listed with OCRS. Regi dropped his résumé to all of them–Citigroup, UBS Warburg, Bank One, Lehman Brothers and Morgan Stanley.

"I'm kind of worried that I won't find anything," said Regi. "I know people applying for everything, even if they don't want the job. I know someone who got an interview with Citigroup and I didn't. They didn't necessarily want to do public finance–they just wanted a job. It's embodied in the Wharton education. If you don't know what you want to do, you go for the security blanket. It's all about hedging."

As the recruiting season progressed, Regi began hedging a little, too. In addition to the public-finance posts, he sent a résumé to Microsoft, mainly because the software giant's Redmond, Washington, headquarters were close to his parents' home in Seattle. No matter what the outcome of his job search, Regi still clung to the hope that he would do something that would make a difference. He spoke about working in public policy for a few years, then perhaps pursuing a PhD in political economy. At times it seemed that the sky was the limit for Regi. That is, until the tensions of the recruiting season brought him back down to earth.

"Everyone is just so focused on finding a job right now," he would say as the leaves began to fall on Locust Walk in early October. "People are nervous. They are keeping all of their cards close. No one wants to appear worse than their peers."

CHAPTER SEVEN

WITS AND NERVES

Sitting in his first interview with one of the top bulge-bracket banks, Regi Vengalil's hands were shaking. He kept them under the table so the two recruiters sitting across from him wouldn't notice. One of the recruiters was an analyst, not more than a year or two older than Regi, who had graduated from Penn. The other interviewer was a vice president who Regi immediately hit it off with. They broke the ice when the VP said he had heard of Regi's small Catholic high school in Seattle.

Regi's nervousness wasn't for lack of knowledge. His mind is like a sponge that soaks in, comprehends and retains vast amounts of information, especially numbers. Yet Regi is far from pretentious about his intelligence. At one point during his interview, the recruiter asked him to pick which bond he would choose if he had a 9.9 percent taxable bond and a 6 percent tax-exempt bond in a 40 percent tax bracket. Without the aid of pen and paper, Regi immediately knew the answer.

"The tax-exempt bond," he replied, proceeding to logically explain the reasoning involved in coming to the decision. For a taxable bond to pay the same interest as the tax-exempt bond in a 40 percent tax bracket, the yield would have to be 10 percent. The slightly lower taxable yield told him the tax-exempt bond was better. "Because you put a 10 percent equivalent taxable yield on the tax-exempt bond and you don't have to pay taxes on it," he reasoned. The interviewer was stunned. Little did he know that Regi had coincidentally gone over a quite similar scenario in his head earlier in the day in preparation for the interview.

"It was one of those times when you know that you nailed it," Regi would say later, bursting with pride.

The other questions weren't as technical. Regi was asked to give his definition of public finance and to explain why he was interested in the field. This was a no-brainer. He had thought long and hard about what he wanted to do, and public finance was one of the leading and most tangible options. It was the perfect mix of the skills he learned in college and the goals he had set for himself. "It has the intellectual rigor of the banking environment, but it also has the sociopolitical and regulatory framework," Regi explained to the interviewer. He was on a roll.

When one of the recruiters requested that he "list five of his strengths and five of his weaknesses," Regi embarked on an uncharacteristically self-promoting sales pitch to convince them that he was the most worthy candidate. At first, Regi listed archetypal reasons why he would be an asset to the firm: his analytical and quantitative skills, his work ethic, and a strong interest in public finance. But it was the last attribute that Regi listed that really caught the attention of his interviewers.

Referring to the lung collapses he suffered in both his sophomore and junior years, Regi added, "My resilience. I've been through hell. I know what hard times are and I know that I can get through it."

"Enough said," the vice president told Regi.

The interview lasted close to forty minutes, almost twenty minutes longer than the normal limit. Regi didn't even have enough time to ask his own questions. It was a good sign. He was feeling more confident, especially in his ability to sell himself.

"I came out at peace with myself this weekend. I did the best I could," he said afterward.

A week later, Regi was invited back for a second-round interview with the bank. Regi thought it helped that his job search was so focused. It had surprised the recruiters when they learned he was only applying to jobs in public finance.

"So if this works out, then maybe the other stuff will work out, too. I was so worried about dropping only for public finance that I thought about dropping for consulting," said Regi, relieved.

He had already given up on the World Bank, and his interest in joining the Peace Corps was waning. Now that he was fully in the thrall of the recruiting process on campus, he had little time to pursue other options anyway.

First-round interviews, especially for the investment banks, usually take place on Penn's campus from late September to mid October. For students who didn't intern at the firm they are vying to meet with, this is their first opportunity to make an impression on recruiters beyond their résumé. They will eagerly log onto Penn-Link's Web site at 3:00 A.M. just to check and see (for probably the tenth time that day) whether they have been invited to an interview or not. If they get the interview, they want to accept it immediately and set up the most coveted time slot—not too early in the day or during an important lecture—before some other interviewee snags it.

Soon after they arrive to these half-hour "screening" interviews, some students end up feeling as though they are undergoing an interrogation rather than participating in a getting-to-know-you chat. The investment-bank interviews are usually conducted by two employees of the bank in a small windowless room close to the Career Services offices. There is often one younger banker, such as an analyst or an associate (usually a recent graduate from Wharton), and one more seasoned executive from the bank, such as a vice president or director. One former Wharton student, who went through scores of investment-bank interviews her senior year, said she was once tag-teamed as soon as she walked in the door for an interview with a bank. As she took her seat, she was greeted with the question, "What's sixty-six times sixty-six?" Scrambling to calculate it in her head, she came up with the answer only to face a litany of more heady, hard-core finance questions that involved calculating corporate valuations.

Students can sometimes log in as many as eight to ten half-hour interviews with recruiters in one day. The sheer number of hours they spend interviewing is so overwhelming that it soon becomes hard to keep the firms' names straight. And in some cases they don't, almost immediately losing all chances for an invite back to a second-round interview. The pressure of recruiting season brings out the best and worst qualities in Wharton students. Sometimes, the crazed pursuit of the perfect job can cause embarrassing lapses in judgment.

A well-known anecdote at Wharton is one of a senior who landed an interview with his first-choice investment bank. The meeting was scheduled at the same time as one of his midterm exams. Distraught about the overlap, the student composed a lengthy e-mail to his professor telling him that he should show him some mercy because an interview like the one he landed was the whole reason anyone attends Wharton, or the professor's class for that matter, in the first place. The student's e-mail continued on to say that this was his once-in-a-lifetime chance and the opportunity he'd been waiting for all of his life. In his feverish state, the student inadvertently sent the e-mail to the class mailing list rather than the professor. His fellow classmates promptly forwarded and distributed the e-mail among their friends on Wall Street. The electronic accident soon turned the student into the butt of several jokes and a pariah on the Street. "This is what everybody tries to live down from the day we walk onto campus," confessed a Wharton grad from the Class of 2000, who was one of the recipients of the e-mail. "A lot of people [at the investment banks] send it around to make sure that they don't hire people like that."

Some students have tried to be more creative with their résumés in an attempt to stand out from the rest of the pack. This can also backfire. One girl created a jigsaw puzzle with the résumé she was sending to Goldman Sachs. On one side of the page were her strengths, and on the other side she wrote about Goldman and what it needed, indicating that she had the skills necessary to fill the needs of the bank. The stunt might have impressed recruiters from an advertising agency, but at the banks the creativity involved went unappreciated, leaving the girl with few if any chances for an interview.

As the recruiting season progresses through second-round callbacks and into the month of October, Whartonites can be broken into three groups: The haves, the have-nots, and the ones searching for something better. Those who accepted job offers early, mainly from their summer internships, tend to keep a low profile at this stage of the game, so as not to rub salt in the wounds of those still anxiously searching for a job. Students who have offers but haven't accepted them yet because they are shopping around are met with quiet resentment from seniors without offers. They see these students as undue competition, taking away interview opportunities and even job offers from them.

Grace Yoon was in anguish. "Every interview I walk out of, I think, 'God! I should have said this or that,' " she would say. As the month of October was rapidly nearing an end, Grace was feeling a little nervous and a little disappointed. A few weeks ago, there was a glimmer of hope. Bain & Co., the consulting firm she really hoped to work for, invited her to a cocktail party. Bain was one of the most well-respected consulting firms recruiting on campus, and as an added attraction they had offices near Grace's hometown in Los Angeles. If Grace could land a job working for Bain, she would not only have a job at a prestigious firm, but she would also have a shot at living close to her friends and family in California. Bain hadn't invited that many students to join them for drinks, and Grace took the invitation as a sign that they would undoubtedly ask her to come in for a first-round interview. But she soon discovered that this wasn't the case.

"They had sixty-eight interview slots," she said in disbelief. "I didn't understand how I was invited to the cocktail party and then didn't get a slot."

Grace was determined to get another chance. So she bid all 1,000 of her OCRS points to get an interview. To Grace, bidding for Bain made more sense than bidding for McKinsey, that Grace declared "everyone bids all 1,000 of their points for."

By mid-October, close to forty companies had received résumés from Grace, and about half a dozen of them invited her to first-round interviews. There was the business management associate program at General Mills, a marketing position at American Express, and a human resources position at Deloitte & Touche. For investment-banking jobs, Grace landed interviews with Citigroup and Credit Suisse First Boston. Grace soon learned that the interviews with the banks rarely focused on the areas that she thought were important, such as teamwork and leadership. Instead, they asked quantitative questions about cash flows and net present values, abilities Grace just hadn't valued as much during her studies at Wharton.

"I was thinking about it. You could get away with a lot of skills [at an investment bank]. You could move up through the ranks, invest a lot of time and energy and still get cast aside after two years," she said. The experience helped her cross one field completely off her list. "I can now say that I'm not at all interested in investment banking."

As she sat in the common area of Huntsman Hall, students she would have had to compete against for those banking jobs surrounded Grace. Knowing that she wouldn't be taking on that particular challenge gave her a minor sense of relief. The offer to return to L'Oréal was looking more and more attractive. If she took the L'Oréal job, she would spend a year rotating through different divisions as a Maybelline Marketing Explorer. From her summer experience, Grace already knew she would like her colleagues, and she could envision a future at L'Oréal that she just couldn't see at the banks. "I feel like I have a better opportunity to eventually become a top person [at L'Oréal]," she explained.

Her L'Oréal colleagues from the summer had been e-mailing her to see where she was in the decision-making process. Grace wasn't ready to say "yes" to them quite yet. She wanted to finish the recruiting process and see if anything more enticing came her way. L'Oréal, however, did seem like a safer option than working for a consulting firm. "There's never a recession in the beauty industry. When you're feeling down, you go get your nails done. There's more stability," she rationalized. The only thing holding her back from accepting the L'Oréal offer right away was the fact that Grace wanted to make sure she chose the job that would be most impressive to admissions officers for the Harvard or Stanford MBA programs.

Now that investment banking was crossed off her list, it was a little bit easier to narrow the field. The consulting interviews were now well under way, and Grace had won the bid for an interview with Bain. She was scheduled to meet with them the following week. She would also speak with reps from A.T. Kearney and JPMorgan's Internal Consulting Services department. Grace didn't want to screw up her chances with the consulting firms, and she worried about facing the complicated case interview questions that consulting-firm recruiters are notorious for. Her anxiety over the questions led Grace to seek help from Career Services. They videotaped her as she practiced sample case-study questions, giving her pointers as they watched the tape. But Grace was disappointed with their feedback. (Career Services has since started to enlist MBA students to help undergrads with case questions)

"They tell you if you're fidgeting," she said. "They focus on appearance rather than the meat of the interview."

Poise and good posture were important, but even more so was the "outside–the-box" thinking that the consulting companies look for when it comes to the case questions. Her answers to the case questions not only had to display her ability to look at problems from an unconventional angle, but also her skill at using an analytical structure to explain her reasoning.

Answering these questions was definitely something that required practice. Grace decided to take matters into her own hands, asking classmates and old study-group partners whether they might start meeting to go over case-study interview questions. To her dismay, no one was interested. Grace had two consulting interviews on Tuesday and one on Wednesday, and she was growing increasingly worried that she was ill-prepared. So she studied Career Services' sample case questions to prepare for them.

- How many skis will be sold in the U.S. next year?
- Estimate the total value of all the personal items on a commuter flight that arrived at LaGuardia airport at 8:30 a.m. this morning from Boston, given that the plane was approximately two-thirds full. (Tip: Don't forget to include checked luggage.)
- You are a manufacturer of toys and you have a product that costs (U.S). $1,000. Estimate how many of those you can sell in Hong Kong.

Her head was buzzing from these questions as she tackled one after another. Grace couldn't help but feel alone in the whole recruiting process. Over the last three years, she hadn't embraced the Wharton culture, at least not socially. Most of her friends were in the College and in her sorority, Alpha Phi. While they were supportive of her quest to find a job, her friends in the College weren't all that interested in hearing about investment banks and consulting firms, and most had no idea what Grace was going through as far as recruiting was concerned. On the other end of the spectrum were her classmates at Wharton, but they were almost too interested to be of help.

"They're very competitive," she explained. "If they went to an interview with a company first, they would never tell you the interview questions."

As November quickly approached, some of Wharton's more competitive seniors would become further obsessed with how they did compared to their classmates during their interviews. Who got asked back for a second round? Who landed what offer with what firm? And how large of a signing bonus did they get? Some opt to remain silent, but the dark suit and ties that students are wearing on a Wednesday morning or Tuesday afternoon are usually a dead giveaway that they are either en route to or just returning from an interview. "The feeling was. 'Forget about schoolwork. What's important is what job you're going to get,' and if you weren't interviewing for a banking or consulting job, you wouldn't even talk about it, because people wouldn't care," recalled Judy Kawaguchi, a graduate of Wharton's Class of 1998.

Recruiting season is a time when friendships forged at Wharton based on the same career goals can begin to crumble in the pursuit of them. The lucky few basking in the glory of a Goldman Sachs job offer are sometimes greeted with criticism from fellow students who believed that they were better suited for the job. "Some people who assumed they'd get an offer, and didn't, would go on rampages. They'd curse other people out or put people down who actually did get an offer," laughed Judy. "They'd say things like, 'I did better than him on midterms, and I can't believe he did so well.' Or, 'It must be because he was better-looking.' "

Judy clearly remembers the infighting and the backstabbing that arose during recruitment season her senior year. At the height of the dot-com nineties, students were landing an average of three or four job offers. The process had escalated to new heights–the competition grew accordingly more heated and the fear of failure more intense. "Were it anywhere else, you would have been ecstatic to get one good job offer. But [at Wharton] if you didn't get three or four offers and if your signing bonus wasn't above $10,000, then clearly you were a failure," recounted Judy, who said few of her Wharton friends were impressed when she landed a well-paying business-analyst position at Accenture, the number-two consulting firm then known as Andersen Consulting.

Shimika Wilder was relieved not to be going through the same pressures as her peers. The anxiety and tension she felt emanating from them was palpable. "Everybody is vying for the same jobs," she said. "People won't even tell their friends who they're interviewing with."

By now Shreevar Kheruka had all but abandoned his efforts to keep his job search limited and focused. Since the second week of October he had dropped more than thirty résumés. He knew it was way too many, but he couldn't help himself.

"It's easy to drop a résumé," he admitted. "All you have to do is click one button and drop it. Many of them are jobs I wouldn't want to do."

In fact, there were only ten or twelve companies that he felt were interesting enough to keep him in the U.S. after graduation. They were primarily the big consulting houses like McKinsey, Bain, and Monitor, and they had yet to really start interviewing on campus. McKinsey was his first choice, because it would give Shreevar a broad exposure to a variety of companies and industries. One of Shreevar's Goldman Sachs colleagues from the summer had introduced him to someone at McKinsey, allowing him a chance to gain some insight into the firm's operations. He attended their information session on campus, hoping it would also prove an advantage come decision time. He would find out in a week or so whether he had won an interview with them.

Shreevar's recruiting track record was looking pretty impressive thus far. Almost all of the firms that he had applied to had asked him to meet them for an interview. The one rejection he got he was relieved to receive. He had submitted his résumé by mistake to the Capital Finance department at JPMorgan. Shreevar had meant to send it to JPMorgan's Private Equity group. When the wrong department invited him to their cocktail party at The White Dog, the critically acclaimed restaurant and bar on campus, Shreevar declined.

"I felt bad because if I got the interview, I'm taking away someone else's interview who really wants it," he explained.

Typically, declining an invitation to attend a firm's cocktail party or dinner reflects poorly on a young candidate. The recruit would need to e-mail the recruiters with a pretty good excuse to gain forgiveness for such an indiscretion. "I would skip a class [for a cocktail party], but not midterms," said Shreevar.

Yet there were always some firms worth taking the risk of missing a midterm for. According to Shreevar, some Wharton professors acknowledge and respect how much time the recruiting process requires of seniors. These professors work with them to accommodate their schedules, sometimes even extending project deadlines or rescheduling midterms. "The ones who aren't understanding are the ones I get frustrated with," said Shreevar. "This is *Wharton*. The *goal* is to get a job."

Shreevar hadn't had to skip any classes for recruiting yet. He passed on most of the investment banks that recruited earlier in the semester and was focusing his job search on the consulting companies. Their interviews were about to begin in the weeks ahead. In the meantime, he had class work to concentrate on. After his bout with malaria and his knee injury junior year, Shreevar had fallen behind in his finance classes and was trying to catch up. In the upcoming week, he had three case studies due, one for each of the upper-level classes he was taking in Venture Capital & Private Equity, Real Estate Investment and Analysis, and Advanced Corporate Finance. The cases were assigned as group work, making the task even harder to accomplish because most of Shreevar's teammates were also in the throes of recruiting season. At times it seemed next to impossible to arrange everyone's overbooked schedules to accommodate meetings.

In general, the case studies that Shreevar and his classmates worked on were actual scenarios that had occurred at companies. The students are given much of the same information about the company that its executives had at the time. They are then asked to determine such factors as whether or not to sell the company, restructure it, or perhaps take it public. The group must review the case together and then come up with a conclusion that they can all agree on. If one student objects, it can become a tedious process that can lead to hours of debate which grows heated at times. Once the group turns in their reports, the professor tells them what actually happened at the company.

In some classes, these case-study projects carry more weight than midterms or finals. One of Shreevar's professors told his class that if they just read the chapters in their textbooks, they would do fine on exams. For Shreevar, his fellow students and even some of his professors, grades had become far less important than they had been in their freshman and sophomore years. "One of my real estate professors said, 'If you care about grades at this point, you should get a life. I just want you to learn,'" recalled Shreevar.

It was early in the morning when Jon Gantman and five fellow Wharton seniors convened on the Amtrak platform beneath 30th Street Station. En route to second-round interviews with investment bank Lehman Brothers in New York, Jon was readying himself for a full day. The train was running fifteen minutes late, and one of the students became overly anxious that tardiness could hurt his chance at getting a job at the firm. He repeatedly asked his fellow travelers if they should call Lehman Brothers and tell them they wouldn't arrive on time. Annoyed by the neurotic display, Jon pointed out that if they all showed up at the same time, no one was going to blame them for something that was obviously out of their control. It made perfect sense, but his classmate couldn't help but call Lehman anyway.

When Jon and his cohorts arrived at Lehman Brothers' offices just five minutes late, no one said a word about the time. Soon after arriving, Jon was met with a schedule of four back-to-back, thirty-minute interviews. The interview questions were more technical and intense than in the first interview he had with Lehman a week and a half earlier. That had been more of a personality screening of sorts to see if Jon would fit in with his potential colleagues. Now on Lehman's turf, the recruiters were all business, firing off one valuation question after another at him. At one of the interviews, the banker decided to play hardball. He didn't even introduce himself to Jon before launching into a series of number-crunching queries. Jon tried to remain unfazed by the banker's tactic, an obvious test of his mettle and his ability to control a situation under pressure.

"He was *trying* to tear me to shreds," described Jon, but he kept his cool. It helped that Jon wasn't as concerned about the outcome of the interviews.

Jon thought he wouldn't get interviews with either one of the banks he had applied to because he wasn't pursuing a concentration in finance. Evidently, he underestimated the power of his résumé, which not only boasted a 3.7 GPA in Wharton's honors program, but impressive extracurriculars as well, including his three-year TA-ship for Management 100, work with Habitat for Humanity and a resident teaching advisor post for the "Leadership in the Business World" summer program.

A week earlier, Jon had met with two recruiters from Citigroup. At the first interview, his questioner took it easy on him. He even doled out helpful résumé and interviewing tips, which Jon took into account and appreciated. During his second-round interview with the firm, though, things weren't as cordial. It all turned with one question, a seemingly innocuous inquiry into Jon's preferences.

"You're about to get on the train to New York, what are the three things you buy at the magazine shop?" the interviewer asked Jon.

Thinking this was a softball question, Jon answered honestly, telling the recruiter that he would get *The Philadelphia Inquirer* newspaper, a copy of *Sports Illustrated*, and an issue of *Maxim*, a men's magazine that often features scantily clad women on its cover.

The interviewer seemed outraged by Jon's response. "*What? What about the Wall Street Journal, the Financial Times?*" Jon recalled the moment, snickering at the thought that any student would honestly opt to buy the business newspapers over his more entertaining periodicals of choice. The interviewer told Jon he was writing down the response, as if Jon had committed some major egregious interviewing error. Evidently, his magazine-choosing faux pas had ruined his chances for an invitation to another round of interviews at Citigroup's offices in Manhattan.

Jon almost felt relieved. He didn't want to waste his time traveling back and forth to New York for a job that he wasn't really interested in anyway. Plus, he said, "I don't want to lead anyone on."

Being honest with himself and recruiters was important to Jon.

During the internship interviews his junior year, Jon practically killed himself to prepare for every one of the thirty companies he met with. "I was very serious. I did all of my due diligence," he said. "Now I just want to be myself."

This time around, Jon took a much different tack to prepare for his interviews. Instead of studying the company and ways to successfully navigate interview questions all night long, he would watch his favorite movie, *Van Wilder*. Jon also liked to watch one of Al Pacino's many motivating speeches in Oliver Stone's football movie, *Any Given Sunday*.

"The speech is about how life and football are both measured in inches. You will only do well in life if you have the passion to pursue that last inch," explained Jon. After his motivational pep talks, Jon then tried to get a good night's sleep.

"When you're taking the SAT in high school, you learn that the test shows where you might fit in best," said Jon. "Why study really hard just to get into a school where you can't keep up?" He looked at getting a job the same way. Jon could keep up at the investment banks, but would he want to work that hard for something he didn't find fulfilling? It was a rational way to look at the recruiting process—and a perspective not often shared by some of his Wharton peers, who were vying for the most competitive and demanding jobs at the most prestigious banks.

After returning to Philadelphia from his interviews with Lehman, Jon had to quickly regroup and get ready for a dinner that Johnson & Johnson was holding for twenty potential hires at the Inn at Penn's restaurant on Walnut Street. There were five representatives from Johnson & Johnson there, each rotating around the room asking the students questions about themselves. Jon loved the fact that the reps took the time to speak with each of the students. Intimate and organized, it wasn't at all like the cattle-call cocktail parties thrown by the investment banks or consulting firms.

After the pricey meals were picked at and end-of-the-evening handshakes exchanged, Jon shuttled over to a cocktail party being held by Bain at a bar on campus. There were five reps to forty students. It was every man or woman for him- or herself, each competing for time with a recruiter. Jon wanted little to do with the whole scene.

The next morning, with the dinner from the evening before well digested, Jon felt more comfortable and confident when he arrived at his first interview with Johnson & Johnson. Surprisingly, the meeting lasted only twenty minutes, partly because the interviewer was exhausted and partly because Jon was such an impressive candidate. After reviewing Jon's résumé and speaking with him about his experience as the head of the Team Advisors for Management 100, the recruiter had no qualms about cutting the interview short. Jon's personality, grades and leadership skills led him to quickly conclude that Jon had "everything we're looking for."

"It was painless," Jon said afterward with a relieved smile.

Jon's next stop on his interviewing tour would require him to return to New York for the second time in three days. He was meeting with American Express for an internal consulting position in their Strategic Planning division. Jon had done first-round interviews with Amex the week before and learned that the position would ultimately report to the travel and financial services giant's CEO, Kenneth Chenault. If he took the Amex job, he would embark on a two-year management-training program at the company's Manhattan offices. The biggest seller was the fact that Jon would only have to work forty-hour weeks on average, giving him enough time to continue pursuing some of his entrepreneurial endeavors and have some fun.

The position at Amex was quickly becoming his most promising prospect. The Johnson & Johnson financial-analyst post was coming in a close second in his mental employer rankings. That job was also a two-year training program, which would entail him spending three eight-month periods of time training in different locations. But before Jon could seriously consider either one of the positions, he wanted to give the consulting firms a shot.

As if the last week hadn't been hectic enough with his two trips to New York, a litany of interviews and a handful of cocktail parties and dinners, the upcoming week was going to be even more heavily booked. The consulting firms were flocking to campus, and Jon's calendar was filling up fast. All of the major consulting firms wanted a crack at him: McKinsey, Bain, Boston Consulting Group, Accenture. He had interviews with four of them on Monday and five on Tuesday. He also had a midterm that week and two papers due, not to mention his duties as a TA to attend to on Tuesday, Thursday and Friday. On top of that, Jon had also volunteered for a charity event sponsored by his fraternity that lasted from Thursday evening to Saturday evening. It required him to sit in a rocking chair for forty-eight hours straight to earn money for the homeless. Between fall break earlier in the month and all of the interviews he'd had in the last couple of weeks, Jon hadn't been to class in two weeks. It was starting to look like he could add yet another class-free week to the list.

Jon was pretty confident that he could handle the load. His laid-back nature helped him take everything in stride, but he was getting frustrated with the lack of time he had for his personal life. He missed hanging out with his friends and his girlfriend. The reality that this was his senior year only intensified those feelings of resentment toward his obligations. It was only a matter of months before everyone would head their separate ways, and Jon didn't want to take the remaining time they had together for granted. Jon looked around at his fellow Whartonites blindly thirsting to be accepted by an investment bank, and was disappointed with the mentality that had overtaken them.

"At Wharton there's this idea that you have to have a job by

October," explained Jon. "You're only in college for four years. To spend time worrying about next year right now seems like a waste to me."

Armed with an offer from Lazard Frères, Jessica Kennedy was much more relaxed than she had been last year going into her internship interviews with the investment banks.

"Every once in a while you get a weird math question, like calculating twenty-six times twenty-seven in your head," she said. "I have a hard time getting stressed out and trying to perform on those now that I have an offer."

Plus, she liked the fact that Lazard wanted her back so badly. Just a few days ago, a third-year analyst who took Jessica under his wing during her summer internship had left her a quick message: "Kennedy, I'm calling to convince you to come to Lazard."

By the end of September, Jessica had been on a full rotation of first-round interviews for positions at investment banks, several of them for jobs in private equity. Jessica was growing increasingly frustrated with interviewers who spent the whole time asking her quantitative questions. When she interviewed with Gleacher Partners, they had asked her leveraged-buyout questions and about what happens to the three major financial statements of a company when bad-debt expense and allowance for doubtful accounts increases. At that point, Jessica couldn't help but think: *Wasn't her 3.9 GPA as a finance concentration in the Wharton honors program enough for them to know that she knew how to define free cash flow and was well-versed in the ways to value a company?*

"Take a look at my résumé! The fact that he saw all of [my credentials] and spent twenty of the thirty minutes asking me technical questions tells me a lot about the firm," Jessica complained.

During her interviews with Lazard's recruiters during her junior year, the questions were more balanced, a mixture of technical questions and those about her experiences and her personality. Jessica felt like they had really been trying to get to know her.

At one of her recent interviews, there was just one twenty-two-year-old analyst on hand to speak with her. This firm didn't even have a senior-level recruiter and didn't seem to care enough about finding young talent for their firm to send more than one banker to vet potential hires. Jessica thought it was indicative of how the firm valued analysts, which at that point seemed to be very little.

"I definitely wouldn't accept another interview," declared Jessica. "They're out."

When Jessica arrived for her interview with investment management firm Blackstone Group, she was impressed with the time they took to lay out a spread of fresh-squeezed orange juice and muffins for students they were interviewing. When she went into the presidential suite at the hotel where her interview was taking place, though, the Blackstone analyst didn't invite her to sit down. It was something a Southerner like Jessica thought should be a professional courtesy, and she noted it in her internal log of pros and cons of the banks she was meeting with. Nevertheless, Jessica thought the interview went well.

Blackstone took longer than most banks to ask her to come back for a second interview and speak with representatives from their Restructuring and Mergers & Acquisitions groups and from their coveted Private Equity group. At that point, though, Jessica was starting to come to the conclusion that the more banks she interviewed with, the more she wanted to go back to Lazard. Her schedule was filling up with projects for classes as well. She decided not to take on any more interviews than the ones she had already agreed upon. "For mental sanity's sake, I'm turning them down," Jessica explained.

Remaining on her calendar were interviews with Citigroup and a small, privately held investment bank, but she didn't feel the same way about them as she did Lazard, so she canceled. There was really only one position that she was seriously considering beyond Lazard, and that was the private-equity analyst position at JPMorgan Partners. Jessica had interviewed with JPMorgan in early October. It was one of the few interviews that left her discouraged. She was convinced that she had "rambled on" with some of her answers to the interviewer's questions about convertible securities. To her surprise, a few days later, JPMorgan asked her to come to New York for an all-day interview session. "It must have been all about presence and personality," guessed Jessica. "There was just no way that what I said was the best out of all the people they interviewed." But the JPMorgan interviews weren't for another two weeks, and Jessica was anxious to give Lazard her answer.

Jessica would head up to Lazard's offices a week later for a "sell day." These days are usually a firm's opportunity to pitch themselves one more time to the young recruits they have given job offers to. Most are lavish affairs, and some sell days turn into sell weekends. Many students travel up the night before (all expenses paid, of course) for an evening of wining and dining with the firm's bankers and human resources personnel. They are put up in four-star hotels and have events planned throughout the day. Some sell days are filled with speeches from upper-level management or tours of the facilities and meet-and-greet sessions. It is a time when the tables are turned between the recruiters and students, when the students can ask every burning question that might help them make a choice between one firm or another.

Lazard's sell day was going to be more low-key than those held by most of the other banks. Instead of bringing all of its potential hires in on the same day, they brought them to the offices on different dates. Jessica was going to have almost everyone's undivided attention. Prior to her trip, the head of recruiting at Lazard had asked Jessica whom she would want to meet with during her time at the office. Jessica told her she would love to meet with someone from each of the two divisions that she wanted to work in most: the Healthcare Group and the Financial Institutions Group (also known as FIG). "There are advantages to going into healthcare," said Jessica. "But FIG would be a good way to set things up and reach my next goal."

That next goal was to become an associate at Lazard within three years. Most analysts work two years, go back to school for an MBA and then return to the banks as an associate. "I really want to make that jump from analyst to associate. Just like I wanted to graduate summa cum laude. I'm obsessive," Jessica confessed.

Lazard's travel agency arranged Jessica's trip, booking her on an 11:00 A.M. train to New York that Friday. When Jessica arrived at Lazard's offices, all of the positive feelings that she had about the firm over the summer came rushing back to her. "I missed it!" she exclaimed, almost surprised at the extent to which she wanted to be back at Lazard. "I wish I had taken a picture!"

Jessica went to lunch that day with an associate and another banker in FIG. Before the plates were put on the table, Jessica laid down the ground rules with her lunch mates. "Don't try to sell Lazard to me," she declared. It was important to Jessica that the lunch be casual. No one talked about Lazard or FIG, for that matter. After lunch, Jessica headed over to the Healthcare Group, where she met with a woman who had worked her way up the ranks at Lazard from analyst to vice president, just as Jessica hoped to do.

In the afternoon, Jessica anxiously awaited the biggest highlight of her day, a meeting with Gary Parr, the deputy chairman of Lazard and the man who had become something of an investment-banking role model for her. Going into the meeting with Parr, Jessica recalled some advice she had gotten from a friend who, five years into his career, was now considered a veteran banker. He told Jessica that if she was going to accept Lazard's offer, she should do so on sell day, and she should announce her acceptance to the highest-ranking person that she could. Parr definitely fit the mold. But when Jessica walked into Parr's office, she hadn't made up her mind one hundred percent. The JPMorgan job was still a slight possibility.

Sitting across from Parr, Jessica couldn't help but be amazed that she had access to such a top-level person at Lazard. She asked him probing questions about the firm and he answered each one fully and honestly. He even took the time to ask her what she wanted out of her investment-banking experience.

"At that point, I just knew," Jessica would say. Later that day, Jessica returned to tell the high-ranking Gary Parr that she, Jessica Kennedy, would love to work for Lazard Frères. Initially scheduled to be at Lazard until 3:00 P.M. that day, Jessica didn't leave until 5:30. She called JPMorgan the next morning to break the news to them. Even on a Saturday, the recruiter was gracious, telling Jessica that while they were disappointed, they hoped everything would work out for her.

Back at school, Jessica hadn't slowed down much at all, not even to celebrate her future at Lazard. Soon after returning, she was back to her old ways. On Monday, she had classes all day and obligations for her post at Wharton Women throughout the evening, after which she studied for an early-morning midterm in legal studies until 3:30 A.M. To Jessica, that was a minor lapse in her work ethic. Usually, she would have stayed up until 6:00 A.M. studying. Jessica's friends were driving her crazy, constantly questioning why she was working so hard now that she had a job in the bag.

"It doesn't work that way," Jessica told them. "It's not until graduation day that I'm done here."

CHAPTER EIGHT

RUNNING ON FUMES
AND ADRENALINE

Jon Gantman was excitedly preparing for the fund-raiser that he and his fraternity brothers from Alpha Epsilon Pi ("AEπ") were staging, and it was hard to focus on anything else. Called "The Rock for the Homeless," he and one of his fraternity brothers were going to spend forty-eight hours planted in La-Z-Boy recliners on campus, raising money for the University City Hospitality Coalition, a local nonprofit organization for the homeless. Yet Jon knew—begrudgingly or not—that he had to refocus his attentions and tend to the demands of the recruiting season. He had grown wary that he wouldn't get the job with American Express. The recruiters had told him that they would be extending offers by now, and he hadn't heard anything yet. So he tried to put his best foot forward with his other options.

Jon had spent the morning at an interview with Boston Consulting Group, then drove twenty miles northwest of Penn's campus to Plymouth Meeting for an exhausting series of five forty-minute interviews with Johnson & Johnson. Sitting before shelves of Tylenol products, one of Jon's interviewers asked him to come up with a new brand of Tylenol that has never been on the market. Jon conjured up "Tylenol Sport," an electrolyte-filled sports drink like Gatorade that included pain relievers and muscle relaxers.

"They told me it wasn't feasible, but that it was a good idea nonetheless," recalled Jon, smiling at his efforts.

Those efforts were enough for Johnson & Johnson to invite him to their sell day the following day. Unfortunately, it was the same day that The Rock for the Homeless began, and Jon was upset about the overlap. After weeks of recruiting and trying to keep up with his busy schedule, Jon was exhausted and just wanted to spend time with his friends. Yet he knew it was important to go to the sell day. Twenty-five students were invited to attend, and only eight of them would be offered jobs. Even if he thought the sell day would be a waste of time, the fact that he showed up would indicate to the recruiters that he was seriously considering their offer.

Jon was running late the next day when he met the bus that Johnson & Johnson had arranged to transport the recruits to Dave & Buster's, a bar/restaurant on the Delaware River waterfront filled with pool tables and video games. The drive to Johnson & Johnson's offices took longer than Jon expected. When Jon climbed onto the bus, he quickly surveyed the scene and discovered that most of the other students had already strategically taken seats next to one another in order to avoid an awkward conversation with one of the Johnson & Johnson reps. Jon had no choice but to sit next to a recruiter. It meant he had to be "on," making conversation and asking well-thought-out questions during the entire hour-long ride. "At that point, I just wanted to be rocking," he confessed. But he quickly found a common ground with the recruiter: sports. The two men shared a love for basketball, and Jon soon got the recruiter talking about the softball team he was on and other sports he played. The ride went by much more quickly than Jon had thought.

Once they arrived at Dave & Buster's, the group shot hoops and played video games as they mingled with the Johnson & Johnson reps. It was far from hard work, but it was eating up pre-

cious time that Jon could be spending at the fund-raiser. Jon returned to campus ready to relax and join his fraternity brother
Bobby in the recliners they had positioned at the edge of Locust
Walk–a choice spot for hitting people up for money. The Rock for
the Homeless was an exercise in living without the comforts of
home: No heat, no beds, no hot showers, and no television. Bun-
dled in navy blue sweatshirts and blankets, Jon and his cohort prepared to camp out for three days and two nights on the College
Green. The charity the boys were sacrificing warmth and the lux-
uries of home for was founded in 1984 by a group of Penn students and local residents after a homeless man named Stanley
Biddle froze to death on campus, and "The Rock" had long been a
fun way to raise funds for it.

On their first night, the recent spring-like October weather
took a nasty turn and temperatures plunged down into the thir-
ties. An empathetic grad student felt so bad for the two trembling
souls that she returned with a Thermos of hot apple cider. Friends
and classmates stopped by to entertain them–several campus a
cappella groups sang songs and one of their frat brothers played
guitar. Even the campus police hung out with Jon and Bobby. After all of their motley crews of companions had left, they shivered
themselves to sleep only to be rudely awakened at 3:00 A.M. by the
icy cold spray of the lawn sprinklers, which–unbeknownst to them–
sprung to life at that time every night.

The next morning brought warm sunshine and heralded the
beginning of Penn's annual Family Weekend. As he did every Friday afternoon, Jon held court with his Management 100 recitation
group. This time, though, they met on the Campus Green, where
the students sat cross-legged in a circle on the grass to discuss
their community-service project. The sun had dried the remaining
morning dew, and Jon's thick hooded sweatshirt absorbed the
heat of its rays as he advised his charges. A few yards away, ven-
dors were lugging in their goods to set up shop for the weekend,

which was a prime opportunity for students to hit their parents up for presents. Small tents and card tables hawking logo T-shirts and beaded jewelry were springing up all along Locust Walk.

By late afternoon, the traffic began to thicken as the parents started infiltrating the campus. They wandered around with their kids, asking them questions about what they've been studying and where their classrooms were located. Occasionally, they stopped their questioning to throw Jon and Bobby some spare change. That night, the two befriended a local homeless man that they had seen around campus from time to time. They shared the meals that were donated to them from local restaurants with him and he told them about his experiences. The campus police would have usually kicked the man off campus after dark, but this time they let him stay.

Saturday was the final day of Rock for the Homeless, and Jon's parents drove up to campus to see their weather-beaten son and visit their daughter, who was a sophomore in the College. Jon's parents lived a quick twenty-minute drive from campus, making it easy to arrange family dinners or outings to the ballpark. Jon's mother was in the throes of her campaign for Superior Court Justice of Pennsylvania. The election was now only a week and a half away, and Jon was happy that she could find the time to visit with him while on the campaign trail. Joining Jon and his family was Penn's mascot, the oxymoronically named Fighting Quaker, who quickly took on the job of holding the inverted water cooler bottle the boys were using to collect donations. By the end of the weekend, the jug had been filled with $1,800.

Jon was thoroughly exhausted on Sunday. He practically slept all the way through to Monday, a day that he hoped to make as uneventful as possible. As he was leaving the fraternity house for campus on Monday morning, he opened the door to find a FedEx envelope awaiting him on the doorstep. It was from American Express. They were offering him a job. At that point, it was the best news that Jon could have received. It was the job he had hoped for the most, and the offer came as a shock.

Jon practically floated to campus, where he picked up that day's copy of the *Daily Pennsylvanian*, the independent, student-run newspaper read by a majority of Penn's faculty and students. On the front page was a color picture of himself and Bobby sitting in their recliners, the headline celebrating their fund-raising efforts. It was quickly becoming one of the best days Jon had ever had. When he returned home that evening, he would receive a phone call from the human resources woman at Johnson & Johnson. They weren't supposed to extend offers for three weeks, but as the recruiter quickly explained to Jon, it didn't take them much time to decide that he would be a valuable asset to their team. Jon had snagged his top two offers in one day. "I've been busting my butt for the last three years," he said. "It's nice now to have other people appreciate it." He quickly called his parents to tell them the news. "My mom started crying," he recalled.

The next day, Jon had five interviews scheduled. He canceled most of them. He had no regrets blowing off one of them because he had been upset with the recruiter's attitude. After his first-round interview with the consulting firm, they had told him they would call him that night with decisions about second rounds. They didn't contact him for a week, and when they did it was in the form of an e-mail addressed "Dear Student"–they hadn't even taken the time to write "Dear Jonathan." Jon thought it was a bad sign. He also canceled two other interviews because he knew that the job offers he received from Johnson & Johnson and American Express were superior. He did, however, hang onto an interview with a local financial services firm, in the hope that he could join them in their box seats at a Philadelphia Eagles game. There was also a meeting with a small consulting firm that had been so nice to Jon in their e-mails that he didn't have the heart to turn them down without meeting with them first.

On top of everything else, Jon had a few remaining interviews with consulting firms that he wanted to follow through on, including an initial four-hour interview with McKinsey he had to reschedule because he came down with bronchitis following the Rock for the Homeless. An interview with General Mills was also in the works. As part of their interviewing process, the company required him to take a 120-question test in twenty minutes. The exam rivaled standardized tests like the GREs or GMATs, with math questions that asked: *What's the next number in the sequence?* There was also a verbal section that tested his knowledge of metaphors and word usage. Afterward, there was an online test designed to assess a candidate's personality by asking questions like: *Do you like to work in groups?* Jon actually enjoyed these kinds of tests. He took them in stride, even as the rest of the people in the room nervously shot glances at each other and fidgeted in their seats.

"Everyone was freaking out, thinking, 'How are we supposed to finish it?' " laughed Jon. "You're not *supposed* to finish it."

Jon wasn't scheduled to meet with the recruiters from General Mills again for a few weeks. It gave him the time he needed to figure out what to do about the job offers he had received. He was planning on meeting with his dad over the weekend to discuss his employment options. Jon found these sessions with his father to be the best way to talk through big decisions in his life, and this decision was one of the biggest he had ever had to make.

Regi Vengalil was trying not to be a slave to his phone or check his e-mail every other minute, but the anticipation was killing him. Even his family kept asking him, "Have you heard anything yet?"

Regi had just gone to a "Super Saturday" with one of his top two choices among the investment banks, and he was eagerly awaiting their decision. Super Saturdays are part of the recruiting process at many of the big bulge-bracket banks. They usually entail bringing the student applicants to their offices (mainly in New

York), putting them up in a top hotel and wining and dining them for a night before putting them through a grueling series of eight to ten back-to-back interviews the next day.

The visit began on Friday when Regi and a friend, who was also invited to the bank's offices for the weekend, made their way to the train station together. They soon ran into six more Penn students, all heading to the same intensive daylong interview. After arriving in Manhattan, they checked into their hotel rooms at The Crowne Plaza in Times Square before meeting for dinner at Guastavino's, a pricey midtown restaurant at the base of the Queensboro Bridge.

The firm had rented out the entire second floor of the restaurant and the young brood couldn't help but feel that they had stepped into a grander world—one not unlike that in Oliver Stone's movie *Wall Street*. It seemed as if money was no object. They mingled with the bankers and tried to restrain themselves from taking too much advantage of the open bar. After the cocktail hour, the group sat down to a lavish three-course meal. Regi was optimally seated right next to the vice president in charge of recruiting. It would have been a great opportunity to sell himself, but the acoustics in the cavernous restaurant amplified the buzzing of the conversations taking place around him, making it next to impossible for him to concentrate or even always hear what the vice president next to him was saying. After dinner was over, the group went downstairs to the bar for more drinks. Regi got back to his hotel room around midnight and managed to fall asleep an hour later.

The next morning, Regi woke up promptly at 7:00 A.M. He had to be at the bank by 8:15 A.M. to begin going through eight half-hour-long interviews. There would be only two half-hour breaks during the entire day. As he stepped into the office of his first interviewer, Regi was nervous. His hands still shook during the interviews, but Regi was starting to learn how to hide it. It helped that the banker he met with first was friendly and immediately put

Regi at ease. The interview was a piece of cake and it readily boosted Regi's confidence. Unfortunately, Regi's good fortune quickly changed when he next encountered a poker-faced interviewer. The poker face was a classic interviewing technique used by bankers to see if a recruit will crack under the pressure of having little to no verbal or visual feedback from his interviewer.

"He didn't give any idea of where you stand with them. The blank expression got me a little worried," said Regi, who was thankful he had his first thirty-minute break afterward, allowing him a chance to pull himself together.

After the brief respite, Regi met with an affable executive director who spent the time talking about what he had done in his career. It was a causal conversation centered more on the banker than Regi, and Regi was happy for it. He didn't have to calculate anything in his head or try too hard to sell himself. It was a huge relief. The pressure was off for a little while longer.

The tables turned in his fourth interview, which was obviously designed to test his quantitative skills. When Regi entered the office where the interview was taking place, he was met with three sober-faced bankers: an analyst, an associate, and an executive director. The executive director asked the questions while the analyst and associate looked on.

The initial question seemed easy at first. The director asked Regi why he wanted to work at this particular bank over the other banks he was interviewing with. Regi replied that the bank was one of the top four banks in public finance.

In a drill sergeant–like tone, the director responded "*What?* So you *aren't* interviewing with the top three?" Regi scrambled to explain further why this bank was better than the other top public-finance banks, but he was made to feel as if he'd just dug his hole even deeper. The director accused Regi of bashing the other banks. If Regi was bashing those other banks to him, how was he bashing their bank to others?

"I wasn't bashing them, though," Regi protested. "I was just saying that they have different perspectives." Regi felt as though he was in a no-win situation.

The interviewer moved onto the quantitative questions that Regi had expected. The first question: *Say you were a computer company and you just bought $5 million in equipment. Would you rather pay $5 million today or $1.5 million over the next five years? With continuous compounding, is it less or more than twenty percent?* Even though Regi was rattled from the antagonistic way the recruiter had treated him, he still managed to get the answer right. "I knew less than twenty percent, but I wasn't sure of the exact amount," recalled Regi. But Regi got it in the end. "I said the rate was 16.6 percent and he was like, 'Do you mean *sixteen and two-thirds?*' So I said, 'Yes, sixteen and two-thirds.'"

A couple of more difficult quantitative questions based on the initial scenario followed. Fortunately, Regi's strength was dealing with heady, number-based queries. He felt he did well, but he couldn't shake the sense that it didn't matter. He had already blown his chance with the executive director. "He swore in the interview," exclaimed Regi. "No one had sworn at me in an interview before."

Near the end of the interview, Regi had the floor to ask questions. It was a good time to redeem himself. He asked the director what he felt were the three qualities that made a good analyst. After the director answered the question, Regi turned to the analyst in the room and asked him if he found those qualities to be true in his experience.

The director was outraged. "Do you think they are going to dispute me to my face?" he demanded.

Regi felt like he had struck out once again.

When Regi left the room, he was rattled. Before moving on to his next meeting, he bumped into the friendly analyst who had conducted his first-round interview on campus and proceeded to tell him how he didn't think he did so well with the executive director. The analyst responded, "Well, if you didn't come out of it feeling like you didn't do well, then he didn't do his job."

That helped Regi to relax. Evidently, the director had been employing the good-cop/bad-cop interview routine to test his mettle, and he had obviously chosen the bad-cop role. Chatting with the other recruits while waiting to go into yet another interview, Regi soon learned that the director had been just as hard on them, if not worse.

The remaining four interviews went off without a hitch. They consisted mainly of "fit" questions, including inquiries into what Regi did for fun or how he would describe his personality. His final interview of the day was with two Penn alumni who worked at the bank. They wanted to know about his experiences at school and why he wanted to work in public finance, both questions Regi had devised well-thought-out responses to prior to the interview.

"I think I finished it well," he said. By the end of the day, Regi was mentally exhausted. "I was thrown off by the quantitative interview. I'm going to pursue final rounds elsewhere. Last week I thought I'd take it [if the firm had made an offer]," said Regi. "Other than that executive director, everyone was extremely nice."

Regi felt that he held up under the pressure of Super Saturday. Now he was just waiting to hear what the bankers thought of his performance. "They said they had a strong applicant pool," Regi noted nervously. "It's not more stressful interviewing. It's more stressful wondering whether or not I'm going to get the job."

Regi was also considering a public-finance position at another large investment bank that had just invited him to their Super Saturday for the upcoming weekend. It would be similar to the weekend Regi had just endured, with another day full of interviews. During his first-round interviews with the firm a few weeks earlier, the conversation with the recruiter had become contentious. The interview had started out as fairly commonplace, with his questioner reviewing Regi's résumé and asking him many of the same questions that other interviewers had solicited in the past. Regi responded with his typical well-rehearsed composure. Near the end of the interview, though, one question got Regi into trouble.

The interviewer asked about his concept of integrity. Regi had just read an article in one of his classes about how this particular bank had steered its client—a major city—toward selling bonds and investing the proceeds in order to fund pensions for certain city workers. The bank had failed to disclose how risky the investments were and as a result the pensions were underfunded. Regi turned the question on the questioner and asked about the controversial article he had read.

"They got really defensive," said Regi skeptically. "The response was, 'The writer [of the article] didn't know what they were talking about.'"

Nevertheless, Regi still wanted to work at the bank. They had a great reputation when it came to public finance, and Regi thought he could gain great experience there. When it took longer than expected for the bank to invite him back for the next round of interviews, though, Regi took it as a sign that he was low on their list of candidates.

"They probably didn't like that I had inadvertently questioned their integrity," he guessed.

Shreevar hadn't let the recruiting process stress him out at first, but now he was starting to break under the pressure. He had just returned from a trip to New York, where he had his final round of interviews with JPMorgan's Private Equity group. It was a day that Shreevar could only describe as "torture," with five thirty-minute interviews back to back.

"It was annoying because obviously the interviewers didn't know what the other interviewers were asking me, so their first ten questions were always all the same," complained Shreevar. "I kept repeating myself."

Unlike typical interviews with investment banks, the interviews with JPMorgan were a mix of both technical and personality questions. At one point the bankers would ask him what his favorite movie was. At another he would be asked how to price options using the complicated Black-Scholes Model, which uses various criteria such as stock and strike prices, expiration dates, the volatility of a stock's return and interest rates in order to determine the value of options. The quantitative questions always frustrated Shreevar, who saw them as a waste of time.

"Given that I went to school at Wharton, I'm capable of learning the technical stuff," he said indignantly.

The JPMorgan interviewers also asked why he didn't want to work for Goldman Sachs, where he had interned over the summer. Shreevar told them he didn't want to be a trader, even if it was at such a highly esteemed bank like Goldman. The self-involved life of traders, who work for their own profits, wasn't for him. He wanted experience working with teams, a crucial skill for anyone who wants to run their own business someday. "I want to be an entrepreneur later on," he told them. "And trading won't prepare me for that."

Shreevar was pretty confident that JPMorgan would make him an offer. Working for their Asset Management team was a prestigious job, and JPMorgan told him that if he performed well for six months to a year, he could then move to the exclusive Private Equity group. The thought of working for the Private Equity group was enticing to Shreevar, but there was no guarantee he would make it there.

So far, all but one of the consulting companies Shreevar had dropped résumés with had invited him to first-round interviews. Interviewing with consulting firms was a much different experience than interviewing with the investment banks. At his first-round interview with Monitor, Shreevar was given a packet with a written case that filled two single-spaced pages along with ten graphs and charts. At the bottom of the final page were three questions. As the recruiter got up to leave the room, he instructed Shreevar to review the information and figure out which information he needed to answer the questions. He only had fifteen minutes. When the interviewer returned, he quizzed Shreevar on the case for close to half an hour.

"The point is not to get the right answer," explained Shreevar. "The point is to figure out how you think."

Monitor was a top-five consulting firm with offices around the globe that had pleasantly surprised Shreevar with its down-to-earth and professional employees. When they took Shreevar and a group of other recruits out for dinner one night, Shreevar had a constant smile plastered on his face. It was enough to put Monitor in the "definitely consider" pile of Shreevar's career options. That was, if they made Shreevar an offer.

Still leading Shreevar's wish list, though, was McKinsey. McKinsey had sent him a prep packet of materials to review before taking the seventy-minute exam that McKinsey required its potential recruits to undergo as part of the first-rounds. Most of the multiple-choice questions on the test were logic-based, offering scenarios and asking the best way to handle certain situations. Following the exam, Shreevar met with two recruiters. Each of the interviewers spent thirty minutes discussing case questions with Shreevar and the remaining fifteen minutes with more personal queries such as, "Talk to me about a time you had to influence someone to get what you want."

His first case question was about a Burger King in a town in Connecticut that was losing money. What information would Shreevar ask the restaurant owner for in order to determine what to do? What are some of the ways that he could help turn their losses around? Shreevar covered all of the possible bases he could think of and left the three-and-a-half-hour interview feeling like he had a shot.

McKinsey soon asked Shreevar to come up to their offices in New York. When he arrived Shreevar knew that he was in for a long day. McKinsey is renowned for its thorough and grueling long interviews, and the interviews that take place at McKinsey's offices are the pinnacle of these. The first of many tests that Shreevar would have to endure that day involved teamwork. It was a classic McKinsey interview scenario he referred to as "McKinsey Day One."

Six recruits were gathered together in a conference room. They were supposed to imagine that they have just started working at the firm and their manager has been called away. One of the firm's big clients is on the way and the recruits have half an hour to prepare for a meeting with them. Shreevar and his peers were then given stacks of information about the client that was so in-depth it would be next to impossible for them to get through it all before the client arrived. Even though these students are competing with each other for job offers, they are forced to work together in order to figure out the most pertinent information to present to the client. All the while, two McKinsey employees are watching the group work through the information and taking notes on their contribution to the team. The "clients" then enter the room, purposely acting difficult to rattle the team. Throughout the exercise, the McKinsey onlookers grade each recruit on how they handle the situation and what they choose to say. With all of this surveillance, though, the recruits rarely act the way they would in a real situation like this. "The problem is, everyone wants to be the leader, and at the same time they don't want to seem too aggressive," explained Shreevar.

During his remaining interviews at the consultancy, Shreevar noticed that the interviewer would often take whatever answer he had given to a question and quickly dissect it for a good fifteen minutes. He had to watch every word he uttered, because it could somehow be turned against him. Luckily, he chose his words wisely and could perform well on the spot. When Shreevar later met with one of the principals of the firm, he was asked a thorny case question that he just couldn't get his head around. The partner kept repeating the question. Obviously, Shreevar didn't properly understand what she was asking and he just couldn't get it. "My brain froze," he admitted.

Leaving McKinsey's offices, Shreevar was "pissed off" at himself for not being able to respond to the question and impress the partner. When McKinsey turned him down a couple of days later, Shreevar felt even worse about it. Intellectual challenges had always come easy to him, ever since he was a child. It was a rare occurrence when he couldn't perform well on something. "I couldn't bear to see myself in the mirror after the McKinsey rejection," Shreevar confessed.

He soon got over the disappointment. He knew it wasn't the end of the world. There were, of course, other jobs. And those interviews were approaching fast.

Grace finally had her chance to interview with Bain, the consulting firm that she had bid all of her points on to get an interview with. But it didn't quite work out the way she had hoped. Grace failed to hit it off with either one of the recruiters. During one of the thirty-minute interviews, she tried to work her way through a difficult case question, but realized she was completely off base. In cases like these, where recruits' answers go terribly astray, the interviewer usually tries to guide them back on track by providing hints or asking leading questions. This recruiter let Grace flounder and ramble for what felt like hours, but was probably minutes. It wasn't a great surprise to her when Bain didn't invite her back for another round.

First-round interviews with the consulting firms were almost always based on case questions and inquiries into one's behavior. Behavioral questions such as *Tell me about a time when you were the leader of a team and you failed* were a breeze compared to the case questions. Case questions really didn't have a right answer, but there were plenty of ways to answer it wrong. Designed to see if a student can logically come up with a way to solve the problem with little or no information, the questions are purposely hard to prepare for and can often befuddle even the brightest of young recruits. During her interviews, the case questions Grace was asked did just that. Many of them were nothing like the ones she had prepared herself for. Grace was disappointed in her performance.

Second-round consulting interviews tend to focus more on personality. For the sake of both parties involved, students and recruiters can get a sense of whether they would like to work with one another. "You get different impressions of people," said Grace. "Some are completely snotty, and you know you don't want to work there. Then others you fit with so well. It's really worthwhile to go on those interviews."

Even though her interview with Bain was disappointing, there were brighter options on Grace's recruiting horizon. She had hit it off so well with the recruiters from global consulting firm A.T. Kearney that they quickly offered her a job. She'd have to work a lot of hours at a firm like Kearney, but the experience would be invaluable. The company had a strong international presence and it would expose her to a variety of industries. Grace had also interviewed for positions with top-ten consulting firm Mercer Management, human resources consulting firm Towers Perrin, and Federated Merchandising Group (FMG), the strategic arm of Federated Department Stores that decides whether its stores should buy more Polo Ralph Lauren or Tommy Hilfiger for their fall collections.

Grace also connected well with one of the interviewers from Mercer. Doing the typical cursory look at Grace's résumé, the recruiter quickly noticed that she and Grace had something in common. They were both sisters of Alpha Phi. The recruiter had graduated from Northwestern University, and the two quickly began exchanging sorority stories and comparing experiences. They also shared a love for basketball, but not for the same teams. The recruiter preferred watching college basketball while Grace, being from L.A., was a Lakers fan. Grace left the interview with Mercer feeling as though she may end up with more options than she had originally anticipated

In order to further expand her career possibilities during the recruiting season, Grace interviewed for a marketing position at Microsoft. She had heard the company was a great place to work, with lots of young employees. They were looking to hire fifty students across the country, and Grace was vying for a spot as a marketing analyst for consumer products—which products, however, she wasn't quite sure. Going into her first-round interview with Microsoft on campus, Grace wore one of the three business suits she had in her wardrobe. She became annoyed when she saw that the recruiter sitting across from her was sporting corduroys, a sweater and sneakers. For the first time in her recruiting experience at Wharton, Grace felt like she was incredibly overdressed. "They could have told me to come in khakis," she said.

When the recruiter asked her if she followed technology, Grace thought she meant technology companies like Lucent and Oracle. Knowing that bluffing could get her into deep water during an interview, Grace replied honestly that she really didn't know that much. Certainly this was going to be a mark against her. She later realized that the recruiter was asking about consumer technology products, not specific tech companies.

Things got easier when the recruiter asked Grace what she liked to do for fun. Grace told her about how she had taken occasional trips to Long Beach, New York, to take surfing lessons the previous summer when she was interning for L'Oréal. Forming a query based on Grace's response, the interviewer asked her what she would do for the product launch of a surfboard. Grace's Southern California roots helped her come up with an extensive marketing plan for a new board. She knew that surfers weren't receptive to mass-market ad campaigns, so she suggested guerilla-marketing campaigns that would include endorsements from pro surfers. She also pointed out that females were a burgeoning market to focus on in the surfing industry. It was then that she believed she had won the Microsoft recruiter over.

As the month of November wore on, Grace really began to feel the weight of the dual demands of recruiting and school. The time needed for all of her interviews had made it harder for her to find time to complete her schoolwork. Her father called her twice a week to see how she was holding up and how her interviews had gone. In his phone calls he would ask, "Why don't you have a boyfriend yet?" or "I thought you were a senior. Why aren't you going out and having a good time?" When Grace first came to Wharton, her father had wanted her to be the next Alan Greenspan. Now that she was about to make crucial decisions about the first steps in her career, he just wanted her to be a college student. It was hard for her family to understand how much work Grace had to tackle and how hard she had to work to get the A's she was so used to getting in high school.

In Korea, where her parents grew up, students work extremely hard at a young age to get into their school of choice. Grace's twelve-year-old cousins endured hours of tutoring sessions each night to prepare them for the entrance exams that would determine the rest of their lives. "But once you're in, it's smooth sailing," explained Grace.

Grace's social life in recent weeks had dwindled down to exchanging instant messages with her friends and occasionally joining them for lunch or dinner. Taking five classes this semester—instead of the usual four—had probably been a mistake. Thanksgiving break was rapidly approaching, and Grace would soon be flying back to California to be with her family. But it was hard for her to get excited about the trip. She had three group presentations and two papers due once she returned. She was beginning to believe that she wouldn't have any time to hang out with the friends and family she missed so much.

"Handling all of this and exams is a bit tedious," Grace admitted. She was starting to agree with the people who thought that classes during the first semester of senior year at Wharton should be graded on a pass/fail basis. "Everyone is having their own meltdowns right now," she declared.

By November, Jessica was relieved that she had accepted Lazard's offer and spared herself from any further involvement in the recruiting rush. She barely had any time as it was. Her extracurricular activities—in particular, her involvement with Wharton Women and Musser-Schoemaker, a Wharton organization that brings corporate executives and political leaders to campus to speak to undergraduates about how they attained their success—had taken on a life of their own and were eating up any spare time that Jessica could find in an already hectic schedule filled with group projects and papers. It made getting a good night's sleep an afterthought.

"Last week I was doing hours upon hours of extracurriculars. I got frustrated because I didn't have the energy to put toward the things I really care about, like classes and schoolwork," explained Jessica. "I am not going to sacrifice my grades for anything."

Jessica played a pivotal role in Wharton Women as the vice president of corporate relations and sponsorship for the group. Wharton Women was founded in the 1960s to help female students network and build their careers. The group is sponsored by some of the premier investment banks and largest corporations, including Merrill Lynch, Bank of America, Goldman Sachs and Morgan Stanley. Jessica had been involved with Wharton Women since she was a freshman and was elected to her current post during her junior year. As part of her responsibilities, Jessica met with several recruiters to see if they would speak at the group's events and helped arrange Wharton Women's annual dinner, a gala affair in November that would be keynoted this year by Judy McGrath, the CEO of MTV.

At times Jessica's responsibilities for Wharton Women had forced her to work late into the night. But as she spoke at the annual dinner in front of all of the other women of Wharton, she felt proud of the sacrifices and commitment she had made to be there. Jessica had helped several younger members by reviewing their résumés and giving them career advice. It was one of the most fulfilling roles that she played in the group. "That's so much more important than raising money or arranging corporate events," she explained.

Jessica also served as a co-chair for a lecture series sponsored by Musser-Schoemaker. She was particularly excited about the group's upcoming lecturer, whose appearance she had arranged: Gary Parr, Lazard's, who Jessica admired so greatly. Jessica could scarcely believe that Parr had agreed to speak on campus given his incessantly hectic schedule.

The room was packed when Parr arrived for his speech in mid-November. Close to 125 people showed up to listen to what he had to say. As Parr gave his speech, Jessica was impressed with his candor and ease. He told the students about his path to success and discussed the investment-banking industry and where he saw it heading. He also gave the prospective bankers in the room advice on how to make it in the industry, telling them to specialize in an area that the CEO of their firm cares about and to avoid being a jack-of-all-trades. Following the speech, the group sponsored a dinner that lasted three and a half hours. Jessica sat across from Parr at the table and took the opportunity to ask him for some advice of her own. She wanted desperately to know the secret of not burning out in the investment-banking world. Parr told her to make sure to exercise and take care of her health. But beyond that, he said he didn't know what other advice to give her–it was a different formula for everyone.

As the semester wore on, Jessica had become consumed with the notion of burning out. She knew that the drive she had within her to succeed at things she was passionate about sometimes came at the expense of her own well-being. "I have a mind-set that I just have to keep going," she explained. "I suspect it's like a personality thing. You're unhappy when you think you're not proving something." Jessica made a pact with herself to avoid pulling unnecessary all-nighters and to take a break every once in a while. "Every person needs to find momentary breaks to make trips to the gym," she conceded. "Or to go to Starbucks."

CHAPTER NINE

AN UNFORGIVING WINTER

Thanksgiving break is a short but much-needed respite between midterms and finals for students, a time to refresh, eat home-cooked meals and relax. Typically, students from America's colleges and universities head to their hometowns in order to see their parents for the first time in months and catch up with friends from high school. It's a four-day period where students can let go of their deadlines and return to the more carefree personalities of their youth.

For Wharton seniors, though, Thanksgiving break can be anything but relaxing, especially if they haven't accepted a job offer yet. Grace was well aware of the fact that her "break" would be anything but, she would be running face-first into a week filled with final projects and time-consuming interviews upon her return. The only way to make sure she could pace herself that week and meet her deadlines was to work throughout her trip home to California. She managed to take intermittent breathers, visiting with her friends and her parents, but the time off almost seemed negated by the weight of her obligations.

Just two days after she returned from L.A., Grace had two papers and three group presentations due in Executive Leadership, New Product Development, and Marketing Research, all subjects Grace hadn't expected to be as demanding as they had become.

And as if the amount of work due that day wasn't stressful enough, Grace had three papers due two days later and interviews with three different companies at the end of the week.

"(That) week probably moved me from an A to a B in most of my classes," guessed Grace. She was getting so little sleep that she wasn't quite sure how she even managed to function. "This is child abuse. It *really* is."

In the midst of all of the demands of her first week back, Grace would head up to New York for a third round of interviews with Federated Merchandising Group (FMG) the fashion merchandising company, for their buyers program. Grace also had a group paper for her marketing class due that day. Getting the work done and making the train to New York was already a concern when, by some sinister twist of fate, things managed to get worse. Grace's partner bailed out on the project at the last minute and she was forced to pick up the slack, pulling an all-nighter the night before to finish it. Without the satisfaction of a minute's sleep to ease the buzzing in her head, she got on the 6:30 A.M. train bound for Manhattan and FMG's offices.

"I felt horrible, and I thought I looked horrible as well," fretted Grace. "FMG is all about fashion. Everyone looked good and they were well-rested."

Close to twenty other recruits were already waiting nervously in the offices when Grace arrived at 8:30. Throughout the morning, Grace went through three interviews and listened to a handful of employee presentations, all the while trying to stay alert. When she had met with FMG the first time on campus, the interviewers' questions were more technical, their inquiries geared toward assessing whether Grace knew how to navigate Excel and was comfortable doing quick and complicated mental arithmetic. Now up in New York, they wanted to learn more about her personality and Grace was mustering up as much charm as possible given her exhaustion. Grace liked the people she met at FMG and was impressed that they treated her as though it were an honor to host her.

"I really like them. But when I walked out I wasn't sure that it was what I wanted to do," she said. "If they gave me an offer, I would definitely consider it."

After returning from New York, Grace barely had time to catch up on the sleep she so sorely craved. At 7:00 A.M. the next morning she was scheduled to meet with Towers Perrin at their Philadelphia office to interview for a position as an executive compensation analyst. When she arrived at their offices, Grace was met with a schedule of six different interviews. It was a long, exhausting morning, and she still had to get back to campus for an afternoon round of two thirty-minute interviews with a brand-management consulting company.

After getting through her morning with Towers Perrin virtually unscathed, Grace returned to campus with only a couple of hours to grab something to eat and regroup for the next onslaught of interview questions. Somehow she was managing to get through this day without having a complete meltdown, but she couldn't help but feel that one was drawing near. As soon as Grace entered the room for her first interview with the management consulting company, she got the vibe that the recruiter sitting behind the table really had no interest in being there. At one point, he even perched his feet up on the desk. Clutched between his fingers was a metal cap from a Snapple bottle. With great regularity, his thumb pushed the indent in the center of the cap, making a loud clacking sound that cut through the awkward silences in the room, as well as Grace's responses.

His first question was, "What do you know about our company?" As Grace went into detail about their business, clients and services, he decided he had heard enough and cut her off. Sporting a facial expression that seemed to signify something between extreme boredom and deep distaste, he began to halfheartedly go through her résumé. "I didn't know if he was testing me or not. He was just going down my résumé saying, 'Tell me about L'Oréal, tell me about Morgan Stanley,'" Grace recalled. "I realized I didn't want to work there." In fact, she was surprised that she even went into the second interview with the firm that day.

Despite her off-putting experience with that recruiter, Grace was growing increasingly interested in working for a consulting firm. So far, A.T. Kearney and Towers Perrin were on her short list. Towers Perrin's recruiter didn't make it sound like an offer was coming her way anytime soon, though. "She told me: 'You're not in the decline pile. We're holding on to you,'" said Grace. Later the recruiter called her to determine just how interested Grace was in the position. Grace, they said, was in a "holding pattern" for a job at their firm. Should a candidate for the job decline their offer, it would be extended to Grace.

The proposition didn't inspire confidence. She was already beginning to worry about the reliability of the consulting firms after seeing them rescind job offers from so many Wharton seniors in the last couple of years. "When I entered as a freshman, the economy was great. The thought was: *They* will be knocking on *your* door," she said. "That changed."

Grace's busy schedule didn't allow for Christmas shopping, let alone a lengthy talk with her parents about her career options. At this point in the school year, most of her fellow Wharton seniors were heading into winter break with some peace of mind. At least for the foreseeable future, they knew where they were going to work after graduation. Many of them had accepted their first or second picks and were happily floating through campus with few cares outside of final exams.

Things were coming to a close all around campus—extracurricular activities, classes, projects and Greek life were all winding down. Grace was trying to tackle it all. She still had one more final to study for, and she needed to make sure that she allotted enough time to celebrate her twenty-first birthday, which was the day before

she would fly home to Los Angeles. Time was also expiring on
the L'Oréal offer. She had to give them an answer by the end of
the month, and she was torn about what to do. Her gut was telling
her that the consulting firm A.T. Kearney might be a better option. It could give her a lot of opportunities, as well as impress the
MBA admissions officers.

Grace debated with herself: "I don't know. I learned so much
at L'Oréal that I know if I go back I'll learn more."

There was also Microsoft to think about. Microsoft invited Grace
to come up to their offices outside of Seattle in mid-December for
another round of interviews. Two days after making the six-hour
plane journey home for winter break, Grace flew up to Seattle to
interview at their Redmond, Washington, headquarters.

During her first-round interview with Microsoft on campus,
Grace had felt greatly unprepared. Even though Grace was pretty
certain that she didn't even want the job, her inner perfectionist
would not allow her to slack on preparing for the next interview.
Her plan was to look up analyst reports and go through the company's Web site to learn about its extensive product lines. But the
recruiter had never told Grace what group she would be meeting
with or exactly what the job was that she was interviewing for. It
made it next to impossible to prepare, since Microsoft had hundreds of products. The end of the semester was so hectic that
Grace was unable to find enough time to do even the broader
research that she had hoped to complete. "I went in blind," she
confessed.

Grace was the only person wearing a business suit when she
arrived at Microsoft's compound. Every one was in casual dress,
and Grace got the sense that somehow her garb made her seem
intimidating or perhaps unapproachable. During her first interview she realized that the job would involve some sort of marketing for the company's Office software division. They asked Grace
what her favorite Office product was and what she would do to

make it better. Grace told them Excel. It was, after all, the application she used most at school, and she had become quite adept at navigating spreadsheets. Yet she found it difficult to determine what to do to improve the software.

Grace would have five interviews throughout her visit to Microsoft's offices. She got along with every one of her interviewers, but she just knew the post wasn't for her. She was also far from smitten with the land of *Frasier* and Starbucks. Walking out of Seattle's Nordstrom department store that evening, a man accosted Grace and asked her for a hug. She thought perhaps the man was dared by friends to do this strange act, but for Grace it was extremely creepy. She soon realized it was a smart move by the company to put her up for three days in Seattle. By the end of her trip, she was convinced that she would never want to live there and was relieved to be heading back to L.A. and her family and friends.

Regi didn't make the long flight home to Seattle for Thanksgiving break. He would be heading back to his parents' house in a month for winter break anyway. So he and his sister, who attended medical school at Drexel University, went to D.C. to spend the holiday with one of their uncles instead. Regi had great news that he couldn't wait to celebrate with his family. Just a week and a half earlier, he had accepted an offer from one of his two top choices among the bulge-bracket investment banks. He was feeling good about the decision, which had actually been easier to make than he expected. In typical Regi fashion, he had sought out many advisors. At first, no one could really help him make the decision because the banks were so similar in so many ways. So Regi decided to heed the words of Craig Carnaroli, the executive vice president for finance at Penn who had formerly worked at Credit Suisse First Boston and Merrill Lynch and served as a sort of mentor to Regi. His advice was simple: Base the decision on where he was most comfortable. "Courtesy, respect: I got all of that there," explained Regi.

The bank Regi chose had made eight offers for public-finance analyst positions that year, five of which went to Penn students. Regi was on his way to Chicago for a Super Saturday at another bank when he received the news via voice mail. Once his Super Saturday obligations were over, Regi hurried outside and called the vice president who headed recruiting for the bank and had just offered him a job. Because Regi was going to be in New York the next weekend, the senior VP suggested that Regi stay in the city a little longer and meet up with him. The next week they met in the lobby of the ritzy Soho Grand Hotel downtown, where the vice president was having drinks with his wife and friends. The banker dropped everything to speak with Regi when he arrived and they chatted for close to an hour.

"They were committed to getting me there," said Regi. "Maybe it was selling time and I won't get the same attention when I'm there, but [the other bank] didn't do this during their selling times. I wanted to be at a place that wanted me."

Regi took a few days to think over his options. When he was convinced that he was making the right choice, he called the vice president to accept the offer. Regi was so elated that he forgot to discuss the terms of his employment contract and the finer details—such as his salary and signing bonus—of his new job. He decided he could hold off knowing for a day or so, but he couldn't bask in his own celebrations quite yet. Now he had a tougher call to make: Turning down the other bank that had also offered him a job.

Students often dread these calls. They have been wined and dined so much by recruiters eager to get them on board that they can feel beholden to them. Picking a different firm feels like cheating on a girlfriend. Luckily for Regi, the recruiter was gracious. It wasn't a messy breakup after all.

After accepting the offer, Regi relaxed some, but he couldn't help but begin to plot out the next ten years in his head. The managing director of the division he'd be working for told him that he could transfer to other divisions within the bank should he prove that he could handle the load and do a good job. Regi envisioned different scenarios like moving from the public finance infrastructure division to the emerging economies debt group someday. If he did that for a couple of years, then perhaps he could pursue a master's degree at Harvard's John F. Kennedy School of Government or Columbia's School of International and Public Affairs. Maybe then he could work for the World Bank or the United Nations Development Program—or perhaps he could pursue a PhD and become an economics professor. "It's more conducive to having a family than public banking," he explained.

As the semester was drawing to a close, Regi would have a couple of finals and a few free days left in Philadelphia before flying to Seattle for winter break. The tension in his face relaxed and it appeared that he was actually enjoying himself once again.

"It's a huge weight off of my back," he said. "I really don't care anymore about anything else. I mean, I still want to do well in school and graduate with honors, but I'm not taking things as seriously any more. I have a great job with people I like."

Regi's grades weren't really suffering, though. His biggest concern was the possibility of getting a B in International Finance. It seemed as if every time his professor had an exam it was right before or right after a job interview, and Regi couldn't concentrate as well as he would have liked. He didn't like getting B's, especially in important courses such as finance. The next semester was going to be much easier. He was going to take only four classes, all of which he really wanted to take. It was time for him to enjoy himself. His job wouldn't start until a couple of months after graduation.

"I have seven months to enjoy my college life," he predicted. "Then I will have to work my butt off."

Jon had rounded up three alluring job offers before the end of the fall semester. It was as though he had navigated a harrowing obstacle course and finally made it to the prize. But the challenge wasn't quite over. When his father took him to a 76ers basketball game as a congratulatory present for getting the offers from Johnson & Johnson and American Express, Jon couldn't help but wonder if he had explored all of his options as thoroughly as possible. He wanted to see the rest of his interviews with General Mills through, and he had a nagging sense that even though he had written off Lehman Brothers' invitation to join them, maybe he should still consider it further.

"As much as I feel investment banking isn't for me, Lehman Brothers impressed me all the way through," said Jon. "They hit a soft spot with me."

Even an inkling of consideration toward the banks was a lot coming from Jon, but he couldn't get over the fact that he really liked the people he had met at Lehman. So Jon sought his father's advice. His guidance had always been helpful, even when his father couldn't (or in some cases, wouldn't) tell him exactly which choice to make. He had consulted his father when choosing colleges, and now he needed his help once again when it came to choosing a career.

"My dad wants to push me to make sure I really think out decisions and to make sure that the thought process makes sense," explained Jon. "As long as I'm thinking things through, he's happy."

At the beginning of the semester, he had been fairly certain there was a strong chance he would end up at a consulting firm like McKinsey, Bain or Monitor. But the jobs at American Express and Johnson & Johnson just seemed to suit him better, and he soon canceled most of his remaining interviews with the consulting firms. The corporate jobs wouldn't entail traveling most days of the week, as consulting firms often required, or working twelve- to fifteen-hour days like the banks demanded.

General Mills had become an interesting prospect. Jon was impressed with how gracious the recruiters were when he had to reschedule his second-round interview because his grandmother fell ill. Upon later meeting with General Mills' interviewers at the company's Horsham, Pennsylvania, offices, he decided that he wouldn't make any decisions on his offers until General Mills got back to him with their decision. Compared to the other companies that Jon received job offers from, General Mills was pretty much on par. But they wanted him to stay in Philadelphia if he took the job, and Jon, who grew up in the area, knew he should take the opportunity to live in another city. Although he loved the idea of being close to his family (who regularly scheduled family outings and supported one another like a tribe) and his girlfriend (a premed student at Penn who, as a junior, would remain in Philadelphia to finish up her studies), Jon knew he'd wonder if he was selling himself short by staying in the region. It seemed almost imperative that he explore other places before he came back to Pennsylvania, where he had always envisioned spending the rest of his life. Jon joked that the only job that would keep him in Philadelphia at this point would be to work for the 76ers.

"I might as well be putting this education to good use," he said with a smirk as he described the job he dreamed up as a "team consultant" to the pro basketball franchise. He imagined leading team activities after practice or serving as a strategic advisor to the general manager. Jon even considered sending a resume to the 76ers with a letter explaining how much they need him but he decided against it. He already had enough choices to make as it was.

Jon went through the list of job offers he had received with his father point-by-point, pro versus con. Initially, Jon was "120 percent sold" on Johnson & Johnson, but he wasn't sure if he really wanted to take the financial track that the job would require. It was like a training program for young chief financial officers-to-be, and Jon was looking for something more creative and strategic. That's where American Express came in. At Amex, Jon would be an internal consultant, working on developing programs and strategic initiatives such as consulting on new-product rollouts or analyzing mergers and acquisitions. Jon would also possibly have the ear of CEO Kenneth Chenault, a well-respected executive in the financial services industry who Jon had heard started out at Amex in the very same division he was going to join. Not only did the Strategic Planning and Business Development post hold the promise of great career potential, but the job itself was extremely appealing, especially the hours. Amex also had all of the perks of working for a consulting firm without the constant traveling or a high risk of layoffs in an economic downturn.

And then there was the fact that Amex had also put less pressure on Jon to make a decision. They had given him until December 31 to accept their offer, and thus far, only two American Express employees had called him to see if he had any questions. When he got the offer from Lehman Brothers it was a different story. Within twenty-four hours Jon had been bombarded with phone calls by everyone he had met throughout the interviewing process, all of them asking when he was going to make a decision. This was a typical experience for Wharton students who were offered investment-banking positions. The banks are notorious for applying more pressure than other employers when it comes to wanting an answer fast. To some students, it was flattering to be called and e-mailed by analysts and vice presidents with such urgency. It made them feel wanted, like they were the one in power. To students like Jon, though, it seemed like incessant hounding and needling.

It was looking more and more like Jon was leaning toward American Express. "It's my first choice, kind of," Jon said with a hint of skepticism. "It's hard to have everyone say, 'Wow! I would kill for that job!' and then you turn it down."

American Express had invited Jon to New York for their sell day in early December, but it fell on the same day as his Management 100 group's end-of-year presentation, an event that Jon was scheduled to emcee. Jon was starting to get nostalgic about his three-year run as a TA and was growing upset that it was rapidly coming to an end. He had become close with his freshman students. They would call him at all hours of the day and night for advice and looked up to Jon as a role model. On the last day that his recitation group met, the students had presented him with a 350-page hardcover edition of quotations. It was a well-thought-out gift. Jon was infamous for blurting out inspiring quotes to his group, and many of them had told him that they had indeed been inspired.

"I almost started crying," Jon admitted. "I will really miss them. They were really a special group. No two of them were alike, and they all came together."

Jon's group was now getting ready to present their community-service project, a diversity day for two hundred local high school students. They had arranged everything, including two speakers who talked about diversity in the workplace. They organized team-building exercises for the kids to show them how similar they are despite their different backgrounds. They even convinced a local radio station to give away prizes and free gifts on campus.

"Now that I'm not crazy interviewing, I'm going to class again. I've also been able to appreciate the process a little more," he said. Heading into Thanksgiving break, Jon was relieved that he was finished with the days of running from one interview to another. The recruiting season had certainly taken a toll on him, though. He now had to play catch-up on all of the work that he'd put on hold for recruiting, including grading papers for his Management 100 group.

Jon usually had ten papers to grade each week, but the papers had piled up. He now had fifty papers to get through by the end of the weekend. Saturday was out because he was going to his grandparents' sixtieth wedding anniversary, where he and his sister were reciting a poem. The papers would have to wait until Sunday. Typically, he spent half an hour going over each paper, but now he was going to grade them in half the time. It still meant he had close to eight hours of work to do. "I'm the head TA and I'm *supposed* to be the responsible one," he noted in a tone of sarcasm.

Jon wanted to get as much done as possible before Thanksgiving. His birthday was coming up later in the week and his friends wanted to take him to the legendary campus watering hole, Smokey Joe's, for "Sink or Swim" night, a weekly drink special that offers twenty-five-cent beers after the patron pays a five-dollar cover charge. On Wednesday, Jon would be leaving for his parents' house to prepare for Thanksgiving. Because the extended family would already be together, they used the holiday to celebrate Jon's birthday as well. Not only would he be stuffing himself full of turkey and all of the trimmings, but he'd also have birthday cake to eat. Somewhere between all of the festivities, Jon really wanted to sit down with his father for what he was calling the "Thanksgiving Summit." Making a decision was becoming increasingly urgent to Jon, who wanted to finally relax and enjoy his senior year.

When Jon eventually had some downtime with his father, it was pretty clear to both of them that Jon had already decided on American Express. The only misgiving that he had about the job at this point was that the downtown Manhattan skyscraper where his offices would be located was not far from the ruins of the World Trade Center. Jon had experienced a dose of what it's like to live in a world of terrorism when he went to Israel for six months in high school. Each child had been armed with a personal gas mask and knew the location of the nearest shelter in case of an emergency. The terrorist attacks on September 11, 2001, had increased his fears. "I guess I'll just have to get over it," he said.

By the time he picked up the phone to call American Express and tell them he had made his decision, those fears had become an afterthought. He called the vice president who had worked hard at recruiting him. She immediately told Jon that he had made her day. She had just come back from a recruitment meeting, and they had discussed how they were worried they were going to lose him to another firm.

Jon then had to call Lehman and Johnson & Johnson to break the news to them. He was nervous that the recruiters he met with would give him a hard time or make him feel guilty. The banker at Lehman asked Jon to give his line of reasoning for picking the job at Amex. When Jon explained, the recruiter seemed to understand. It was the next call to Johnson & Johnson that Jon was truly dreading. "When I was rushing fraternities, I hated deciding between two groups of friends," Jon recalled. "I don't want to call Johnson & Johnson. They sent me a huge Halloween package with chocolate-covered pretzels and saltwater taffy."

Johnson & Johnson and American Express had been neck-and-neck in Jon's mind throughout most of the semester. (Amex had sent him Godiva and Ghirardelli chocolates). Jon knew that whichever company he chose, it would be a great choice. For his peers, though, that didn't seem to be the case. "So many of my friends are out there still searching for what they want to do. And they're stressed because all of these people have offers from banks," he said. "The Wharton kids that don't have jobs, they are the most stressed."

For Jon, making those calls in early December was like ripping a three-hundred-pound gorilla off his back. He could now concentrate on his finals and the remainder of his obligations—and perhaps have some fun with his friends again. Jon didn't have many final exams, but he did have two monstrous group papers due the second week of December. One was for a political science class guest-taught by Pennsylvania Governor (and Penn alum) Ed Rendell called "Who Gets Elected and Why." Jon found the class especially interesting because his mother was now awaiting a recount of the votes cast a month earlier for her candidacy for a seat on the State's Superior Court because the results were so close. For their final project, the class was given information on a fictional election that was based on a real scenario. The groups had to present their plan for campaigning, funding and legal strategies, among other factors. Jon was stuck with three sophomores who weren't pulling their weight when it came to getting their presentation together, and he ended up carrying most of the burden.

The other paper was for Jon's entrepreneurship class. Jon loved the class because he and his friends were working on the One Stop College Shop in it. The paper was actually a thirty-page business plan for the endeavor. The cover of the plan was the infamous photo of John Belushi wearing his "College" sweatshirt in the movie *Animal House*. Jon and his group then presented their business plan to two venture capitalists. The experience was made even more anxiety-ridden for Jon than other presentations because he truly hoped that the One Stop College Shop would become a reality someday.

After turning in the papers, Jon was done with schoolwork for the semester. He now turned his attention toward his other obligations. Jon had been asked to speak at the Management 100 year-end event, which takes place after each of the Management 100 groups present their projects. Penn's president Judith Rodin and Wharton's newly appointed Vice Dean Barbara Kahn were scheduled to speak before him. There were seven hundred students and faculty in the audience. Stepping onto the stage, Jon encountered the first bout of stage fright he had ever endured in his life. But as he started speaking about giving back to the community and how fitting it was that Management 100 is the first course that students take at Wharton, his nerves eased and Jon spoke with the confidence that he normally conveyed.

After the speeches were over, Jon, his friend Mark, who had also been a Management 100 TA and was head of the Wharton Council and another TA named Rose, broke through the rigidity of the night with a skit for the students. "It was one big sexual innuendo using management terms. It was a lot of fun," laughed Jon. The skit entailed a scene where Jon and Rose played a couple who were trying to deal with their relationship problems. Jon's character urges Rose's character to work through them:

Rose: It's going to be painful, Jon . . .

Jon: I can submerge my ego.

Rose: Okay, fine. If you want to know, fine. I cannot handle your lack of energy.

Jon: What?

Rose: That's right. You've lost your physical stamina, baby.

Jon: What are you saying?

Rose: I'm saying I need a man who is a Creator-Innovator, Jon! It's just been so routine lately.

Jon: But what about last Sunday . . . you know . . . with the . . .

Rose: Oh, Jon!

All the while, Mark, who was playing "Wharton Man," a superhero well-versed in management speak, urged the couple to continue communicating. By the end, Jon declared to Rose:

Rose, not only will I be more affiliative, but from here on out, I will also be your Organizer. Your Thruster-Organizer.

The couple embraced and the skit concluded in a roar of laughter from the crowd. It was a hit.

Once the skit and the rest of Jon's responsibilities were over, he felt renewed again. It had been a tough semester, but he had managed to get through it while keeping a cool head and not jumping at the first job offer that crossed his path. He felt he had stayed true to himself, as he had pledged to do at the onset of recruiting season. Although Jon was done with his work for the semester early, he stuck around to relax with his friends for a few nights before heading home.

"Last night I just felt like myself again," he would say as the semester drew to a close. "I wasn't doing job stuff. The TA stuff was over. I love my boys. We feel like freshmen again."

But he knew that feeling would subside all too soon.

The release of tension that Jon and other Wharton seniors who had accepted jobs were experiencing was lost on Anthony Sandrik. He had been invited to a couple of final-round interviews, but none of them ended up yielding offers. Anthony had limited his job search to trading positions, and he soon discovered that not only were the positions few and far between, but many of them weren't exactly what he was looking for.

The Chicago Trading Co. had flown Anthony to Chicago for a round of interviews. After a couple of sit-down meetings, Anthony was escorted onto the floor of the Chicago Board of Options Exchange with a couple of the firm's younger employees. It was a madhouse, with guys screaming at the top of their lungs, their arms flailing. Anthony became immediately uninterested at that point.

"You don't need a business background for that type of work," he explained. "You just have to be good at math. The kind of stuff I want to do is more intellectual. There everything is 'sell high, buy low.' "

Anthony wanted a position closer to what he did over the summer at the hedge fund he worked for. He wanted to be the "right-hand guy" to some of the big-time traders at a firm and learn the ropes from them. He didn't want to be screaming his lungs out on some trading floor. Morgan Stanley's trading positions sounded a little better, but when Anthony learned they were moving their operations to Westchester County, New York, a suburb north of New York City, he knew he didn't want the job. He wanted to live in the thick of things, and Westchester was a far cry from Manhattan.

"If I had known it was going to be *this* hard to find the job I want at the beginning of recruiting season, I would have applied to the consulting firms," said Anthony.

The Chicago Trading Co. and Morgan Stanley most likely sensed Anthony's lack of enthusiasm for the posts he was being interviewed for, because neither of them offered him a job. The act of getting rejected had its own term in the Whartonite lexicon. It was called getting "dinged." And Anthony had just gotten "dinged" twice.

There was an infuriating formula to the rejections that Anthony and other Wharton students received. Oftentimes, it came in the form of an e-mail or letter. To Anthony, it seemed as if the rejection letters always started out with a compliment like "You're really smart," or "You're very intelligent." And then there was always the inevitable, "But..." "As soon as they compliment you, you're out," joked Anthony. "I would appreciate them being straight up. If they say I'm really qualified, then why don't I have a job?"

Anthony was growing increasingly nervous about heading into the second semester without a single offer in hand. He began to feel he needed to broaden his options beyond trading positions. "I think I shot myself in the foot," he said. "I only applied to twenty companies, and that's really not that many."

Anthony typically took things in stride and often joked about the hysteria that had hit his fellow Wharton students during his stand-up routines with campus comedy troupe, Simply Chaos. In the student-run newspaper at Wharton, he occasionally wrote witty columns poking fun at Wharton students most consumed with recruiting season—which often seemed to be nearly all Wharton students. But now he was starting to feel a bit envious of those who had pushed themselves so hard to secure an offer early on.

"It's frustrating," he explained. "In high school, I was accepted early [to Wharton]. I knew early what I was going to do in the next four years. Now I want the security of knowing what I will be doing over the next two years or so."

Those feelings didn't defeat Anthony's confidence, though. He knew that he could get a job for the sake of getting a job. But he also knew that his degree from Wharton gave him the luxury to look for a job that he really wanted. "You don't know what unemployment feels like here [at Wharton]," he said. "They told us 'even in the Depression, people got jobs.'"

Anthony was also clinging to something he had heard from the career counselors at Wharton. They had told him that if the economy continued to improve, then the recruiters would come back to campus in the second semester to fill the spots they were unsure they had the budget for during the first semester. Seeing that many of his peers were already landing higher signing bonuses than the seniors the year before them was also an encouraging sign. For the time being, Anthony decided to just focus on finishing his coursework for the semester. He was heading to his parents' home in Paris in a few days and then flying to Lebanon to see the rest of his family during winter break. He would continue his job search when he returned in January.

As the fall semester draws to a close at Wharton, the night encroaches earlier and the days, while shortened, feel longer because there is so much to get accomplished before nightfall. The early sunsets only made things worse for Jessica, who felt like she was running on fumes. Her eyes looked uncharacteristically tired as she entered the Starbucks on Walnut Street to get a drink and decompress for a minute in one of the coffeehouse's oversized armchairs.

The night before, Wharton Women had held elections. Jessica

would hand over her spot as vice president of corporate relations to her successor within days, and she had wanted to make sure it was going to go to someone competent. In the upper floors of Huntsman, Jessica and her fellow board members had sat in the MBA Café interviewing candidates and later debating over which ones seemed best suited to take over their posts. Jessica pounded the table in support of a candidate who she felt displayed the strongest leadership skills out of all of the those nominated to take over her post. It was a quality that Jessica felt you just couldn't teach someone. One of the other board members supported another girl for the post, and the debate was heated. Eventually, Jessica's choice won. "You realize how passionate you are for Wharton Women when you're going to bat for these girls," she said proudly.

The elections had dragged on late into the night. Although Jessica was anxious to get home and finish working on a fifteen-page paper due the next day, she also wanted to make sure that solid candidates were chosen for the leading roles for Wharton Women. She felt some of them just didn't have what it takes. One candidate told her that she thought it would be a great idea to get pop singer/actress Mandy Moore to speak at the group's annual dinner. Another runner-up suggested a charity ball. "I was like, 'Ya'll, we have worked too long and too hard to be taken seriously. We are not a sorority, we are career women,'" Jessica recalled complaining.

Once all of the offices were filled, Jessica had turned her attentions to her paper. She was already sleep-deprived, having worked throughout her time in Texas over Thanksgiving break. Her parents had friends over the day Jessica flew in. Jessica hung out with her mother's and stepfather's friends for a couple of hours and then went back to work. The next day, she had skipped out on the LSU football game her parents attended with her sister in order to get work done and she missed dinner that night, too. Now looking at the paper she had worked on with such determination, Jessica was happy she had put in the time. It was an analysis of a potential merger between General Electric's NBC and Vivendi Universal, which had been announced a couple of months earlier. The report was bound in a black plastic binder and the cover page was complete with the color logos of both companies. Jessica worked hard to figure out the competitive advantages the company would have once the merger was complete. It was the same type of work she would be doing at Lazard, and she couldn't help but put her all into it.

Now Jessica still had to work on several other projects, and she was growing concerned that her body was starting to revolt. She didn't even have time for her regular visits to the Pottruck Health and Fitness Center. The stress was starting to overwhelm her. "I don't have time to get sick right now," she exclaimed. "At the end of freshman year, I was so sleep-deprived that I was always sick. And last night I wigged out on all of these cookies."

After Jessica turned in her paper, she had a much heftier assignment to face. Her Security Analysis professor had assigned her and her partner Rob a project that was eating up much of her time. "Rob and I spend ten times as much time together than I do with anyone I hang out with socially," revealed Jessica.

The two were putting together a report on Belk, the largest private department store chain in the country, which had been founded 125 years ago. The professor always picked a private company, making it harder for the students to just look up analyst reports or public information. The assignment was a monster, and it was now due in a couple of days. She even skipped out on the MBA charity ball that she was invited to in order to work on the project. "This is like real banking. There will always be other balls," she rationalized.

Exhausted, Jessica and her partner turned in their Belk report on Monday morning. Jessica's sorority, Delta Delta Delta (known as Tri-Delt), was having its Winter Ball that evening. Even though Jessica wasn't all that active in her sorority, she felt she had to go. She was at the point in her college career where she was now handing off all of her board positions and memberships, and she felt it was imperative that she at least get some closure with them all.

It had also been close to a month since she had really hung out with her friends, and she thought the ball would be a good social break, a time to catch up and unwind a little. Until recently, Jessica had even considered a coffee break a luxury. Partying was not high on her list of priorities. She wasn't a big drinker, because she felt it only caused people to waste time sleeping in or being hungover, and she couldn't afford that.

On the contrary, Jessica always seemed to need something to work on. As a member of the Joseph Wharton Scholars Program, she was now setting out on establishing the topic for her senior thesis. Started in 1988, the Joseph Wharton Scholars Program is an honors program that incoming Wharton freshmen and a select few rising Wharton sophomores can apply to for admission. Each year about fifty students are admitted. These students typically are in the top ten percent of their high school or freshman Wharton class, and they must maintain a minimum 3.4 GPA, which means graduating at least cum laude. Throughout their college careers, Joseph Wharton Scholars students are required to complete eight honors courses, three of which must be taken at the College usually through the Benjamin Franklin Scholars honors program. The biggest hurdle of the program comes in their senior year, when they must research and complete a senior research project. In the summer before senior year, the students are supposed to begin formulating and researching their thesis, but it's a rare few who can get such an early start.

At first, Jessica was going to do her thesis on what she felt were alleged gender differences in communication. Jessica believed the differences were more a result of socialization rather than something hardwired. For her, it was the classic nature-versus-nurture argument, and the subject was something Jessica had encountered personally. "It's the stigma women face: the work/life balance," she would explain.

Jessica knew she wasn't a typical "girl." Her career came first, and at this point, she didn't want to get married until much later in life, and she couldn't imagine having children. She had fought against the labels that came along with her long blonde hair and cheerleading background, and she hadn't included her involvement with Tri-Delt on her résumé for fear of being typecast. But even with all of her precautions, people still tried to stereotype her. Recently, one of her fellow summer analysts from Lazard e-mailed her to congratulate her on taking the full-time job at the bank. He asked, "Now that you have a job, are you going to spend your time going to the tanning salon and the gym?" It was that kind of attitude that outraged Jessica and only made her want to prove herself more.

Given experiences like these, it was understandable how the thesis topic on gender communication was compelling to Jessica. But then she started thinking it may make more sense to write about something more beneficial to her career. She decided she should do something financial. She scrapped her original thesis and decided to investigate the subject of valuing financial institutions. Most of the students enrolled in the honors program don't start working on their thesis until second semester, when the bulk of recruiting season is over and they have completed all of the more taxing classes. But Jessica wanted to start working on it right away, even though she wasn't even done with her fall-term finals yet. She arranged a meeting with the head of financial institutions at Wharton and planned to spend her entire winter break becoming well-versed on the matter. She was joining her family in the Turks and Caicos islands for five days over Christmas, and Jessica didn't envision herself snorkeling or drinking mai tais.

"I'll be sitting on the beach in the Turks and Caicos studying the history of M&As," she explained. "I'll be so far ahead of my analyst class!"

An early December snowstorm was moving toward the East Coast as Shreevar Kheruka packed his bags for a weekend in Boston. The meteorologists were calling for three to five inches. It would take a lot more snow than that to keep Shreevar from getting on the plane. He was one of twenty-five college seniors being offered a job at the consulting firm Monitor. Now Monitor was bringing these recruits up to its offices in Cambridge, Massachusetts, for "Choice Weekend."

The label made it sound a lot less forced than "Sell Day," but that was exactly what this weekend really was: an opportunity for Monitor's recruiters and employees to persuade these young prospects to choose them over the Bains and McKinseys of the world. Monitor told the recruits that it was a chance for them to determine whether or not they felt comfortable in Monitor's environs. It was also a chance to ask any outstanding questions that might help them make a decision. Before he left for Boston, Shreevar had received a call from the head of recruiting; she wanted to see which divisions Shreevar would like to learn more about. It gave Shreevar another opportunity to put his hat in the ring for the Private Equity division, which he wanted to work in most. He was soon enjoying the special attention that the firm was lavishing upon him.

Shreevar arrived safely in Boston on Thursday evening, and hailed a cab to the Eliot Hotel in the trendy Back Bay neighborhood where Monitor was putting him up for the next two days. Shreevar swiftly unpacked before he joined the rest of the students and a cross-section of Monitor's employees at the Armani Cafe, an Italian restaurant amid the high-end shops of Boston's Newbury Street. Mingling with Monitor's top brass during the cocktail hour, the recruits were stunned to see that even Monitor's

CEO was there. As they shuffled toward the table for dinner, the recruits realized that they were assigned seats near the senior-level members of the divisions they were interested in working for. Shreevar was happy to have the ear of one of the power players from the firm's Private Equity division. He turned on his subtle charm and they quickly broke the ice.

The dinner lasted for close to three hours. Sated with food and wine, the older executives of the firm left for their homes. Some of the recruits did as well, wanting a good night's sleep before a long day at Monitor's offices the next day. Shreevar chose to join the gaggle of twenty-one-year-olds who weren't ready to turn in yet. Along with the head of recruiting, ten of the recruits ventured out into Boston's wintry climes to hang out at a local bar. For Shreevar, it was a great chance to bond with his peers; after all, they might be his coworkers someday soon. He didn't get back to his hotel room until close to 3:00 A.M.

Shreevar cursed the alarm clock when it shocked him awake the next morning at 8:00 A.M. He knew he had to get up. Monitor had prepared an event-filled day that would begin at 9:00 A.M. Luckily, the first part of the day entailed listening to people speak about various aspects of the firm. It gave Shreevar some time to wipe the sleep out of his eyes and gather his wits. One of the first people to speak to the recruits was the allocations manager, who talked for an hour about how he doles out projects to first-year analysts. He would try to meet their requests to work on specific projects, but there wasn't always a guarantee. Shreevar thought about cornering the market on private-equity assignments or perhaps getting assigned to an international gig so he could do some real traveling. A partner of the firm was up next, and the way he addressed the group helped push Shreevar over the edge in making his decision.

"It was very impressive," described Shreevar. "People asked him about Monitor's weaknesses. He didn't give the usual B.S. answer.

He was genuine." Shreevar's opinion of Monitor was improving by the second.

The senior-level employees then left the recruits with four analysts who were just finishing their first year at the firm. It was as if their parents had just left them home alone for the weekend. Breathing a sigh of relief, the recruits felt they could be more candid and ask those niggling questions that may appear unseemly to upper-level executives. *How many hours will I work? Who is the best person to work for? What can I expect?* The recruits learned that they would normally work fifty-five to sixty-five hours a week, but during crunch time, an eighty-five-hour week wasn't out of the question. They should also expect to pack their bags on a regular basis—as is common in the consulting industry, there would be plenty of travel involved. They would be on the road at least two days a week, if not more.

After lunch, each student embarked on a series of half-hour "conversations." Shreevar met with the heads of the three divisions that he had expressed interest in: Private Equity, Manufacturing, and Marketing. He found all of them to be genuine. Monitor, one of them told him, wasn't as structured as the McKinseys of the world. As a first-year, he wouldn't be allowed to speak with clients, but once he proved that he could handle himself, those responsibilities would follow. Shreevar took it as a personal challenge. He wanted to quickly prove himself.

Shreevar and the rest of the group then took a tour through Monitor's offices. While the firm has offices in more popular cities like New York and Paris, its Cambridge office serves as headquarters and houses close to five hundred employees. It was an architecturally stunning brick-and-glass building with atria throughout.

"It's the best office I've ever seen. Everyone has access to natural light. Working at Goldman Sachs there's no chance of that," explained Shreevar.

He wouldn't be stuck in a cubicle, either. Instead, he'd share an office with one of his coworkers. There was no doubt that the Cambridge office was where Shreevar wanted to work, even though most of his friends would be heading to New York. The Private Equity group was based in Cambridge, and so were all of Monitor's most influential executives. Like any good Wharton student, Shreevar knew it was important to be as close to the power players as possible.

That evening, the group met for dinner. Comprised mainly of the recruits and analysts, the median age of the crowd was a lot younger than the previous night. There was a sense of jubilation in the room, especially among those who had already made up their minds to join Monitor. Shreevar, a vegetarian, ate pasta primavera and sipped glasses of wine throughout the three-hour dinner. Even after a jam-packed day, the group wasn't ready to call it a night. They made their way to The Big Easy, a nearby nightclub with a cavernous interior that often played host to local bachelorette parties. Despite '80s music he called "cheesy," Shreevar was having fun. He just wasn't compelled to hit the dance floor.

The snow began falling around 11:30 that night. By the time the group left The Big Easy for another bar, the streets were carpeted in glistening white crystals. Around 2:00 A.M., they decided to head back to the hotel. There were twenty-five of them and not a single cab in sight. Shreevar used his charming smile to convince a local woman to give five of them a ride back to the hotel. As he and his traveling companions left in her car, the remaining students were left to fend for themselves. Many of them ended up walking as the snow continued to fall.

The next morning Shreevar made it to a breakfast for the recruits a half hour late. Looking out the window of the hotel, he saw that more than a foot of snow had accumulated on the streets of Boston. US Airways soon called his cell phone to tell him his flight was canceled. Shreevar booked himself on a flight for the next day and spent the rest of Saturday relaxing and watching TV on Monitor's tab. He had brought the books he needed to study for a final scheduled on Monday, but he wasn't motivated to crack them. Something about the quiet that the snow brought and being in a different place made him feel like it was okay to take this break. Shreevar also had a group project for his Real Estate Finance class due on Monday, and one of the other group members was also stuck in Boston. They would need to work a marathon of hours when they returned to campus in order to catch up.

When Shreevar awoke Sunday morning, the snow was still falling. It seemed as though there was an unending supply of the stuff. Shreevar's flight was canceled once again. Now the workload he was facing seemed more real, and anxiety began to set in. He had to get back. He and some other students made their way to the train station, only to find that the train to Philadelphia was running three hours late. "I was screwed," he proclaimed. On his return to campus, his Real Estate Finance group would have to work until 6:00 A.M. Monday morning to complete their project—and he still had a final to take that day.

In the next week and a half Shreevar would also have to turn in four papers and complete a take-home final. But that seemed like the least of his cares. He now had two offers in hand that he was seriously considering. There was the offer from Monitor, where he felt so comfortable, and there was also the offer from JP Morgan Asset Management for a position that the firm had said they had never before invited a person his age to take. Both were so attractive to him that he believed accepting either would be a smart move. In ten days, Shreevar was going home to Bombay for winter break, and he wanted to be certain of his decision before he'd have to break the news to his grandfather and father. He was nervous that they would try to talk him out of it, and he wanted to have the proper mind-set to convince them.

"If you're committed to something, it's easier to go to bat for it," he explained.

PART IV

AFTER THE RUN

CHAPTER TEN

A NEW SEASON BEGINS

Grace returned a few days early from winter break to help out with Alpha Phi's rush, a two-week period of theme parties that the sororities throw to find the best girls for their upcoming pledge class among Penn's freshmen and sophomores. Grace was happy that she wasn't one of those sisters in the sorority who had completely checked out by second semester of their senior year, but she wasn't one of those inordinately active sisters, either. She had never lived in the sorority house on Walnut Street. Opting to live alone in one of the graduate-student apartment complexes made more sense to her, given the amount of work she always had to do. Nevertheless, Grace did try to attend as many events as possible, and rush was one of the most important events to be a part of. Throughout the process, girls rushing the sororities are assessed by their personality, style, approachability, intelligence and extracurricular activities. Almost everything is open to scrutiny. The sisters were looking to select only the best girls to create the next generation of Alpha Phi.

Rushing wasn't unlike the recruiting process Grace had just gone through. She had spent the last semester trying to impress the banks and consulting firms, navigating their queries and obeying their schedules. She had, in essence, rushed to be a member of their upcoming analyst pledge classes. Grace, too, had been under a great deal of scrutiny and pressure. She, too, had to compete with her peers. It almost seemed possible that the Greek system was a caricature of life in the financial-services industry. Once a person gets a job with a bank, for example, they are treated like pledges. They are handed most of the dirty work, and they put in the longest hours. As with fraternities and sororities, there is a hierarchy among the banks and the consulting firms, and each of them has a signature personality that defines the type of people that they are looking for. Alpha Phi was somewhat of a fun-loving group that liked to get involved in campus activities. Other sororities, on the other hand, were more renowned for their sheer ability to party.

Watching the freshmen eagerly trying to make a good impression on the sisters of Alpha Phi, Grace felt a great sense of relief—her own "rush" was now over. She had finally made a decision about her career over winter break. She was going to join A.T. Kearney. As much as she loved L'Oréal, she wasn't fully convinced that working for the cosmetics maker would be the strongest starting point for her career. Before getting her MBA at some point in the next two to four years, she wanted to gain exposure to a variety of industries in order to figure out where to focus her studies and her postgraduate job search. A.T. Kearney would expose her to all types of companies and even some government agencies—ranging from aerospace to utilities to sports and entertainment. "It's a taste of everything so I can see what it is I really want to do," she explained. Perhaps after getting her MBA, she would decide that L'Oréal really was where she belonged after all, but she wanted her experience at A.T. Kearney to confirm whether or not that was the case.

While debating her decision, Grace sought her parents' advice. Her father, a construction developer, kept a hands-off approach despite his jokes about wanting her to be the next Alan Greenspan. He knew that Grace would figure out what was best for her career on her own. His faith in her bolstered her own confidence in her decision-making abilities. Her mother, on the other hand, embarked on a dialogue about how much she missed her only daughter during the years she spent in Philadelphia. It was a not-so-subtle push for Grace to return to the West Coast. Over winter break, a recruiter from A.T. Kearney called Grace out of the blue and sweetened the pot for their offer. They asked her if she'd like to work in their Southern California office in Costa Mesa. It was as if A.T. Kearney was perfectly tailoring the position to Grace's (and her mother's) desires.

"I got *everything* I wanted," she said in disbelief.

The hard part came when Grace had to let L'Oréal down. The people she had met at L'Oréal had been extremely supportive throughout Grace's job-hunting experience. They never pressured her for a response. They had even encouraged her to go through the recruiting process to ensure she was making the right decision. Grace called them on December 30, the day before her deadline expired to accept the job. She was getting ready to leave for Las Vegas, where she and her friends were going to celebrate New Year's, when she made the call.

"It was really difficult. I had to tell the person I loved most at the firm that I wasn't going to work for them," she said with a touch of guilt. "I'm sure that they have fabulous people that signed on."

Grace's sponsor at A.T. Kearney called Grace soon thereafter to see if she had any remaining questions about the job. "I told her I was ready to come on board and sign. She was so excited," recalled Grace, her tone shifting from sorrow to glee in seconds.

Her new title was going to be Business Analyst. Grace was the only undergraduate student from Penn hired by A.T. Kearney for its Costa Mesa office. She didn't know much about the office; not even how many people worked there. It made her a bit anxious, but she now had months before she really needed to think about it.

Grace's course load for the spring semester was a liberal arts overload. She only needed one more course to graduate, but Grace couldn't stand the idea of taking the easy route, or for that matter allowing her mind to lie almost idle for the remaining four months of her college career. So she signed up for five classes, three of which she took on a pass/fail basis. While Grace was appreciative of her Wharton education and what it had done to prepare her for a career, she felt that she had missed out on a broad liberal arts background and now she was going to play catch-up with classes like Victimology and "Japan in Contemporary Literature," which only required three book report–type papers and a presentation.

Like Jessica Kennedy, Grace also needed to start her senior research project for the Joseph Wharton Scholars Program. Wharton finance professor Dr. Martin Asher, an approachable and well-liked mentor among the undergraduates, was the advisor for the program, and he generously devoted his time to help students come up with research topics and guide them through the process. After some debate on her topic, Grace and a friend chose to team up and look into the various ways that popular fads such as Beanie Babies and Mr. Potato Head had been successfully marketed, and to see how those methods more often than not differed from traditional marketing efforts. Asher helpfully suggested people that Grace could speak with to aid her in her research. The partners were due to present their idea to the class in March. By mid-January they hadn't even started doing their research yet, but Grace was little concerned.

"After all that I went through last semester, this is nothing," said Grace matter-of-factly. "I am really glad it's over. And hopefully I will never have to do anything that stressful again."

Grace's friends in the College were in a different boat. Most of them were just starting to think about their résumés and getting a job. They were hoping to benefit from Grace's early recruiting experience and guidance.

"Wharton students are more prepared for the job market," said Grace. "The College students don't know how to do presentations, résumés, things like that. Maybe the competitive level isn't there to get internships and jobs."

Shreevar spent three weeks in Bombay, India, with his family over winter break, his first return home since August. Usually, these trips were a much-needed time for him to relax and recoup between semesters. But this time, Shreevar's mind was heavy with the burden of telling his family about his decision to take the job at Monitor. Shreevar hadn't officially accepted the offer yet, for fear that somehow his family would convince him not to.

"It's different for Americans," explained Shreevar. "In America, once you go to college and you graduate, then you are sort of on your own." In India, he explained, most kids return home and live with their family after college. "It's more of a cohesive family unit. You might think it's an infringement on your privacy, but when the chips are down, it's really beneficial."

It took Shreevar a few days to bolster his resolve before sitting down with his grandfather and father to discuss the matter. They conversed, argued and debated for close to four hours. It was far from easy for Shreevar to prove his point.

"I had to tell them that me staying in the U.S. for a little bit was the best thing for the family," said Shreevar. His argument revolved around the experience that he would gain at Monitor and how it could prove helpful to the growth of the family's glass import/ export business when he returned to India someday. "Monitor will put me on different cases over the year. It will help me get a good understanding of what is going on with other industries in the world. When I go back home, I can apply the problem-solving aspect to my own firm, or if I feel like we need to start something new in the family, we can start doing that," he explained.

He was already thinking about all of the different places the family business could go. The company already made everything from drinking glasses to sheet glass for windows to laboratory glass for high-precision science experiments. Primarily it exported its goods to Africa, but Shreevar saw many opportunities for expansion across the globe. He could possibly learn how to go about doing that at a place like Monitor or at least make some good connections.

Eventually, Shreevar's family came around. Once he got the conversation over with, he could breathe easier. His father wasn't one hundred percent behind the decision, but he seemed to understand. Shreevar ended up having a great time in India and the remainder of his trip seemed to fly by.

When Shreevar returned to campus, he was met with a handful of messages from Monitor's coordinator of recruiting. They had extended offers to four other Penn students and it seemed as if Shreevar was probably the last holdout. A couple of weeks later, Shreevar formally accepted the offer. He immediately knew he had made the right decision. Not only would his work be relevant to his goals, but he also felt like he could be completely himself at the firm. Throughout his interviews, he had never tried to put on a show for the recruiters, because he had never felt the need to.

Shreevar could now enjoy his final semester at Penn. "I'm really relaxed. It's second semester of my senior year and I haven't done any work so far," he said at the end of January. "I'm totally chill and I'm just looking to enjoy myself and travel around a bit."

Unfortunately, he had so many course requirements for Wharton remaining that he had to sign up for a full course load—and none of the classes were what could be characterized as easy. Shreevar hoped his experience from last summer as a commodity trader would help him out in his International Finance class. He was also taking a course on family-controlled businesses that he was sure would keep him interested given his background. The remaining classes included Legal Studies, Management, and his International Relations thesis, none of which would be considered a cakewalk.

After her last fall semester final in Legal Studies, Jessica still couldn't let go. Just a matter of days until she left for winter break, Jessica awoke in the middle of the night with the words "Misappropriation theory!" resounding through her mind. It was part of an answer to one of the questions on her Legal Studies final that she hadn't been able to remember during the exam. Now it was haunting her in her dreams. Winter break would be the first extended period of deadline-free time that Jessica had had in close to a year—yet she still set out to find work to do.

During the five days she spent in the Turks and Caicos islands, Jessica divided her thoughts between wishing the late December rain would cease so she could wear her new bathing suit and what she was going to do about her thesis for Joseph Wharton Scholars. Prior to leaving for the vacation, Jessica discovered that there was very little research available on valuing financial institutions, and definitely not enough on which to base her thesis. She would have to revisit her topic on gender communication in the workplace, and she couldn't stop thinking about the work she needed to do. It was as though having free time made Jessica uncomfortable. She wasn't happy unless she was accomplishing something, and island life wasn't about accomplishing things.

Instead of going back home with her family to Austin after the trip, Jessica headed back east for New Year's. First-semester grades were going to be posted on January 5, and Jessica was waiting "on pins and needles" for the 5:00 A.M. deadline when they went live on the school's Web site. She was overjoyed to discover that she had received an A in Professor Holthausen's Securities Analysis class—the one that she and her partner Rob had practically killed themselves working on the paper about Belk for. That A was one of many. She had earned a perfect 4.0 GPA for the semester. Jessica now had a cumulative 3.9 GPA. Unless she really slacked off during the spring semester, there was no doubt that she would be graduating summa cum laude, which required a student to have a cumulative 3.8 GPA.

"I guess I'm just aiming to get a few solid numbers behind that point-nine for my own joy," she wrote in an e-mail.

In mid-January, Lazard Frères was named lead banker for the merger between JPMorgan Chase and Bank One. It was a $58 billion deal that Lazard's financial institutions group (or FIG), led by Gary Parr, had secured. It was estimated that the deal would bring in $20 million in advisory fees for Lazard. FIG was the group Jessica hoped to work for once she got to Lazard, and she was extremely excited to see they were doing so well. "I bet my MBA mentor who told me I was making the wrong choice not to pursue Goldman is biting his tongue now," she added, referring to one of the many MBA students she had befriended and sought out for career advice.

With no official posts at Wharton Women to tend to, Jessica soon found herself with more free time than she knew what to do with. So she began rigorously embarking on what she liked to call "wise old woman extracurriculars," which entailed mentoring and conducting mock interviews with juniors who were heading into their first interviews with the investment banks for internships.

In mid-February, Jessica received word that she was one of three finalists being interviewed for the Dean's Award for Excellence, arguably the highest honor a Wharton undergraduate can receive. Other dean's awards included one for Service to Wharton, Service to the Community, and Innovation. (Jon Gantman, with his three years of Management 100 leadership under his belt, was a finalist for the Dean's Award for Service). Jessica had spent hours on the required essay, explaining her roots and her achievements at the school.

"Neither of my parents had graduated from high school and I grew up with a very young, single mother," she wrote in the essay. "So when I arrived at Penn years later, I felt that I had come a long way and I was determined to take every opportunity to push my limits and to live in full this dream that had once seemed so lofty and that many had told me was unrealistic."

To Jessica, receiving this award would be the pinnacle of all of the achievements she had earned during her time at Wharton and yet one more lofty goal for her to achieve.

Jon Gantman joined his family in New York over the holidays to see a couple of Broadway shows and do some shopping. It had become a ritual for the Gantmans, who had been making their annual pilgrimage to the city for more than a decade. Usually Jon viewed the bustle and lights of the holidays in Manhattan as a periodic escape from his more peaceful suburban Penn Valley roots. This time, he looked at the city from a new perspective. Since he accepted the job with American Express, he had been envisioning what it would be like to live in Manhattan—and to his surprise the city was starting to grow on him.

"I see living in New York as a two- to five-year commitment," he said. "But I wouldn't be shocked if I moved in and lived there forever."

Just one day after the revelers in Times Square watched the ball drop to ring in 2004, Jon's mother learned that she had won the race to become Pennsylvania's next Superior Court judge. The results of the election were so close that they had been tied up for two months in recount deliberations and state and federal court proceedings. Finally, with a slim margin of twenty-eight votes, Jon's mother had won the election. It was one more accomplishment for the family to celebrate.

In another coup, the One Stop College Shop had been the only business plan from Jon's entrepreneurship class last semester chosen for a feature story in *Get It Started*, a quarterly newsletter published by Wharton Entrepreneurial Programs that went to 5,000 alumni, entrepreneurs and small-business owners. Jon and his friends had been working tirelessly on the venture for months now. They met each week for dinner and divided up the tasks: Jon would speak with house deans about what students needed most and gauge the demand for such a business, one of his partners would talk to suppliers, another would focus on potential marketing initiatives. At one point, they dreamed of getting MTV to sponsor the venture and renaming the business "College Cribs." To make sure her students' heads weren't getting too bloated (or that they expected to get an easy A in her class) because they had been chosen for the article, their entrepreneurship professor had e-mailed them with a warning: "Being chosen for this doesn't mean you're doing well, you're just newsworthy."

But the guys couldn't help but hold out hope that the article might pique the interest of a venture capitalist or some other interested party with deep pockets. When first-semester grades came out, Jon discovered that he had received what he called a "well-earned A" in the class. He and one of his friends decided to take the entrepreneurship class again for the spring semester, just so they could continue working on their plan.

Otherwise, Jon was trying to do as little work as possible during the second semester. "I feel like I've been up to absolutely nothing," he would say contentedly in February. In addition to his entrepreneurship class, Jon was taking a course in photography with his friend Mark. The professor told the duo that it was obvious that they were Wharton students because they were so excited to go out on photo shoots that they were acting like they had just been released from the zoo.

"You have a beer or two before you go out and take pictures. It's more in touch with your creative side," said Jon, who discovered that he had quite an eye for the craft. By the end of the semester, he was making copies of his black-and-white photos and framing them for his friends and family as gifts.

Jon also spent several hours a week doing independent research for Kenneth Shropshire, the head of Penn's Legal Studies Department, who was writing a book on the art of contract negotiations using professional sports as his framework. Jon was helping Shropshire conduct research, and he was going to write about it for his senior thesis for the Joseph Wharton Scholars Program, which he, too, was a part of.

In February, Jon was invited to speak to a group of Wharton alumni at the luxury Trump Tower high-rise in Manhattan. It was an event held for some of the school's largest donors. Jon was on the roster to speak, along with a Wharton MBA student and Wharton's dean, Patrick Harker. "I was wearing my Sunday best," laughed Jon. But the fancy duds couldn't hide his nervousness. It was one thing to speak to a roomful of students. It was another to speak to a group of older, wealthy Wharton alums.

Jon had memorized his speech almost verbatim, spending a handful of minutes talking about the Joseph Wharton Scholars Program and Management 100, both programs that the benefactors in the audience had helped fund. Jon would also thank the Wharton alums who had helped current seniors by giving them career advice or helping them get jobs.

"They provide a great example with their support," said Jon after the event. "Even if we can't provide the same financial support that they have, we hope to emulate the type of efforts they put in for us."

A couple of weeks later, Jon traded in his "Sunday best" for his swim trunks. He was basking in the sunshine of Puerto Rico with ten of his friends. One of those friends had generous parents who allowed the group to take over their vacation home for spring break. They had even stocked the fridge with beer and food. The weather was a perfect respite for a group of students from West Philadelphia's frozen streets. It had been an especially harsh winter, with single-digit wind chills, and it was nice to thaw out on Puerto Rico's sweltering beaches, where temperatures danced toward ninety degrees each day. The island also proved to be a wonderful place for Jon to practice his new skills with the camera. When he returned from break, he couldn't wait to get back into the darkroom and see the pictures that he had taken.

When Jon returned to Philadelphia a week later, the air had thawed and he and his fraternity brothers decided to fill their free time by starting a Wiffle-ball league. They painted a catcher on a piece of wood and propped it up on the wall bordering the wooden porch of Jon's house on Locust Street. The house soon became a veritable Grand Central Station, with guys showing up to practice their swing at all hours of the day. In addition to perfecting Wiffle-ball strategies, Jon was contemplating his postgraduate life, studying the neighborhoods of New York and wondering where he and his potential roommates might want to live.

"Most of my good friends will be in New York," he said. "Now it's just a matter of picking who I'll live with."

"Career Services is dead for me," proclaimed Anthony.

Two months into the spring semester, he was still looking for a job. By March, there were fewer than thirty postings on the OCRS Web site, and most of them were "bottom-of-the-barrel–type jobs" that Anthony had no desire to pursue, including one for a company that markets products to new mothers. "I'm not going to apply to that no matter if the economy is hot *or* cold," said Anthony.

By the end of January, there had only been three posts that he even bothered to send a résumé to, and two of those firms canceled their visits. "For me, it feels like it's very late in the game. At Wharton, it's all the first semester," he said. "In a sense, I feel like I'm kind of behind at Penn, but at other colleges they're just starting."

He was trying to remain undaunted. "Maybe in about six weeks I'll start coming up with an emergency plan."

In addition to his hopelessly regular logins to the OCRS Web site, Anthony started perusing the want ads in the *New York Times*.

None of the jobs were of the caliber of those that had flooded the OCRS Web site during the first semester. Most of the trading jobs Anthony found in the paper were for "chop shops," he said. He also started trolling MonsterTRAK, a college-targeted job search Web site created by the online employment behemoth, Monster, Inc., which surprisingly proved more helpful to him. The problem was that many of the jobs posted on the site needed to be filled immediately, and Anthony had four months of school left. Eventually, he found two promising posts on the OCRS site. One was an analyst position with the Wall Street consulting firm Orion Consultants, and the other was for a training program with Maersk Sealand, an international shipping company based in Europe. He thought he'd also try contacting the hedge fund he'd interned for over the previous summer to see if they possibly had an entry-level space to fill even though he knew those spots tended to be a rarity.

Anthony landed his first interview with Orion in late January. The job he was vying for would entail conducting research and writing reports for Wall Street firms on certain investments. It would require personal skills as well as analytical ones. It was the first time he'd met with recruiters from a consulting firm, and it was vastly different from what he had experienced during his interviews with the banks first semester. "In finance, they only interview you twice. After two sit-downs they're willing to throw $70K in your face," said Anthony. "Because you're going to be working tons of hours, they're not taking that much of a risk."

He found that the interviewing process with the consulting firms was weighted more heavily on the candidate's personality, with questions that didn't have cut-and-dried answers. "Consulting interviews are three rounds. The first one is to determine that you're not psychotic or socially inept. The second and third interviews are to see if you can do the job," he explained.

The problem with the personality interviews was that Anthony wasn't quite sure how they went. At least in the interviews with the banks, the questions have right or wrong answers, making it easier to determine whether or not he was on point.

Anthony felt that the interviewers at Orion were trying to figure out if he had the kind of personality that the job required. Looking at his résumé, the interviewer became focused on Anthony's involvement with the Penn stand-up comedy troupe Simply Chaos. Anthony was often asked to tell a joke at the interviews. It always made him nervous. Most of his routines weren't exactly appropriate for the discriminating ears of recruiters. Actually, most of his routines made fun of the interviewing process and the type of people the recruiters were searching for.

"It's a problem, because (my jokes) are all offensive," explained Anthony. "Pretty much everything is about Wharton." A recruiter from Morgan Stanley once requested a joke from Anthony and upon hearing it, made some sort of odd noise that Anthony couldn't quite decipher. But he knew it wasn't good. "It was a complete disaster," he said. "Needless to say, I got my ding less than twenty-four hours after that interview. In retrospect, that was a great thing."

Throughout his years at Wharton and months of recruiting, comedy was Anthony's way to cope with stress. "The only way to get through this pressure stuff is to find the humor in it," he explained.

He got a lot of his material for his shows in the fall after seeing his fellow students clamoring for the attentions of recruiters at the information sessions hosted by Morgan Stanley and Goldman Sachs. In April, Simply Chaos was having its last big show of the year at the Iron Gate Theater on campus. Two hundred and sixty people were in the audience and Anthony was one of a dozen performers. It was his last show at Penn and Anthony wanted one last hurrah. One of his final jokes had to do with interviewing.

"I once got an interview question where I was asked, 'What would your enemies say about you?'" Anthony told the crowd.

"What kind of stupid question is this? *Enemies?* I don't have enemies. I'm a twenty-one-year old senior from Wharton. What am I, a superhero? The Hobgoblin isn't after my ass. Rappers have enemies. I'm no rapper. Do you see me rockin' ice, showin' off my bling bling? Am I rolling on dubs? I don't know [if I have enemies] ... because I don't even know what the hell that means!" His delivery was perfect and so was the response from the crowd.

After leaving his interview with Orion it was much harder to gauge their reaction. Anthony felt like he had a seventy percent chance of being invited back for another round. He was more dispirited by the fact that the campus was now swarming with recruiters, but none of them were looking for a student like Anthony. These recruiters had diverted their attentions since the first semester. Now they only had eyes for juniors seeking internships for the summer. It was like pouring salt in his wounds.

"I saw this kid jumping up and down on the sidewalk. I was like, 'What is this guy's problem?' He got a job offer, and I'm a senior and I *need* a job," exclaimed Anthony. "The worst is seeing a junior complaining that they don't have an internship yet. You're a junior. You're coming back to school next year! I'm a senior. What will I do? Watch French TV for a year?" The thought of moving back to Paris and living with his parents started to become a startling possibility.

Anthony soon began to come up with that emergency plan. Many Wharton students had become engrossed in the reality TV show *The Apprentice*, which had just embarked on its premiere season in January. Wharton alum Donald Trump produced and starred in the show, which pitted groups of ambitious young people against one another in a series of business-related tasks. Among the challenges the contestants had to excel at were selling lemonade on the streets of Manhattan, running a theme restaurant for a night, and trying to rent out a luxury penthouse within twenty-four hours for the largest sum of money possible. At the end of each show, Trump regally sat at the glossy, dark-wood table in his infamous "boardroom" and brusquely announced to the loser that week, "You're fired!" as he sliced his hand through the air. It was a gesture that had become synonymous with the infamous billionaire. The goal of the show was to be the last man (or woman) standing at the end of the season. Whoever won would get a six-figure salary and become president of one of Trump's companies for a year.

It wasn't surprising that the show was such a hit among Wharton students. Even if they were reluctant to admit it, they knew that they were cut from the same cloth as many of the participants. They were driven overachievers eager to prove that they were the most aptly suited to be a leader. The corporate dynamics they had been studying at school played out in front of *The Apprentice*'s viewers' faces. It was a game of survival of the fittest, and it drew Anthony and his friends in like a drug. They had heated debates about their favorite and most-hated participants and how they could have done the tasks better. Anthony began to think it wouldn't be such a bad idea to make his own audition tape for the show in the hope of being cast for the second season. Then maybe he could put off his job search for a little while longer.

The idea was sounding increasingly feasible to Anthony, who was surrounded by excited juniors in business suits on the sidewalks of campus and seniors who were now absorbed in making postcollege living arrangements. It seemed as if everyone had a job. His nerves were starting to win the battle over his resolve when Orion called and offered him another round of interviews at their offices in New York.

"I guess things are looking up," he wrote in an e-mail. "Maybe it's that recovering economy."

It was late February when Anthony went up to New York to meet with Orion. All of the great things about the city that he remembered from his younger years in Manhattan came rushing back, and he knew that he wanted to live in the culturally diverse metropolis again. Over the course of the day, Anthony met with so many people at Orion that he was pretty sure he had spoken with everyone who worked at the firm. This round of interviews was a hybrid form of banking and consulting interviews. At one point, Anthony was asked analytical questions and, at another, he was providing examples of times he worked on a team. One recruiter handed Anthony a page of material and asked him to quickly decipher the main issues and write brief bullet points that encapsulated the information. It was similar to what they would want their first-year recruits to be doing on the job, which entailed speaking with traders and directors from brokerage houses about certain investments, gleaning the most important information and writing long- and short-term reports.

"For me that was really easy," he said, "because in business school that's what they teach you. In liberal arts you write thirty-page papers. I'm taught to write memos, which really helps with this job."

Anthony returned to Philadelphia with a renewed air of confidence. He thought that if he couldn't get this job, then he wouldn't be able to get any job worth having. A few days later, Orion invited him back for a final round. Through MonsterTRAK he had also received an application for a job as a financial advisor at Morgan Stanley in California. He wasn't sure yet if he was going to go after it, but at least he had another option. He also abandoned his backup plan to make the audition tape for *The Apprentice*.

"I was so disillusioned with the job-finding process that I needed to regroup and focus on finding a job, not trying to get on a TV show," he said. "I also realized that the only winner on the show now is Trump. Everyone else is a lackey."

Anthony left a few days later for Cancun with two of his friends for spring break, and he was relieved to escape the stress of hunting for a job. To Anthony, who had traveled all over the world with his family, Cancun wasn't exactly the most exotic destination. It seemed as if there were more Americans in Mexico than Mexicans. "It was like Middletown, U.S.A.," he laughed.

Anthony soon grew tired of the muscle-bound spring breakers constantly thirsting for beer on Cancun's beaches. He needed better entertainment. The racy men's magazine *Maxim* was holding a promotion where they were dyeing people's hair. To entertain himself, Anthony decided to get his dark brown hair dyed bright red. It looked cool in Cancun, but when he returned to campus, it was a whole different story.

Tanned, relaxed and redheaded, Anthony went back up to Orion's offices in New York the day after he returned from Mexico. "I wanted to wear a red tie or something to deflect the redness of my head," said Anthony. "I looked like a jackass."

Over the course of the day he met with ten people, many of whom were the same people he had met before—none of them said anything about his hair. The encounters were much more relaxed this time. "Now they were seeing if they could stand you very much," he said. "They see if they can tolerate you, in a sense."

Anthony also got a better idea of what it would be like to work in their offices. "The environment is very laid-back. It's like a college dorm," he described, noting that most of the associates were under twenty-four. "Coming from Wharton, if you work on Wall Street, you get the complete opposite environment."

Orion was looking more like a feasible option when Maersk Sealand called and invited Anthony to an interview. Anthony had always hoped to work for a company with an international presence. He wanted to put his joint degree in International Relations and Business to work, and the shipping firm fit the bill. If he got the job with Maersk he would work in the U.S. for two years, and then he could choose to move to one of the company's 325 offices around the globe. It was the best job Anthony felt he had seen thus far.

The night before his first interview with Maersk, Anthony attended the company's preinterview information session in Huntsman Hall. During the ninety-minute presentation, the crowd learned exactly what it was this humongous European shipping company did. At the presentations for banks such as Goldman Sachs or Morgan Stanley, they would never waste their time explaining to Wharton students what the company does because it's a given that Whartonites already know. But this wasn't an investment bank. Near the end of the session, the woman hosting the session told the group that in the previous year, the company had close to two thousand applicants for three spots. It felt like the odds of getting a job at Maersk were close to those of winning the lottery.

"The lady scared the hell out of us," Anthony admitted. After the presentation, all of the students who still held out hope for the job were given an IQ test to take. "This is a shipping company, what the hell am I taking an IQ test for?" pondered Anthony as he read the first question on the test: *What is the third day of the week?* As an exit prize, the test takers were given a deck of cards and a pen.

Anthony's interview with the Maersk recruiter the next day lasted all of twelve minutes. He felt that the interviewer's questions lacked insight and didn't gauge his talents very well. When she didn't have any further questions to ask, he began asking his own questions and answering them so he could prove himself to her. "What is Huntsman?" he would ask. "Well, Huntsman is a dual-degree program..."

It was probably one of the oddest experiences the interviewer had encountered all day, but at least Anthony stretched out the interview for a couple more minutes to make a deeper impression. Anthony considered it a debacle and a major disappointment. He would have taken the job in a heartbeat.

In early April, with just under two months of college left, Anthony received a job offer from Orion. He had until the end of the month to make a decision, and he felt like he should make sure that he had tried all possible avenues before he accepted. There was no doubt that he felt better now that he had an offer in hand, but he wanted to continue investigating trading jobs. "At this point, I'd trade fertilizer," he would say.

But after encountering a trading firm that–in lieu of a salary– would only pay him a percentage of the money he earned for the company, Anthony decided Orion was looking like a much better (and safer) bet. He ended up accepting Orion's offer a week later.

Regi visited Vancouver and the windswept beaches of Oregon with his family while he was on winter break. He tried to soak it all in, making sure not to waste one second of precious time with them. Now that he was going to be working at an investment bank, Regi knew that any time spent with his family now would have to carry him for quite a while. His job would soon take over holidays and mark the beginning and ending to most of his days. It could be two years again before he'd get a chance to pay them an extended visit in Seattle.

As one Wharton MBA student explained, her experience at a leading boutique bank was typical of the commitment the banks required. "Nothing ever prepares you for the life of an analyst," she said. "The first time you stay until 2:00 A.M. you think: 'What have I gotten into?' Then you stay until 2:00 A.M. the next night and the next night."

Upon starting at the firm in July, she had requested a day off during Presidents' Day weekend–eight months away. All requests were put on a board for everyone to see. Within hours, the young analyst was pulled aside and given fair warning that her request was inappropriate for a first-year. "They told me first-years shouldn't take vacation," she said. "No one ever told me that." The longer she worked at the bank, the more she was made to feel that her personal life was of no consequence to anyone at the firm. After working there for three years, she decided to redirect her life and pursue an MBA.

Even though Regi was sanguine about the demands of his future job, he was still excited to start. So much so that he wanted to look for an apartment in Manhattan months before he would even move there. His friends calmed him down, telling him he was jumping the gun. As part of his employment agreement, the bank Regi was going to work for agreed to pay a real estate broker to help him secure an apartment. In Manhattan, brokers can sometimes charge a fee of fifteen percent of a total year's rent, easily adding many thousands of dollars to a rental in what is already one of the most expensive residential markets in the world. With a broker working for him, Regi wouldn't have that hard of a time finding a place anyway, his friends advised.

The great sense of relief and anticipation that Regi felt after accepting his new job was still extremely palpable. It was even getting hard for the consummately studious Regi to concentrate on schoolwork. "I'm definitely slacking in my classes," he confessed, admitting that he had been filling up most of his free time watching movies and playing poker online.

Regi had signed up for four courses in the spring semester, three of which were geared toward skills that would prove helpful in his new job. When he returned from winter break and realized how much work he had to do, he decided he would have to forgo his senior thesis. "My friends advised me to just relax and bag the thesis," said Regi. "It's kind of disappointing."

Doing so freed Regi up to participate in some of the rites of passage that seniors tend to enjoy. He went to Honolulu with five friends over spring break and, a few weeks later, made up for lost partying time by attending Spring Fling. The unseasonably cold weather had disappeared just in time for the weekend's parties and concerts, bringing warm sunshine for the first time in what seemed like years. The prior year, Regi had been laid up in the hospital during Spring Fling. Now he could take in the spring air and watch the jousting contests on campus, eat the fried Oreos being sold at one of many concession stands, and laugh at all of the drunk people staggering around campus.

A week later, Regi was preparing to attend "Hey Day," another Penn tradition involving booze and bad food. Hey Day marked the last day of classes for the year, and the point at which juniors are inaugurated as seniors. Each year, juniors march down Locust Walk with a traditional straw hat and cane toward the College Green, where the school's president delivers a speech officially declaring them seniors. Before they reach her, however, the juniors are subjected to some friendly hazing by the upcoming graduates. Like lambs to the slaughter, the juniors are coated in tossed ketchup, eggs, mustard, shaving cream, and flour as they make their way through campus. It's a collective party, with burgers and chips being served on the playing fields and keg parties launched at frat houses. "It's one of the few days where it's okay to be drunk by 11:00 or 12:00," explained Regi, who was planning to buy the messiest shaving cream he could find for the event.

Once he recovered from two weekends in a row of debauchery, Regi needed to tackle his last round of finals. It wasn't going to be easy. He had two exams, two ten-page papers, and a simulation project due. It would be a somewhat bittersweet end to his time at Wharton.

CHAPTER ELEVEN

THE FINAL MARCH

Come all ye loyal classmen now
In hall and campus through,
Lift up your hearts and voices
For the Royal Red and Blue.

Fair Harvard has her crimson,
Old Yale her colors too,
But for Dear Pennsylvania, we wear
the Red and Blue.

Hurrah! Hurrah! Pennsylvania!
Hurrah for the Red and the Blue;
Hurrah! Hurrah! Hurrah! Hurrah!
Hurrah for the Red and the Blue!

"The Red and Blue" by William J. Goeckel, Class
of 1896, and Harry E. Westervelt, Class of 1898

For some seniors at Penn, the final days leading up to graduation, called "Senior Week," can turn into one alcohol-laden event after another. There was a night out to a Phillies baseball game, a trip to the Six Flags amusement park, and reunions for seniors who lived on the same hallway freshman year. Then there was the senior formal at the Bellevue Hotel, which featured an open bar. Free drinks and college students can be a particularly entertaining mix at times. Grace Yoon witnessed the inhibitions of some students fly out the window at the event. "People were saying whatever they wanted to people. There were guys telling girls, 'I've had the biggest crush on you for years,'" she laughed.

The next day, many of the seniors embarked on a twelve-hour bar crawl down Walnut Street in an annual rite of passage called "The Walnut Walk," in which seniors proceed from Philadelphia's Society Hill near the Delaware River, through Center City, back onto campus and ultimately to Smokey Joe's on campus, hitting every bar along the way. It had been hot and humid that day. The bars along the street offered drink specials as the sweaty seniors popped in and out of their establishments from two in the afternoon until two in the morning.

Shreevar Kheruka spent Senior Week reconnecting with friends from freshman year. He had fallen out of touch with many of them as his workload at Wharton had become increasingly demanding. He regretted not going out more freshman year. By the time Shreevar had begun taking the relentless Wharton "core" classes his sophomore year, it was next to impossible for him to forge new friendships. "I tried making up for it by joining a frat," he said.

While bumping into his old friends at the bars around campus, it seemed like he and the guys he met four years earlier had never skipped a beat. "Even if I meet them ten years later, there will still be that connection there," he proclaimed. "If someone from Penn asked me for help ten years down the road, I would help them."

Jessica Kennedy skipped the Senior Week festivities to hang out with professors and friends that she knew she would miss once she left Penn. When Jessica had her last meeting with Professor Holthausen about her finance project, she was struck with a deep sadness that her time at Wharton was coming to an end. It was the last project Jessica would ever pull an all-nighter for at school.

"When this is done, college is over," she thought as she was leaving his office. "I've been sincerely sad, flat-out sad. I don't want to leave," she admitted.

Graduation was soon upon Jessica and her classmates. To keep her company while she got ready, Jessica's mother arrived at her daughter's apartment in the luxury Left Bank building just off Penn's campus at 7:30 A.M. It was Wharton's graduation day, and perhaps one of the most important days in Jessica's life. As they shared the morning rituals of fixing their hair and makeup, Jessica thought about how grateful she was to her mother, who without a high school degree had worked so hard to give her daughter this opportunity.

"I'm at the point where I've always dreamed to be," said Jessica. "I'm so far from where I was as a little girl."

Jessica had butterflies in her stomach. She was going to find out at graduation whether she was deemed worthy of the Dean's Award for Excellence, the highest honor that the Wharton School could bestow upon her. Getting the Dean's Award would be further evidence in Jessica's mind that she had successfully navigated her time at Wharton to the highest degree possible. She already knew she would graduate summa cum laude (in the top five percent of her graduating class) with honors (as a Joseph Wharton Scholar), and the award would distinguish her even further. Jessica fastened her graduation cap on with bobby pins, arranged her tassel and grabbed her gown, checking herself one last time in the mirror. As she prepared to leave the Left Bank for campus, she grabbed her red golf umbrella. There had been a nasty thunderstorm the night before, and the skies today were filled with the threat of another. She didn't want the rain to ruin her big day.

Each of the schools within Penn has its own graduation ceremony the day before the much grander, university-wide ceremony.
These sub-ceremonies allow the schools to more personally celebrate their students' accomplishments. They allot enough time for
each graduate to be called out by name to receive his or her
diploma, and for the announcement of the beneficiaries of scholarships and awards. Wharton's ceremony was the earliest of the
bunch, scheduled at 9:00 A.M. at Franklin Field, Penn's 52,593-seat
football stadium, which most notably hosts the Penn Relays track
meets.

As the Wharton students lined up in alphabetical order before
proceeding to their seats, Jessica eagerly thumbed through the
graduation program, searching the names of those awarded various scholarships and recognitions. She quickly found the listings
of Dean's Awards and, to her dismay, discovered that she hadn't
been chosen for the honor that she had coveted so much. Realizing that the two other finalists she was up against somehow
both received the award made her feel even worse.

"Not only did I not get it, but *two* other people got it!" she
would exclaim.

To her surprise, though, she was given another honor: the
Beverly Kushinsky Virany Memorial Award. It was a venerable
tribute given to a female senior who had demonstrated all-around
academic merit, leadership abilities, integrity and strong character
and was an overall "good person." Yet, for Jessica, it still wasn't
enough to outweigh the blow of losing the Dean's Award.

In her disappointment, Jessica turned to one of her fellow graduates who was standing in line in front of her and told him that she
was going to need some cheering up when they announced the
Dean's Award recipients at the ceremony. Even though she didn't
know him, he graciously turned to her and said: "I bet you're a lot
cooler than them, and you will always have that." Jessica smiled at
his words, imagining the day when she would become a vice

president or even a managing director at an investment bank and laugh at how upset she had been that she didn't win the Dean's Award when she was a senior at Wharton. She continued to smile as she marched out with her fellow graduates onto the field.

Roughly an eighth of the bleachers at Franklin Field were filled with friends and family members of the graduating class, many of them bearing balloons or roses along with their umbrellas. The rain had gone and the sun could be seen glowing from somewhere behind the gray-and-white cloud cover. As the graduates circled the field in two single-file lines, wide screens on either side of the stage projected close-ups of their relieved and smiling faces. Every so often, the cameras captured a student with one arm waving violently in the air in an attempt to stand apart from the sea of black caps and gowns and capture the attention of his supporters in the stands.

After the students took their seats, Wharton's faculty made their entrance and moved toward the stage as the students clapped vigorously. Some of the professors now walking onto the field had consoled them during periodic meltdowns—while others had incited those meltdowns by assigning one weighty project after another, making the students' lives a living hell. Now that it was all done, though, the graduates seemed thankful for being pushed so hard. These professors' legacies would be borne out in the months and years to come, whether through a shortcut used to figure out a complicated corporate valuation late at night or the recital of an inspiring quote to coworkers in a Manhattan bar.

Just nine months earlier, Wharton's managing director, Suzanne Kauffman DePuyt, welcomed the incoming freshmen of Wharton's class of 2007. Now she was bidding adieu to the Class of 2004. The annual Wharton student cycle had come full circle. DePuyt greeted the group and introduced Dean Harker, providing a laundry list of his admirable accomplishments.

In a maroon robe and striped royal-blue hood, Harker congratulated the Class of 2004, telling them how proud the faculty was of the group and how much they looked forward to seeing their accomplishments in the years to come.

"Nearly half a million business degrees will be awarded (in 2004)," he told the students looking up at him. "But you will carry the distinction of having a Wharton degree." The training that they had undergone over the past four years and the piece of paper that marks the successful accomplishment of that training will define them throughout their careers, he explained. "Today you become the Wharton that the world sees.... You are the brand image of the school."

Many of these students knew that the Wharton name had much to do with preparing them for the world beyond college by helping them to secure the jobs that they would embark on in the months to come, and they were moved by his words. As Jon Gantman would explain: "Wharton opens lots of doors for you. You just have to walk through them. It's one step to get to the door, but once you're there, it's you."

Harker told the students to uphold business values, to do what is right even if it is not the popular thing to do, and to believe in what they are bringing (and selling) to the world. "In the years ahead, you will be tested more than you have [been] here in school," warned Harker. "Leaders lead. They must move away from the herd because the herd is a safe place ...," he said. "Leaders spend more time in the crosshairs."

The young Wharton graduates of the Class of 2004 already knew this to be true. Their group projects taught them about the trade-offs of leadership and how it sometimes can serve as an alienating force. And those who underwent the recruiting rush in the fall were well aware of what it felt like to be in the crosshairs of interviewers and their own peers.

The vice dean of Wharton, Barbara Kahn, followed Harker. A well-respected marketing professor, Kahn had just completed her first year as vice dean, and this was the first commencement speech she would deliver. With her straight, walnut-colored hair flowing from under her cap, she looked much younger than her years. Before introducing the student speaker, Kahn told the group to try to use their talents to improve the shape of things. "You are better prepared than any other undergraduate in the world," she declared.

Amal Devani had been chosen by his class to speak at the ceremony. Standing on stage now before them, he wittily poked fun at the group. "How many of us find ourselves wearing business casual to class?" he asked. "How many of us have more than one Palm Pilot?

"Wharton is a place that has one thousand male college students talking about curves," he said. But, as he explained, they aren't talking about what one might imagine. "They're talking about their finance midterm."

A communal wave of laughter burst from the crowd. During the last seven days of celebrations, many of Wharton's graduates realized that they could have spent a little more time during their college careers having fun.

Jessica's spirits were improving by the time Harker got around to announcing the winners of the Dean's Awards. In fact, she was happy that one of the recipients of the honor was a girl named Daphne Tong, who Jessica saw as a formidable opponent from the beginning. Daphne had a near-perfect GPA; she was the captain of the school's women's rugby team and an active member of Wharton Women. Jessica truly believed that if anyone was fair competition for her, it was Daphne.

"I was happy that I was happy for her," Jessica would later declare. That afternoon, she would send Daphne a congratulatory e-mail. "It wasn't like a good sportsmanship thing. If someone was going to get it, I wanted her to get it."

As the graduation ceremony progressed to the conferral of degrees, the students were asked to stand up when their concentration of study was announced. They were all receiving a bachelor of science in economics, but their concentration was what defined them within Wharton. At times, only one student stood amidst the crowd as concentrations in fields such as Environmental Policy and Management and Insurance and Risk Management were called out. At other times, particularly when the finance and management concentrations were announced, it seemed as though almost all of the students rose up. Once they individually crossed the stage, shook hands with (and in some cases hugged) the deans and professors who had guided them through their years at Wharton, and moved the tassels on their mortarboard caps from right to left, the students could now tell themselves that their long and sometimes grueling run at the school was definitely over.

As Penn's alma mater, "The Red and Blue," was sung, Grace said her own private goodbye to the world that had been so foreign to her four years earlier. That world—for a fleeting time in her life—had at some point become her home.

Wharton students who pursued joint degrees, such as Anthony and Shreevar, would attend multiple graduation ceremonies that day. The College of Arts & Science's graduation began at 7:00 P.M. The ceremony seemed to drag on forever as the daylight turned to darkness as more than 1,500 names were called out. Even though the faculty were rushing through the names, the process still felt like it took an eternity to Anthony, who just wanted to get out of there and relax before the university-wide ceremony the next day.

That night, eight of Jessica's family members gathered together at her Left Bank apartment building at 32nd Street and Walnut for a fully catered party in her honor, complete with Veuve Clicquot champagne. Jessica was excited, anxious and a little disappointed.

"I think that I did build up this day," she said. "Between the ceremony and not getting the award, it was not exactly the picture I had in my mind."

Nevertheless, there was no doubt that she was proud of her accomplishments and happy to have had the experiences that

Wharton had afforded her. And the next day's ceremony promised not to disappoint.

On Monday morning, the graduates of the University of Pennsylvania gathered in Hamilton Village, the area between the undergraduate high rises (the Harnwell, Harrison and Hamilton College Houses) lovingly called the "wind tunnel" for the incessantly strong breeze that pushes through this "super block" of high-rise dormitory apartments. Groups of friends were convening and helping each other to secure their caps as they lined up for their final walk down Locust Walk as the Class of 2004. Shuffling down the path leading through campus, the stream of black robes seemed to stretch forever. Occasionally, one of the graduates would spot their mother or a friend in the crowd and leave their place in the slow-moving herd to stop and take a picture. Shreevar made sure that he would be easy to find in the crowd. He had used masking tape to write out "Will work for food" on the top of his cap.

As the graduates moved slowly into the heart of the campus, they were met by "The Old Guard." Similar to an honor guard, the Old Guard is comprised of alumni who border each side of Locust Walk and arch red-and-blue class flags over the heads of the graduates. Lined up according to the year they graduated, the youngest alums greet the group first. A member from almost every Penn graduating class dating back to 1934 stood on the sidelines. In his robe and trendy sunglasses, the representative for the Class of 2003 didn't look any different than the graduates walking past him. But as the graduates progressed down the line, they noticed that the young alums had morphed into middle-aged women and men (some with slightly protruding guts), who then morphed into elderly alums bearing down on canes or seated in metal folding chairs. It was as though they were witnessing the cycle of life in some condensed form.

The ritual was a moving experience for all who witnessed this display of support from those who had treaded on this walkway in years and decades past. Penn's graduation weekend is also the alumni weekend for the university, with reunion ceremonies held for every fifth anniversary of a class's graduation year. This year, the classes of 1999, 1994, 1989 and others were being honored. Alums from other years were also there to participate in symposia, hear lectures and attend award ceremonies at the university. Now standing along the sidelines as the most recent graduating class was parading before them, the Old Guard illustrated the sense of community that Penn engenders among its former students—even those who graduated seventy years earlier—and hopes to engender among this new group of graduates. Also dressed in the flowing robes of academia on the College Green was Penn's faculty, who greeted the students next with a round of applause. Occasionally, a professor offered an outstretched hand to congratulate a student of whom they were particularly proud.

As some of the graduates made their way onto Franklin Field, the projector screens next to the stage allowed parents to spy their sons and daughters among the masses as they moved toward their seats with the other graduates. Facing stage left were two large sections reserved for those graduating from the School of Arts & Sciences. On the opposite end of the field were the Wharton students, who comprised a much smaller quadrant. Encircling the shoulders of Wharton's graduates were red, blue and mustard-colored hoods that identified their pursuit of business studies. In 1896, Penn had adopted the "Intercollegiate System" of academic dress for commencement ceremonies, which uses specific colors and markings on the robes and caps to signify the distinction between bachelor's, masters, and doctoral graduates and various color combinations on the hoods to signify which institution the graduate studied in. Graduates from other disciplines also had Penn's trademark red-and-blue silk lining in their velvet hoods, with a third color to signify the type of degree they were receiving.

While waiting for everyone to file in and take their seats, a group of Wharton students instigated a short-lived "wave." As the Old Guard entered the stadium, the volume of ongoing applause from the bleachers exploded, especially when the graduate from 1934 was helped onto the field. Penn president Judith Rodin's entrance harkened the arrival of the faculty, garnering an even more exuberant ovation. After a ten-year run as president of the school, Rodin was about to present her final commencement address at Penn. She had made history as the first woman president of an Ivy League institution, and during her reign, she changed the face of West Philadelphia by initiating a series of urban-renewal projects that tied the fortunes of the school more closely to those of the neighborhood adjacent to campus. The improvements were indeed a renaissance for the once poverty-stricken area. Accordingly, many people stood up in their seats to applaud her accomplishments.

The cheers in the crowd reached a fever pitch as the occupants of the stadium realized that the commencement speaker that they had been anxiously awaiting had entered the field. Bono, the lead singer of the rock group U2, strutted onto the football field in a flowing black commencement gown and his signature blue-tinted sunglasses. He waved to the crowd and raised his fingers up in the peace sign. Young women began screaming: "We love you, Bono!" from the stands.

The pomp of the ceremony quickly turned into something akin to a raucous rock concert. As if perfectly orchestrated, men in uniforms from various divisions of the armed services soon followed in the procession. It was a sobering reminder of the ongoing war in Iraq, and the throng quieted down.

Once on stage, a handful of smiling faculty members gathered around Bono like teenage fans. Eventually the excitement abated and the ceremony began. After taking the podium, Judith Rodin welcomed the new group of alumni sitting in front of her. Penn had close to 300,000 alumni worldwide—including Rodin herself, who graduated in 1966 from what was then the College of Women, but has since been fully incorporated into the university–and these graduates could be proud to be part of that group, she said. Rodin began reminiscing about the things that she would miss most about Penn and its campus, namely spring days on Locust Walk, the infamous wind tunnel of Hamilton Village, and Floyd Johnson, the whistling traffic cop. She would be nostalgic for those signature charms of the university, but as she had decided, sometimes it's time to move on.

"As the Red Queen says in *Alice in Wonderland*: 'It takes all of the running you can do to stay in the same place,'" she said. "But we haven't trained you to stay in the same place." Rodin beseeched the students to make the future their business, to make real and positive change in the world. In the 1950s and 1960s, Penn had turned its back on West Philadelphia and its plight, she told them. Now new relationships had been forged.

"We became a better neighbor," declared Rodin. "You will now have to go out and define your roles as neighbors and citizens." Not just neighbors in cities or towns, she warned, but global neighbors: "Think about China and India! Think about Africa! Think about Iraq and the Middle East!" In the crowd before her were students from dozens of different nations. It was Penn's own global community, and they had the power to heed her call.

After her speech, Rodin was awarded an honorary doctor of laws degree from Penn's Chairman of the Board of Trustees, who proclaimed, "If Benjamin Franklin is the first citizen of Penn, you are a close second–and only by virtue of seniority."

Bono was Rodin's fellow graduate for the day, also receiving an honorary doctor of laws degree. Rodin introduced him, telling the crowd that not only had Bono's voice helped U2 win fourteen Grammy Awards in twenty years, but it had also become an important voice of change. In 2002, the rock star had established an organization called DATA (Debt, AIDS, Trade, Africa) to help combat the AIDS epidemic and the economic crises that had un-relentingly plagued Africa. His organization had raised more money for Africa in the last year than any other organization had done before.

As Bono took to the stage, the crowd exploded once again. "My name is Bono," he said, smiling. "And I am a rock star."

With his long brown locks tucked behind his ears, Bono continued to charm the crowd as he reminisced about the last time he had visited Franklin Field. Seven years earlier, U2 had performed at the stadium during their POPMART Tour. Unlike the conservative robes he was currently wearing on stage, Bono had worn a mirror-ball suit. For the encore, the band had emerged from what he described as "a forty-foot revolving lemon that was sort of a cross between a spaceship, a disco ball and a piece of plastic fruit." "I like to think it was at that point that your trustees decided I deserved a high academic honor," he joked, punctuating the point by adding that he never attended college. Like many of the people sitting in Franklin Field, Bono also found it peculiar that he was now receiving a doctor of laws, especially since he had broken so many laws himself, including those of nature, physics and the Commonwealth of Pennsylvania.

As Bono proceeded to get into the meat of his speech, it became increasingly clear that the message he had hoped to relay to the students was similar to the challenge Rodin had laid out before the young graduates earlier: Take the gifts you have and make a change. "What's your big idea?" he asked the group. "What are you willing to spend your moral capital, your intellectual capital, your cash, your sweat equity in pursuing outside the walls of the University of Pennsylvania?"

Bono told the audience how he discovered what he was willing to spend his cash and sweat equity on. He and his wife were nearing the end of a month-long visit to Ethiopia for Live Aid in 1985. As they were preparing to leave the country, a man handed

Bono his baby, pleading with him to take the child back to Ireland. If the child stayed in Ethiopia, the man explained to Bono, he would surely die.

"At that moment, I became the worst scourge on God's green earth: a rock star with a cause," he announced. But what is happening in Africa isn't a cause, he clarified. It's an emergency, with seven thousand Africans dying every day from AIDS, a disease that is preventable and treatable in wealthier countries like the U.S. "Equality for Africa is a big idea–a big, expensive idea," he said. "I see the Wharton graduates working the math out on the back of their programs, and the numbers are intimidating."

As Bono further illustrated the scope of suffering that the people of Africa have been subjected to, his words were lost on a handful of graduates from the College who began booing the Wharton students because Bono had mentioned them in his speech. After all, almost all of the Wharton graduates had jobs, most of which had been nailed down months earlier, while many of the College graduates were facing unemployment as soon as they left campus. (Close to 40 percent of Penn's 1,528-person graduating class–including Wharton students–did not receive job offers until June or later).

"Now go forth and build something!" Bono exhorted as he prepared to close his speech. "This is the time for bold measures. This is the country. And you are the generation. Love and luck to you, Pennsylvania. Thank you."

Bono had wowed his audience. Grace was sad that her parents couldn't be there to hear his motivating words. They had spent a couple of days in Philadelphia over graduation weekend, but had left early Monday morning to return to Los Angeles, missing the pageantry of the school-wide graduation. In her parents' eyes, they were there for the most important part: to see Grace graduate from Wharton. They were beaming with pride after Wharton's graduation ceremony on Sunday. Her father smiled at her with the biggest grin she had ever seen and asked, "What are you going to do next? Are you going to get your PhD?"

Finally it was time for the university-wide awarding of diplomas. Deans from each school rose to present their graduating class to Dr. Rodin, who then officially declared them graduates. For each school, the deans try to say something clever about their students and their disciplines. The dean of the engineering department introduced his students by saying "Tech rules the world, and these kids are in the driver's seat." As Dean Harker moved to the front of the stage to introduce Wharton's young brood, students from the College began booing yet again, this time making it hard for those in the audience to hear what he had to say.

Luckily for the Wharton students, they were front and a little off-center to the stage, so they could hear Harker. It was also fortunate that the College students were on the opposite side of the field, making it harder for the Wharton grads to hear their jeers and catcalls. "If anything, it makes us feel better," Anthony would say of it later. "I mean what kind of person would actually boo us? You can boo us as much as you want, but that is just *sad*."

Shreevar admitted that there was some animosity between the College and Wharton students, but he was surprised at the degree it had risen to during the ceremony. "They think we're snobs," he would say. "But I don't think that's representative of Wharton overall. Most of my frat brothers are Wharton students, and they are the most down-to-earth people I know."

The commencement ceremony closed with one final rousing round of the university's fight song, "The Red and Blue." Soon, masses of lost-looking family members clogged the sidewalks outside of Franklin Field, many of them on cell phones trying to find their newly graduated kin. Bouquets of flowers and hugs were being bestowed on graduates at every corner.

Shreevar met his family and moved toward College Hall, where they awaited their turn to take pictures in front of the giant bronze statue of a seated Benjamin Franklin. Wearing his black cap and gown and a pair of sunglasses, Shreevar's grin was huge as he posed with his family. His parents, sister and brother-in-law had flown in from India four days earlier, and they were all proudly singing Shreevar's praises. His father couldn't help but extol the virtues of his once-wayward son who used to care too much about sports and too little about his future when he was younger. Now he was listing his son's accomplishments in chronological order, causing Shreevar to cringe and blush with each sentence. "My family is so happy," Shreevar said. "For my parents, it's like they are reliving their childhood."

Looking out toward the College Green and all of his fellow classmates draped in black gowns, smiling and carrying on, Shreevar would take a somber tone. "You know, I'm looking around at this stuff and I know I won't see it again," he said. "I think back and I curse myself for that extra night of working instead of going out. Enjoying this is so much more important to me than getting a 3.9."

While everyone was congratulating Shreevar, he was having a hard time feeling an overwhelming sense of accomplishment. For him, college wasn't the pinnacle of his lifetime achievements. It was what he would accomplish with his degree that was most important to him. Wharton, he said, pushed him to perfect his innate abilities, to work harder and think things through in a logical manner. But now he was ready to move on and put those talents to work.

"It's akin to taking a raw material and making a finished product out of it," he explained. "Coming to Wharton was a good decision. I didn't come here with set expectations. I just wanted to make friends, learn a lot and accomplish a lot—and I've done all three of those things."

While most kids were taking pictures with their family at the various landmarks around campus, Grace had already shed her cap and gown and was relaxing in the sunshine at the Au Bon Pain outside of Huntsman Hall. She had a renewed air about her. It was as if all of the stress of the last year had completely left her body. As she sat in the outdoor café where she had spent so many hours studying and hanging out with friends, she began to come to terms with the fact that her four-year run at Wharton had actually come to an end.

"It hasn't hit me yet that I graduated and that I'm leaving. I am feeling a sense of accomplishment. I mean, for four years of hard work. I guess I feel lucky and privileged because not everyone gets the opportunity to get a higher degree," she said. "Bono doesn't have a degree, and look at him. I'm coming out of Wharton and I should be able to do something with that."

A.T. Kearney was paying for Grace's cross-country move. The movers had arrived a few days earlier to pack the trappings of her college life into boxes. Now all Grace had left to do was to pack a suitcase and gather her laptop together for her flight home to Los Angeles the next day. She wouldn't be starting her job at A.T. Kearney until mid-September. Beyond a week-long trip with her friends to Miami's South Beach, Grace wasn't planning on filling that free time traveling to Europe or lying on the beach. She was looking for something to keep herself occupied. At one point, she even thought about asking A.T. Kearney if she could start her job a couple of months early. Instead, she applied for an internship at an advertising agency, just to check out one more career option.

"I know I'm an overachiever," she said with a sheepish smirk.

As much as Grace sometimes hated to admit it, that overachiever in her was perfectly suited for a school like Wharton. When Grace had first arrived on Penn's campus and started attending her Wharton classes, she had felt as though she would never make any friends. There were times when Grace felt distanced from the whole experience, but deep down inside she knew

Wharton was the best place she could have gone for her degree. Over the last four years, Grace had learned a lot about herself and how to deal with various types of people. It was not only an asset in her social life, but it would help her out in her career as well.

"My parents were looking out for me in the long run," she said. "Wharton is a really good school."

Many of the other new Wharton graduates were planning trips to Europe or other more exotic locales during the time they had off. Jon wasn't starting his job at American Express until September, and he was busily planning a backpacking tour of Europe with a group of friends. Shreevar was heading to Norway and England with his family before returning to India for the remainder of the summer. Other students had plans to hike the mountains in Nepal or trek through China and Thailand.

But in Jessica's mind, traveling just wasn't a priority. She had planned to move to New York by mid-June. "I don't want to mess with things that aren't important," she said. Perhaps once she made associate at Lazard, then she would take a break and go somewhere. Right now, Jessica was more interested in getting to New York as quickly as possible and settling into her new apartment. She imagined that the experience would be similar to becoming a freshman again. This time, though, the concept was a bit more daunting. She wouldn't have much free time to maintain friendships and have the time she needed for herself.

"I'm used to having a lot of people to call if I want to hang out. Knowing that I won't be able to maintain all of those relationships is going to be hard," she predicted. "The people I'm close to will probably understand, because they will be doing a similar thing."

Close to twenty of Regi's friends were moving to New York in the months ahead. He had been told Manhattan was like "Penn in New York." One of the largest financial capitals in the world, the city served as kind of postgraduate satellite campus of Wharton, where a majority of newly minted Whartonites annually transplanted themselves.

"I think it's both good and bad," explained Regi. "Part of leaving college is reestablishing yourself and having the opportunity to be who you want to be. There are a lot of people who aren't close to you, and I think certain people bring certain assumptions with them about you."

In his final days at Penn, though, Regi was more consumed with the thoughts of the friendships he had forged. The last four years had been a roller coaster. He not only had to deal with the demands of Wharton but also the recoveries from his lung collapses, an experience that made him greatly value the people in his life. "My four years haven't been the *most* fun," he admitted. "But it's not so much about the time here, but more about the friendships I have made."

Anthony, on the other hand, was mourning few if any attachments. He wanted to escape Wharton and its students. Even though he was leaving the school, he knew he wouldn't be able to achieve the kind of freedom from Wharton that he had hoped for. Anthony was scheduled to begin training at Orion's Park Avenue offices in July. Moving to New York meant that he would have plenty of occasions to run into his fellow Wharton alums, even those he didn't care for much. But first he would spend a month in France with his family and hopefully gain the distance he needed from Wharton.

While Anthony acknowledged that it was Wharton that helped him land a job, he wasn't quite sure he'd see the payoff of his pricey Ivy League education anytime soon.

"Wharton kicked the crap out me for the last four years," he said. "You go to Wharton to get a good career. The payoff at Wharton really comes out in the next five to ten years, when you see where it gets you."

EPILOGUE

IN THE ARENA

Instead of relishing the idea of days spent on the beach near her parents' house in West Hills, California, or sleeping in, Grace lined up an internship with RPA, an advertising firm in Santa Monica, to fill in the remaining weeks that she had free. It would be one more field that Grace could try her hand at—and yet another experience to add to her laundry list of internships. Even at this late date, Grace still felt as though she was looking for something that "fit" just as comfortably as the sweaters that she had bought to shield herself from Pennsylvania's unforgiving winters. The ad agency was hesitant to put Grace on any long-term projects for fear that she wouldn't be able to see them through before she started at A.T. Kearney, so she became more of a gofer, pitching in wherever a fire needed to be put out or whenever copies needed to be made. The lack of demands gave Grace enough time to study for the business school admissions test, the GMATs, which she took on September 10, just three days before she reported for work at A.T. Kearney.

Grace barely had any time to settle into her new cubicle once she arrived at the consulting firm's offices. Instead of stocking her new desk with supplies and getting to know her colleagues, she was soon packing her bags for a two-week training session in Illinois. It was a precursor to the life she would lead in her new job.

In the months to come, Grace would quickly learn that a consultant's life is one lived out of a suitcase. With her mobile devices and her wheeled luggage, Grace headed to Kearney's headquarters in Chicago.

The first week of training was called the "Business Analyst Skills Development Program" and it required Grace and her twenty-four fellow trainees to spend most of their days in a classroom. Senior members of the firm taught them about Excel spreadsheets, PowerPoint presentations and the analysis of financial statements. All of it was information that Grace had learned in her classes at Wharton, and she was happy to sit back and relax while others struggled with the definition of EBITDA and creating an Excel spreadsheet that calculates the proper rate of return.

Being ahead of the class also provided Grace with the luxury of exploring Chicago at night. In fact, she and her fellow business analysts (BAs, as they are referred to in the consulting industry) went out every night. Grace got to know several of her peers and she grew increasingly confident that she had made the right choice by accepting A.T. Kearney's offer. Grace even started to get enticed by the charms of the Windy City and was somewhat disappointed that she hadn't considered working at A.T. Kearney's larger offices there. Given her climatological experiences in Philadelphia, though, Grace knew that the warm autumn months in Chicago would soon take an ugly turn.

As the first week of training in Chicago came to a close, Grace packed her bags once more and headed to the Chicago suburb of Lisle, Illinois, for "New Consultant Orientation." All of the BAs from the first week of training were there, too. Fifteen more trainees, who had been hired as senior business analysts fresh from MBA programs, also joined them. This part of the training program focused on the skills specifically related to dealing with a client, including interviewing skills and what to ask in order to ascertain where problems lie, and how best to remedy them.

The trainees were also armed with interview guides that served as a type of cheat sheet for consultants with questions like: *What's your background? Are there any problems in the office that we should know about?* Grace wouldn't be able to conduct interviews right off the bat, but it seemed like a fun part of the job and she was looking forward to getting to the point where she could spend some face time with the clients. Armed with two weeks of training and the skills she learned at Wharton, Grace headed back to A.T. Kearney's Costa Mesa offices with a renewed sense of confidence.

In October, Grace was assigned to her first long-term project, working with a large aerospace and defense company in Southern California. There were six consultants assigned full-time to the project, and Grace was the most junior person on the team. She didn't know much about aerospace or consulting yet, but she was excited to be exposed to something new—even if it meant constantly asking her colleagues a barrage of questions.

Grace was initially assigned to the project for an eight- to ten-week stint at her client's offices. She and her colleagues had moved into a hotel nearby and was spending five or six nights a week there. "It's like a college dorm. You work all day with them and then you go back to the hotel," she explained.

Grace usually arrived at the client's offices by 7:00 A.M. and finished around 9:00 P.M. She often worked closely with her colleagues throughout the day. Upon their return, though, most of the A.T. Kearney troops would take the hotel's elevator to different floors and plug in their laptops to finish their day's work alone. On two rare occurrences, Grace had to pull all-nighters, once finding herself making copies at a local Kinko's at 5:30 A.M. for a presentation that she wouldn't be allowed to sit in on. Grace's job was to stay behind the scenes for now. She was a number cruncher, spending most of her time gathering sales and other financial data and then synthesizing it into charts and graphs for her senior team members to use in their proposals. "Excel and PowerPoint have sort of become my children," laughed Grace. "I think I'm going to have to name them soon."

There were times when an especially exhausting day would cause Grace to wonder what her life would be like if she had taken the job with L'Oréal, where the hours were pretty much 9:00 A.M. to 5:00 P.M. But the longer she worked with her team, the faster the hours passed. Even when the group had to work through the excitement of the presidential elections and the Red Sox winning the World Series in early November, Grace had joked about it, saying how she had grown closer to her colleagues because they were all stuck in "the cave" together. "I'm getting a taste of different things and I'm never bored," she explained, smiling. "I'm just tired and overworked. But I'm also young. I can do this for a year or so and then go back to school."

At the end of each week, Grace spent a couple of hours in traffic driving back to her parents' house in West Hills for the weekend. At first, she thought the weekends would be a great way to catch up with her friends and family, but she soon discovered that all she could really allow herself to do was catch up on was sleep.

Grace returned to her alma mater in December, which allowed her to take a brief respite from her computer and Excel spreadsheets. She had flown to Philadelphia to help A.T. Kearney lure in a couple of recruits from Wharton who had yet to accept their job offers over a sell dinner. She took the two young prospects to Morimoto, a high-end Japanese restaurant on Chestnut Street named after founding chef Masaharu Morimoto (the "Iron Chef" of television fame). Grace entertained her guests for five hours, all the while enjoying being the person on the other side of the recruitment table. She knew all too well what it felt like to have been the one under scrutiny. "I didn't know them, but I was really sympathetic," she said.

Grace hadn't spoken with any of her fellow Wharton classmates since graduation. She really didn't feel the need to. It was her other friends from the college that she cared most about keeping in touch with. Yet Grace couldn't help but feel a strong connection to Wharton that almost surprised her. She was grateful for the opportunities Wharton had given her, and she knew that whatever path she ended up taking, whether it was the pursuit of an MBA or another career years down the road, the Wharton name would support her. "I feel like my Wharton degree is more important now. People in the industry actually know what it is," she said in a tone of disbelief. "It's almost like this silent killer."

Grace suddenly felt a sense of urgency to get her diploma framed.

In the first week of July, Jon Gantman returned from his backpacking tour of Europe with three friends. The group had covered six countries and nine major cities in five weeks, staying in hostels and traveling by train. Jon had never experienced anything like it before. In Barcelona, they stumbled upon a free Sting concert, and in Rome, the group saw superstar celebrities Matt Damon and Brad Pitt filming *Ocean's Twelve*. There were also some mishaps, including a grueling train ride in which the crew was crammed into a sleeper car with five other people and a hyperactive heater. To get some air circulating, they opened the window. As the train pushed forward, a steady stream of seeds blew into the car that evidently sparked an allergic reaction in one of Jon's friends, who was temporarily blinded in the ordeal. All of it was worth it, though, especially the $1.50 liters of beer in Prague. "I grew up a lot," said Jon. "I had never traveled like that before."

When Jon returned to Philadelphia, most of his Wharton friends had already moved to Manhattan and started their jobs at the investment banks. They were all too busy to be regaled by Jon's backpacking stories or play catch-up. Jon figured he would get a chance to see them once he made his own move to the Big Apple anyway. Instead, he spent the rest of July in Philadelphia, in order to spend time with his girlfriend and his friends from home. There was also plenty of time to be with his family, allowing him to spend hours comparing notes with his grandfather on their respective travels in Europe.

While Jon was traveling, some of his future colleagues at American Express had called him to tell him how excited they were for him to start in September. Jon took it as a good sign that the recruiters were continuing to court him even after he had signed on with them. He was growing increasingly excited about starting his new job.

"I'm pretty pumped and I'm excited to try something new, but I think I'm more excited to go to New York than work," he said with a grin. "I miss school, but sort of in the same way I did the summers before. It hasn't clicked that I'm not going back. It will hit me in September, but right now it still feels like just another summer."

Jon took the first step into his new life in August when he packed up his things and moved to New York. His roommate, a Wharton grad who worked at an investment bank, had already been living in the city for close to a month. Their new apartment was in a high-rise building in Manhattan's Chelsea neighborhood. It had been referred to them by some of Jon's friends from Penn who had moved there a few years earlier.

The lobby of the building was paved in marble. There was a doorman and a gym downstairs, the membership of which was included in his rent. It was perfect except for a space issue. He and his roommate were sharing a seven-hundred-square-foot, one-bedroom apartment. But, as Jon reminded himself, this was New York after all, where space is a precious and expensive commodity. To create another bedroom, they had a makeshift wall built that cut the living room in half, leaving just enough room for a couch and a wide-screen television. It was really all that either of them needed. Jon was getting the "real" bedroom and his roommate got the other half of the living room. It made sense since his roommate was barely home as it was. "It's not that big for two people. It's basically a very nice shoe box," joked Jon.

Jon's start date at American Express had been pushed back to the second week of September because the Republican National Convention had come to town and shut down several parts of Manhattan for the week following Labor Day. The U.S. Open had also begun that week. Even though Jon hadn't started working at American Express yet, they bestowed on him the first of many perks—coveted tickets to the semifinals of the world-renowned tennis tournament. All thirty-five of the employees in Jon's division went, giving him a chance to get to know his coworkers early on.

When Jon finally reported to American Express's office downtown, he expected to be inundated with information and to be furiously scribbling down notes, trying to absorb as much as possible. Instead, his employers eased him in slowly, introducing him to his colleagues and showing him the cubicle where he would work. Pretty much the only thing Jon had to scribble down were the "fifty million passwords" they assigned to him for access to things like databases and e-mail.

By Jon's second week on the job, formal training had begun. He spent the first three days learning about each of American Express's different business divisions and how the financial services behemoth makes money, including the intricacies of the sometimes complicated (but very lucrative) credit-card business. And then, of course, the dynamic duo of software programs was discussed. "I never thought of myself as someone who is good at Excel and PowerPoint. I mean, I was average at school. But now people think I'm really good at this stuff," Jon said. "Wharton is the closest thing to a vocational school at the undergraduate level."

The remainder of the week, Jon participated in a consulting workshop, which went through the different stages of problem solving and the proper ways to structure one's thinking when dealing with an issue. The group was frequently broken up into teams to go over case problems and other consulting exercises. Many of the new hires had just received their MBAs and were willing to help guide Jon through some of the more difficult problems, giving him a sense of immediate camaraderie not unlike what he felt in his Management 100 groups. Throughout the training period, there were events scheduled that allowed Jon to get to know his colleagues in a more social way. Amex sprung for the group to take a cruise around Manhattan that allowed for a prime view of landmarks such as the Statue of Liberty and, of course, New York's famous skyline. Then there was the occasional happy hour at a nearby bar, and a poker night where Jon won $60.

Jon knew there would be a lot of bonuses to working at a place like Amex, including a corporate credit card, tickets to ball games, and a fancy dinner here or there, but there was one perk he wasn't anticipating, and to him, it was perhaps the best of them all. On two occasions during the fall, Amex sent Jon to Penn's campus to help recruit new talent. Jon could go back to his stomping ground with all expenses paid and even get a chance to hang out with his girlfriend in the premed program there.

Jon helped the Amex recruiters sift through the heaps of résumés they had received. He knew some of the students who had applied to Amex, and his colleagues thought it would be good to have his input on them and other applicants as well. "It was so weird going through the résumés. You see all your friends and you are trying to figure out how to separate between what makes a good candidate or not," said Jon. "It's a lot less stressful than going through the interviews and it's good for a couple of laughs. You see all of the stupid things you did like addressing cover letters for a different company and misspellings."

Jon wasn't allowed to sit in on the interviews on campus. Instead, his role was the "greeter" who welcomed students as they arrived for their interviews pumped up and eager to impress Amex's recruiters. Jon would sit in the waiting area with the recruits and make small talk with them. He noticed that the Wharton students, in their typical overachieving way, always showed up early to their interviews. They were the ones he had to entertain the longest. Not that it was a chore for Jon, who was rarely ill at ease with anyone. After the interviews were done, Jon would report back to human resources about who he thought would fit in best at the company.

By early October, Jon had sufficiently settled in to his new cubicle in Amex's offices and was ready to start doing the job he was hired for. His first assignment was to work with the small business network division, which provides small businesses and start-up companies with corporate cards and other financial services. Jon's mission was to help them determine better ways to make the division more profitable by researching initiatives such as cutting spending on certain initiatives or putting more money into others. In the upcoming months, Jon would be assigned to a series of projects such as this one. Each time, Jon would interview the heads of the group, as well as the employees working for them, to ascertain what had worked well in the past for that division and what hadn't. In some cases, he would search for areas that needed improvement and evaluate their five-year plans to determine whether they were feasible.

Jon was impressed with the amount of respect that he was getting from higher-ups at Amex's other divisions. They didn't treat him like a kid fresh out of college. "I think people really respect the work that this group has done in the past and, because of that, they are very receptive," he explained. "Because we are part of the same company and we are working toward the same goal, it gives us a little more foundation to work with these people."

Overall, Jon loved his new job, and the hours made it even better. He was in by 9:00 A.M. and was almost always out by 5:30 or

6:00 P.M. Only on one or two occasions did he stay past 8:00 P.M. For him, it was perfect. But when Jon got home, the apartment was eerily quiet and empty. He barely ever saw his roommate, who was working so many hours that he would come home long after Jon had ended his day. Occasionally, Jon would see him in the early mornings before work or for a couple of hours on the weekend. They had hoped to take boxing classes at the gym downstairs, but that idea was soon quashed when the two realized it would be next to impossible to find the time. Jon encountered his other friends who were working at the investment banks even more rarely. "I haven't seen one of my best friends who works at a big-bulge bracket bank in a month and a half, and he lives just three blocks away!" marveled Jon.

In order to get out of his apartment and socialize, Jon would explore the many great restaurants of his neighborhood at night, almost inevitably gravitating toward Murray Hill, a neighborhood on Manhattan's East Side that seemed to beckon Penn grads to its taverns and bars. "I would be lying if I told you I didn't miss college," admitted Jon. "It's tough trying to keep in touch with everybody. You go from having fifty of your closest friends on the same block as you, to being spread out and being busy. You find out who your closest friends are and the rest fall away. I miss college. I was so happy at college."

But Jon was happy in New York as well. Surprisingly, corporate life wasn't as tedious as he had feared. In February, Jon got his first review and it was glowing. In the weeks to follow, he was given more responsibilities. He felt as if the job was living up to all of his expectations, and he was truly enjoying the work that he did and could see himself staying with the company for five years or so. Yet, ever the entrepreneur at heart, Jon still clung to his dream of starting his own business someday. "If an opportunity ever comes along where I can start up my own company or do something with a group of friends, I don't think I can ever pass that up," he would say. "I mean, I love Amex. It's a great corporation. I just don't know how long I will last in corporate life. As of right now I don't see it as me, but that can change."

Shreevar Kheruka took the long route back to Bombay following graduation. After going on a cruise in Norway with his family, he then stopped in England with his sister before returning home for the summer. While on the cruise ship, Shreevar could tell that his father was proud of him. His father had always wanted to attend some prestigious university in the United States, but he'd never managed to leave India. Instead, he worked full-time throughout college and didn't have the time to get involved in his studies to the extent his son had. "I think he's living vicariously through me," Shreevar said.

But in a matter of weeks, Shreevar found himself vicariously living his father's life. Shreevar wasn't going to start working at Monitor until September 7, so he spent the summer working for his father. For three months, Shreevar shadowed his father and learned the ropes. They were putting in a furnace at one of the company's three glass-manufacturing factories, and Shreevar was there taking notes on the furnace's design and the logistics of building it, knowing that someday the decision whether or not to build a new furnace in a factory would be his to make.

By the end of August, Shreevar was fully entrenched in the family business, and it was hard to put an end to it in order to prepare for his new life in Boston. "My dad and I definitely had disagreements and so forth," explained Shreevar. "But it was really nice working with him."

With just two weeks until he started at Monitor, Shreevar flew back to the States, stopping in Philadelphia to meet some friends before moving into his new apartment in Boston's Back Bay. It was then that Shreevar's prospective roommate called with some bad news: He wasn't going to live with Shreevar after all. Very apologetically, his friend explained that his summer visit home to Delhi, India was enough to convince him that he needed to stay close to his family and work for his own father's business. It was a dilemma Shreevar knew all too well.

"He was very torn," described Shreevar with a note of sympathy. "Given the situation, it made a lot more sense for him to stay there and take care of stuff."

Now Shreevar was moving to Boston knowing only one person–a friend who graduated from the College at Penn–and without a roommate. But Shreevar's didn't have time to mourn the loss of his roommate; training day was quickly approaching. He was hoping that he would be placed with the private-equity group so that he could gain experience in the financing of companies. The head of the group had called Shreevar a couple of times over the summer and told him he was looking at four or five résumés, Shreevar's included, to fill the sole entry-level slot in the group.

When Shreevar embarked on his eight-day training period at Monitor, he was amazed at how easily everything came to him. "You take for granted that other people don't know this stuff," he said. "The Wharton kids were almost excused from training at some points."

When Shreevar followed up on the private-equity position, he realized he didn't want it. The analyst they would hire for the post would spend their entire first year doing research. It seemed to Shreevar he'd get a lot more out of his experience at the firm if he was meeting clients and working with a team to create solutions to problems. Eventually placed with a group that focused on marketing initiatives, Shreevar was soon assigned to his first client, a home-building-supplies company that wanted to launch a new decking product, but had next to no consumer marketing expertise in-house.

Shreevar was charged with the task of doing an extensive marketing analysis of the broader decking industry. There were two main groups: the do-it-yourselfers and the contractors. So Shreevar and his team created surveys to learn more about the two groups, including how much they pay for materials and why they buy one material over another. The placement and wording of questions on the surveys had to be just right, or the results could be skewed, explained Shreevar. "Writing a survey is a pretty tough job," he admitted. "It's very scientific."

Once the results were in, Shreevar was in charge of analyzing the data, which meant hours upon hours alone with his computer. At times, this "grunt work" frustrated him. He had to console himself with the fact that it was all part of the job and he would soon be moving on to the next task. After crunching the numbers, Shreevar started working on the client's business plan for launching the new product. He spent days going through stacks of SEC filings to understand the industry's financials, as well as making dozens of cold calls to competitors and customers in hopes of ascertaining their reaction to Monitor's client.

Throughout his three-month stint on the project, Shreevar reported his progress to his manager. Beyond these periodic updates, however, Shreevar was often left to figure things out for himself. He liked the autonomy, although he admitted at times it would have been nice to have a little more direction. It was probably the only complaint Shreevar could muster about Monitor and it really didn't matter after he got the hang of things.

Shreevar didn't travel as much as some of his peers at other consultancies. Even when he did travel, he was rarely in one place for more than two days. Monitor placed an emphasis on its employees having lives outside of the office, and that meant keeping the hours and the travel time reasonable. Shreevar rarely worked on weekends, and he had only put in two exceptionally late nights in the office, for which his boss apologized profusely the next day.

In just six months, Shreevar had built a whole new life in

Boston. He had made some friends at Monitor and spent Sundays during the football season watching games with his new companions. He also took weekend trips down to New York to visit his friends from Penn. Once the weather warmed up he was planning on taking sailing lessons on Boston's Charles River. But Shreevar tried not to make too many future plans. He was well aware that this new life was fleeting.

Shreevar joked that his family had become so supportive of him living in Boston and working for Monitor that he believed they were using reverse psychology on him—and it was beginning to work. He began plotting out the number of months before he could return to Bombay. Shreevar's father was looking to expand the family business and build a new factory in India, and Shreevar felt he should be part of it. "If it happens, it would be a big investment, and I think he would need my help for sure," said Shreevar. "Economically and career-wise, I think it would be the best move for me to be there."

Shreevar had taken the job at Monitor hoping that the exposure to different clients from various industries he would gain would give him a breadth of business knowledge. But what he found the most useful in his experience was not what happened at the clients' sites, but inside Monitor's offices. "When I go back [to India], I'm going to be viewed as the boss's son or the boss. I will be in a managerial role from day one," explained Shreevar. "This experience has given me the perspective on what it's like being the junior-most person and how one manager is able to motivate me to work and how the other one isn't."

Shreevar viewed the fact that he acquired two degrees at Penn the same way. He was happy that he didn't spend his four years at the university focusing solely on business with his fellow Wharton students. Instead he felt he gained a wider perspective by pursuing his International Relations degree and taking classes at the College, where he got to know all types of students. All of these experiences, he believed, would prove beneficial when he returned home to India—a move that was looking like it was going to happen much sooner than Shreevar had originally planned.

Following graduation, Jessica Kennedy couldn't wait to start her new life in New York. She cut her trip home to Texas short and decided that her wisdom teeth—which she wanted to get removed before she started work—could be extracted by her dentist in Philadelphia instead of one in Texas. That way she could take the train to Manhattan after her surgery and recuperate there. Part of the reason that Jessica was in such a hurry to start her new life was the fact that she only had six weeks until she started at Lazard Frères, and she wanted to be completely settled in by then. Once she started at Lazard, she knew she would have little time to do things such as get teeth extracted, decorate her apartment or scope out the neighborhood Starbucks (she would quickly find there were two of these caffeine purveyors just blocks from her apartment).

Jessica had looked at apartments in Manhattan for months prior to graduation. She asked her friends who had graduated before her which neighborhoods were best, and more importantly, most convenient to her new office. In April, Jessica had fallen in love with a large studio apartment in the East 60s, just blocks from the high-end shops lining Madison Avenue where she hoped to be able to afford the $800-plus dresses in the storefront windows some day. Known as the "Gold Coast," the neighborhood hosted multimillion-dollar co-ops and condos nestled in prewar mansions, much of it supported with Wall Street money.

Jessica loved the area and the building, which came complete with a doorman, but the rent was higher than she was planning to pay. Taking the apartment would mean that Jessica would have to really watch her spending. But it was hard for her to forget the apartment's gargantuan windows that faced south and allowed her to gaze upon the gardens growing on the rooftops of neighboring penthouses from nine stories up. She started creating a budget to figure out how she could afford the place during her first couple of years at Lazard. She knew that she wouldn't be racking up that much in utility bills—or, for that matter, food—because most of her time would be spent in Lazard's offices anyway. After doing some tricky cost-cutting, she decided she could make it work. She would only have to watch her pennies for a short while, anyway. If she moved through the ranks at Lazard as quickly as she hoped, then affording this apartment wouldn't be a big deal in a year or two.

By June, Jessica had moved the stately cherrywood furniture that she had inherited from her mother into her apartment. Jessica tucked her canopy bed into the alcove reserved for her bedroom, and situated her impeccably clean, cream-colored couch against the living room wall, where she could look out the windows of her apartment. Her artwork had been hung on the walls just so, and pictures of her friends and family had been tastefully framed and placed around the room. Soon Jessica had created her new home—and it was a far cry from the piecemeal hand-me-downs and IKEA furnishings that most twentysomethings tend to decorate their first apartments with.

During her time off, Jessica also allowed herself some pleasure reading. *The Fountainhead,* by Ayn Rand, was quickly becoming the voice that expressed Jessica's work ethic. It was the second book she had read by the Russian-born author. Rand's *Atlas Shrugged* was Jessica's favorite book, which—as Jessica describes it—focuses on the love of one's work. To her disappointment, *The Fountainhead* seemed to revolve more around greed and selfish motivations, and Jessica wasn't enjoying it as much. Once she put *The Fountainhead* down, Jessica cracked open *Financier: The Biography of André Meyer* yet again, hoping to finish the tome by the time she started at Lazard so she could discuss it with Gary Parr.

As the month of June wore on, Jessica became increasingly anxious to start working. Training wouldn't start until the second week of July, and Jessica decided that she should at least stop by and visit

Parr and a female vice president she had grown to admire. She managed to get some time with both of them, and—as if it weren't already evident—she reiterated how excited she was to start her career with them. Jessica had returned to her apartment that humid afternoon even more excited to start than she had been before.

Now the only thing bothering her was whether or not she'd be able to forge a better bond with her fellow analysts during training than she had during her summer internship a year ago. While Jessica knew she couldn't betray her die-hard work ethic, she wanted to come off a little less competitive than she had the summer before in hopes of appearing less intimidating to her fellow analysts. "During my internship, I was pulling all-nighters and I turned in all of my work on time. Once one of the VPs said to me after I handed him some work that he asked for, 'You're a star, and I'm going to make sure everyone knows it,'" recounted Jessica. "And I think that bothered people. Part of it is me being overly ambitious and part of it is being misunderstood."

Jessica didn't necessarily want to be best friends with the people in her analyst class or spend every free night going out with them. She just wanted to relate to them better and hopefully prevent the whisperings and rumors that had been generated by one of her peers last summer (who she noted wasn't offered a full-time position by Lazard). "People don't understand that I love my social life, but I love my work more," she declared. "It can be misinterpreted as me being antisocial."

Jessica approached her training as if it were the calm before the storm. She had imagined that most of the time would be spent sitting in a classroom going over information she was already all too familiar with. The project deadlines and demands of higher-ups wouldn't be there, and Jessica assumed she would be able to leave the office by a semi-decent hour. But the one thing Jessica didn't account for was all of the social events she would be expected to attend and the rigorous structure of Lazard's intensive training program.

Typically, Jessica would arrive at the conference room where classes were held by 8:45 A.M. for the first of a series of classes in Excel or finance or some other topic that lasted well into the evening. Occasionally, speakers from Lazard's various divisions, such as the Alternative Investments Group or the Capital Markets Group, would provide a welcome respite from accounting class by regaling the new analysts with stories from the trenches or simply just explaining what they did. It beat sitting through a seven-hour session on accounting topped off by a couple of hours learning about corporate valuations again. "It's like being in Security Analysis class for twelve hours a day," Jessica described with a sigh. "I can't even imagine how hard it is for people who didn't go to business school."

On top of the long days of training, it seemed as though there was an event scheduled every night, whether it was drinks at the Rink Bar in Rockefeller Center or at the Rainbow Room upstairs. No one wanted to lose face by skipping out to get a good night's sleep. In fact, during the first day of training, Jessica and the thirty other first-years put in a fourteen-hour day and then went out afterward. Jessica didn't get home until well after midnight. By August she was averaging four hours of sleep a night and was exhausted. "I feel like I've been on for twenty hours a day for weeks at a time," she said, noting that she couldn't even remember the last time she had been able to drop off her laundry.

There was also a less material reason why training took an unexpected toll on Jessica. It wasn't so much the energy and effort needed to complete the work assigned to her, it was the energy she had devoted to establishing her rank among her peers. Even though there was less of a sense of rivalry between the members of this analyst class, the pecking order was something that Jessica believed was inevitably being established. She wasn't sure if the other people in her analyst class perceived the clear lines that were being drawn in the sand between those who knew what they were doing and those who didn't, but she couldn't help but feel it palpably. "I'm probably more sensitive to it than anyone else. I should be ahead of the game because I was here for a few months last year," said Jessica. "I'm so on that I can't fall asleep."

Once Jessica was assigned to her first project in late August, all of the pecking-order issues quickly took a backseat to the work she was facing. She had wanted badly to be placed in the Financial Institutions Group, one of the most demanding divisions in a legendarily demanding firm. She had even made sure to introduce herself to everyone working in the division, so if her name came up as a candidate to join them, they would remember her. Jessica believed that if she ever wanted to run an investment bank someday, working in FIG would provide her with the perfect training for it. "I knew FIG would have a good deal-flow," said Jessica. "It's supposed to be real intense, and I thought I would do best in an intense environment. Some people come into banking and they try to avoid the intensity."

Soon Jessica had been granted her wish and was assigned a desk in FIG's "pod" with one second-year and two third-year analysts. Jessica rarely encountered her fellow first-year analysts, who worked on different floors. Only occasionally would she bump into them in the elevators, or downstairs when she was dropping off a package to be mailed out.

At first, the assignments trickled in, but they gained momentum rapidly. She was soon assigned to a big project headed up by some of the most senior people in her division, including Gary Parr. Jessica took the assignment as a vote of confidence in her abilities. By mid-September, Jessica was up to her old work habits from the summer before, taking on as many projects as possible, staying up all night long and working well into the weekend (and into the next week) to finish everything on time. In fact, she was working so much that her only expenses were rent, lunch, and getting her hair done. Everything else was either expensed to Lazard or avoided completely because she didn't have the time to buy anything, no matter how badly she wanted to go shopping in the stores lining Fifth Avenue. "The urge to spend money (especially across the street at Saks) is coming back with a vengeance," Jessica wrote in an e-mail. "I keep reminding myself that I can't do that until I make associate, though."

When her mother visited from Texas one early October weekend, Jessica could barely steal away for three hours to spend time with her. They had to cancel some of their plans, an inconvenience that Jessica had warned her mother might happen. It was during this time that Jessica began to feel that she was experiencing first-hand the horror stories people had related to her about working at an investment bank. For three weeks in a row, Jessica never left the office before 5:00 A.M. and barely clocked in more than a couple of hours of sleep a night, if that. "I don't burn out easily, but 140 hours a week is enough to start me on that track," she said.

Jessica had been working on an unusually large project analyzing a takeover target for a client book for two weeks when the managing director who had requested it changed his mind about the way the presentation should look and ordered the whole thing redone. Jessica grew frustrated. She couldn't believe that all of the hours she had spent on this book were practically in vain. She began questioning why she was in the office at 7:00 A.M. on Saturday mornings and whether the zealousness that she showed for the work was really worthwhile. It was hard to reinvigorate herself and start again, but she managed to, because deep down she knew that there was nothing she could do about it. The day after the pitch book was handed in and approved, the staffer who doles out projects to analysts called Jessica and assigned her to yet another massive project from the same MD. She thought about saying "no," but she knew it wasn't a possibility. The work had become relentless. "I kind of need to have the attitude of doing whatever they need whenever they need it," she said with resolve.

It was during those especially trying couple of months that Jessica became consumed with the notion of burnout yet again. Part of her hated admitting that burning out was even a possibility. At the same time, though, she wanted to be honest with herself. She knew she was different from most people her age. She didn't need to take time off or spend time with her friends socializing to feel good about herself. What she needed to feel fulfilled was to prove herself through her work. "If you're going at an average pace and doing a good job you cannot burn out, but if you're going to stand out you can't go at an average pace," she explained.

And Jessica wanted to stand out. She steadfastly clung to her goal of making associate as quickly as possible. It would be quite a feat—most analysts take three or more years to do so and Jessica dreamed of getting promoted even more quickly than that. "If they promoted people all the time in less than three years, then it wouldn't be a cool thing," she remarked. "I need to be the perfect analyst, then demonstrate that I can deal with clients."

Jessica knew that striving to be the perfect analyst meant making certain sacrifices, and in her case it meant sacrificing friendships. It seemed as though the only people she ever saw were those she worked with. Even when she was overburdened and working throughout the night at Wharton, she still managed to meet new and interesting people. Since she had been working at Lazard, she really hadn't met anyone outside of the office. Even if she did have plans to meet her non-Lazard friends, she often wouldn't have the energy to stay out too long or even go out at all. On most nights, Jessica was so tired when she got home from work that sleep seemed more essential than partying. Jessica wasn't happy about her social life, but she accepted it as "the way it is."

"My early twenties are probably going to be like this. Rather than being all depressed about it, I have to accept it," she said. "What comes to mind are all of the quotes I have about 'never, never, never quitting' and determination. In a way, I guess I took those for granted."

With time, Jessica knew that she would get better at managing her job, her personal time and her social life. Work would always take precedence, though, no matter what. She just had to keep up the pace at Lazard for another year or so as an analyst and then things would be a little easier (although not by most people's standards).

"You're not great at it yet," she explained. "You haven't seen all the fruits of it all. It won't mean that much in the end if you don't get through the rough time at first."

Perhaps Regi Vengalil had taken his friends' advice to wait to find an apartment in Manhattan too much to heart. In the spring, he had started looking around at different neighborhoods and inquiring about apartments, but his friends told him he was jumping the gun and should hold off for a little while. Now in June, with only two weeks before starting his job, he was scrambling to find a place—even with the help of a broker. An influx of fresh college grads had taken most of the available apartments and had overwhelmed the real-estate agencies. When he and his roommate finally found a place, Regi was greatly relieved. He knew that his focus needed to be on his job and didn't want to be distracted by apartment hunting.

Nine months into his fledgling career, Regi would say that choosing public finance had been the right decision. After all of his internal debates, he had picked a field that satisfied his interests and stimulated him intellectually. The hours were long, but it was a job he truly enjoyed.

Anthony Sandrik couldn't believe his luck—good and bad. He and his two prospective roommates, one of whom was a recent hire at an investment bank and the other at a hedge fund, were in the final stages of landing a three-bedroom duplex apartment with a deck in the West Village. The place was a palace, especially for three twenty-two-year-olds. In early June, everything seemed to be all clear for the boys to snag the place, when the real estate broker received an offer from a couple of lawyers who had a little more cash to spend on the place. The great apartment coup was even written about in the Real Estate section of the *New York Times*. Anthony wasn't mentioned by name in the article, but he liked the celebrity of it nonetheless. Within a couple of weeks the guys found a new three-bedroom apartment in SoHo, a high-end downtown neighborhood filled with pricey restaurants, designer shops and art galleries. The apartment was almost as decadent as the one they had lost and came fully furnished, complete with antiques and artwork hung on the walls. Everything they needed was there, so the guys used the money they were planning to spend on furniture on a fifty-inch television instead. The mix of the antiques and the big screen gave the apartment a schizophrenic air that seemed appropriate to these young Wall Streeters living in a nouveau-riche neighborhood built on the backs of artists.

Anthony wasn't going to start training at Orion until the second week of July, so he had plenty of time to explore the restaurants and cafés of his new neighborhood and beyond. He tried to avoid the bars that many of the Penn alums flocked to. He just wasn't ready to be thrown back into the world that he had been so relieved to leave only weeks before. "There's nothing about Penn that I miss," admitted Anthony. "I don't miss midterms. I don't miss Huntsman Hall. And I never really made any contacts with professors."

One of Anthony's favorite pastimes while at Manhattan's bars was figuring out who the bankers were in the crowd. According to Anthony, they always traveled in packs, had a certain cockiness about them and drank heavily. "You can tell that drinking beer does nothing to them. The fact that they are trained to operate efficiently for eighteen hours a day will help them through life, I guess," he observed.

Anthony was more than ready to get to work by the time training rolled around in July. His new offices were in the Helmsley

Building on Park Avenue in midtown. Including Anthony, there were eight people in the training class, and all of them came from Ivy League schools or their academic equivalents–Stanford, MIT and Oxford. In some odd way it seemed as if the group was on a level playing field, but Anthony had one distinct advantage–he was the only business major that Orion had hired. While the job entailed a great deal of finance-related knowledge, it also required a lot of writing, and the firm traditionally hired those who could write well over those who knew about asset-backed securities. "The biggest difference is that I won't panic on the phone if someone drops a finance term," he said modestly.

During training, the group went through tutorials on derivatives, mortgages and loans–most of which Anthony had covered the summer before while interning at the hedge fund or while sitting in his classes at Wharton. All of it was pretty straightforward, or at least Anthony had thought. It seemed as though the writing style in Orion's research reports was pretty formulaic and easy to emulate. When they gave him his first writing assignment, Anthony had soon discovered that it was a lot harder than he had expected. Thankfully, one of the managers was always there to make sure everything was in order before any clients had seen the new associate's work.

Anthony had plenty of time to practice his writing and get the format down. He and his fellow trainees probably wouldn't be put on a client team for another few months, and that's when the heavy lifting would begin. At first they would just handle one client, but then they would graduate to covering whole industries. Anthony knew that he probably wouldn't be sticking around long enough to cover too many industries. He wasn't quite sure where he was going to end up–perhaps a hedge fund or trading somewhere–he just knew that this type of work wasn't something he would spend his entire career doing. It seemed as if most people went on to do other things after two or three years at Orion, making room for a fresh crop of faces like Anthony's each summer.

Yet, working at Orion was a lifestyle that Anthony soon acclimated to nicely. Unlike his investment banker roommate's, Anthony's hours were pretty much set and predictable. He would get into the office at 9:00 A.M. and leave by 7:00 P.M., and he always had some spare moments to grab a cup of coffee during the day. While his roommate got paid a handsome bonus at the end of the year, Anthony wasn't guaranteed one. Yet, Anthony would enjoy other perks his roommate would never have time for–such as a weeklong, all-expense-paid ski trip and a free gym membership. In addition, Anthony shared an office with two other people he liked and worked under two managers and a boss, all of whom were young and easy to work with. "Everyone is right out of college and there's no pressure," he added. "There's free breakfast, and no one ever gets pissed. The guy who runs the shop is laid-back and that trickles down."

Orion was perfect for Anthony's sensibilities. He still wanted to try his hand at trading, though. Orion could help him there, too. Most of Anthony's sources for his research were traders, and he could start building a relationship with them over the phone. All of it seemed too good to be true, and Anthony was truly happy that he had spared himself from the banking life. He finally felt that he appreciated where his education had brought him.

"When I was at Penn I never saw it as an accomplishment. It was like, I did well on the SAT's and in high school, so what?" said Anthony. "This is the first time I ever felt as if working my ass off is finally paying off. And I'm so glad I'm in New York."

Shimika Wilder was happy to be back home in Maryland after graduation. She had close to two months to catch up with old friends and chill out with her family before training commenced at Goldman Sachs. During her last semester at Wharton, Shimika had taken the courses necessary to attain a minor in forensic science at the College. She had enjoyed the classes so much that she even kicked around the idea of joining the FBI someday. She still held on to her hope of going to law school, too, but she needed to pay off her college loans first, and working at Goldman was certainly going to help her do that—even if it meant sacrificing the next two years of her life to the bank. Her stay in Maryland would have been an ideal time to study for the LSATs—something she swore she would do during senior year—but relaxing and having a good time while she had the opportunity seemed more important. This would be one of those rare periods when she only had to be concerned about her own life and catching up with friends and family, and she was going to take advantage of it.

The early summer days flew by, and in mid-July Shimika headed north with her worldly possessions. She was set to live with a young woman who had just graduated from Yale and was also going to be a first-year analyst at Goldman. The two had met during their internships at Goldman the previous summer. While they weren't necessarily great friends, they had hit it off well enough and Shimika thought it made sense to live with someone who was going to be leading a similar lifestyle to her own. The two women had signed a lease for a one-bedroom apartment in a high-rise building near Wall Street (and the Goldman Sachs offices) called The Crest, which had been going through some massive renovations. (Several other new Goldman analysts were planning to move into The Crest as well). Shimika and her roommate would have to build a wall and split a room in half to make another bedroom. Space would be tight, but at least they would have an easy walk to the office.

With just two weeks before training was scheduled to begin at Goldman, the women received some shocking news: The overhaul at The Crest was not complete, and their apartment wouldn't be ready for them to move into for several weeks. They would be left homeless for their first weeks of training at Goldman. During their lunch hours and intermittent breaks Shimika and her prospective roommate would call the complex's management office and fight with them to get their money back. They still needed a place to stay. Luckily, Shimika found a friend to crash with. Her prospective roommate wasn't so lucky: She moved into a hotel room during the first week of training.

On the advice of a second-year analyst at Goldman, the women went to look at a two-bedroom apartment in Liberty Towers, a new high-rise building in Jersey City, across the Hudson River from Wall Street and a short ferry ride into the city. Not only would they each have their own bedrooms, but they would have their own bathrooms as well. Even better, they would have their own washer and dryer, *and* receive a Goldman Sachs discount that waived their amenities fees and paid for their ferry rides for a year. Without hesitation, Shimika and her roommate pounced on the place.

While the commute would be longer than at The Crest, Shimika was happy that she and her roommate would have the space that they both needed. She was quite certain that they wouldn't see each other much anyway because their hours, while they would be undoubtedly long, would probably differ. Once Goldman's five-week training period was completed, Shimika was placed in the Technology, Media, and Telecommunications Group that she had worked with during her internships. Her roommate was placed in the Healthcare Group, which Shimika explained was a little less demanding than her division and required fewer hours of its analysts.

Shimika was soon seated in a cubicle among the other analysts, associates and assistants in her group. There were about twelve other first-years assigned to the division, and Shimika immediately hit it off with most of them. Goldman soon armed Shimika and her cohorts with BlackBerry wireless devices that would access their e-mail so they could be plugged in at all times. Cell phone bills, they were told, would also be taken care of by the bank. The tradeoff was that Shimika and her peers had more or less become Goldman's indentured servants. They now had to be reachable at all hours of the day, no matter what they were doing or where they were—even while they were on vacation (an indulgence that is a rarity for a first-year) or on the weekends. Of course, they were expected to be in the office every weekend anyway.

Shimika would soon discover that the hours she worked as a full-time analyst (about 110 hours a week) felt longer than the hours she worked during her internship. At least when she was an intern, she knew that the long days would eventually subside when she returned to Wharton at the end of the summer. But once she was on the track of Goldman's two-year-long analyst program, the days and months weren't passing as quickly as she had hoped, and the end seemed nowhere in sight. At times, it left Shimika discouraged and her exhaustion only compounded matters. "Doing this job I've come to the realization that I'm going to break down a few times," she explains. But for Shimika there was no giving up: "In your heart you're so driven that you just can't quit."

To keep charging ahead, Shimika clung to the fact that she had a broad range of responsibilities as an analyst, including attending client meetings, building financial models for mergers or leveraged buyouts and putting together road-show presentations and pitch books that sometimes led to multimillion-dollar deals. At times, those responsibilities gave her a sense of empowerment, as if her voice was being heard and her work was being seen by some of the most important people in the corporate world. "In no other job coming out of undergrad would you have this amount of responsibility," she declared.

As her stint progressed, Shimika's personal log of phone calls to return kept getting larger. She made an effort to speak with her best friend and boyfriend on a regular basis, but it was her mother who took the utmost priority. Shimika made sure to call her mother every day, and soon her ten-minute morning walk from the ferry to the office became the only predictable free time for those calls. As she told her mother about how late she'd worked the night before or about a project that was taking weeks to put together, her mother was in a state of disbelief. She just couldn't understand why Shimika was staying so late at the office and couldn't just go home at a reasonable hour and finish up her work the next day.

By the spring of 2005–nine months in to her job–Shimika was increasingly thinking about what she was going to do when her time at Goldman came to an end. In April, she enrolled in an LSAT prep course that required three hours a week that Shimika swore to herself she would find time for. She was planning to apply to law schools in the fall, and acing the LSAT the first time around was imperative. Shimika was finally starting to feel like she had embarked on the path that she had laid out for herself during senior year: paying off her college loans, boosting her resume and using her Wharton degree to do what she really wanted to do with her life.

In April 2004, Wharton's Dean Harker announced that the school would no longer make its alumni e-mail lists available to newspapers and magazines such as *BusinessWeek, U.S. News & World Report, Forbes,* and the *Financial Times,* which use the information for surveys that help them compile their business-school rankings. "There is a very strong consensus among all of the parties I've consulted that the ranking methodologies are severely flawed," wrote Harker in a letter to the not-for-profit Association to Advance Collegiate Schools of Business (known as AACSB International). Another prominent (and highly-ranked) business school–Harvard's– announced a similar dictum.

While the publications' rankings will continue to include Wharton and Harvard, the ranking data will not incorporate all of the familiar polls that are traditionally used to ascertain a school's rating (although some publications still have contact with alumni and will be able to do some polling). The move has stirred debates: Would not having all of the surveys hurt Wharton's ranking and therefore impact enrollment or the school's prestige?

So far, the decision hasn't seemed to hurt Wharton at all. In October 2004, six months after Harker wrote the letter to

AACSB, *BusinessWeek* ranked Wharton's MBA program two spots higher to third place in their biannual rankings. It hasn't deterred applicants, either: Wharton's undergrad program saw an almost nine percent increase in applications for the Class of 2009.

But perhaps another, more effective way to gauge an institution's effectiveness is based on how its students fare in the world outside of campus. As far as Wall Street's recruiters are concerned, Wharton would be ranked highly. Almost 340 employers came to Penn's campus in the fall of 2003 and spring of 2004 to recruit members of Wharton's senior class. The Class of 2004 went on a total of 12,364 interviews, averaging fourteen interviews each and receiving an average of two to three job offers. Following graduation, an estimated sixty-three percent of Wharton's Class of 2004 was working in the financial services industry, with forty percent of that group doing investment banking. Another nineteen percent of the class went into consulting. In their first year out of Wharton, this group made an average salary of $52,300 a year–the highest average since 2001 and $2,000 more than the Class of 2003–and landed average sign-on and year-end bonuses of $6,800 and $14,870, respectively. According to Career Services' Barbara Hewitt, who now oversees all of On-Campus Recruiting at Penn, the recruiting season for the Class of 2005 was turning out to be a good one. There were almost fifteen percent more employers on campus searching for young talent than the year before. Accordingly, the investment banks were courting more students and even the consulting firms had increased the number of protégés they would hire (albeit that number was far from the levels they hired in 1999 and 2000).

It's safe to say that the Class of 2004 is doing all right for themselves. And there is no doubt that–barring a major economic upheaval–Wharton's next generation and the one after that will have accordingly impressive track records whether as captains of industry, real estate moguls, financial titans or whatever else they put their well-trained minds to.

AUTHOR'S NOTE

It was a sweltering day in late August 2003 when I first weaved my way through the clusters of students standing in the sunshine outside of Huntsman Hall. I had come to the University of Pennsylvania's campus to meet with a group of Wharton faculty and administration members to explain the project that I was embarking on, in the hope of gaining their blessing. Before entering the building (which I would later come to know as the "Tower of Greed"), I took a moment to survey the landscape. There was something intoxicating about being back on a college campus, a feeling of energy and of clean slates. As I would tell Wharton's staff that day, it was the school and its students—raw and full of passion—that I had come to learn about. I wanted to chronicle the pinnacle of the Wharton experience: the notoriously competitive recruiting frenzy, when seniors take their first steps toward finding their place in the most prestigious financial hubs and corporate boardrooms of the world.

Over the course of the fall semester of 2003 and well into the spring semester of 2004, I regularly met with more than a dozen seniors from Wharton's Class of 2004. Not only did I seek to learn about these students' experiences at the school, but I also wanted to understand what drove them, both collectively and personally. I sought to discover what made this school so alluring to some of the top students in the world and a hotbed of talent for hungry recruiters. I also wanted to demystify the infamous Wharton stereotype, one that was both Darwinistic and masochistic—qualities that were evidently attractive to Wall Street's top brass.

While on campus, I often met these students at one of the Penn's two main coffee shops, Starbucks and Cosi (these are highly caffeinated kids), or in the common areas of Huntsman Hall. For some of them, our meetings became the only nonschool, nonrecruiting event they had scheduled on their calendars for days. I grew to know each of them quite well and have continued to stay in touch with most of them through graduation and well into their post-Wharton lives. Throughout our time together, these students recounted a number of their experiences, whether it was a job interview or a night out with friends. The pages of interview notes that I took have provided a majority of the material in this book, and in writing this book I strove to present the student's opinions and their stories as accurately as they had presented them to me.

Over the course of my interviews, a couple of students fell by the wayside when they decided to put off the recruiting process for one more year and stay at Penn, either to finish up a dual degree or embark on a sub-matriculation program that would award them a master's in addition to their bachelor's degree. Other students that I met with became nervous about the impact that their involvement with this book might have on their future careers. Some of them asked me to change their names or not to name the banks they were speaking about for fear of getting a job offer rescinded or being "blackballed." During this time of corporate scandals, in which some analysts and traders were seeing more of the courtroom than the trading floor, banks had become especially cautious and tight-lipped about even the most innocuous information. Many of these students had provided me with valuable insights and anecdotes, some of which I have not used, others of which aren't attributed in this book. Although the identities of all of the students in this book are genuine, at times, the names of employers and other institutions have been left out at the students' request.

When I first spoke with Wharton's faculty and administration about cooperating with this project, I was met with some reluctance. A few people were concerned that by allowing me to observe the recruiting process, Wharton might lose credibility with recruiters. To ease their minds, the administration sent out a letter to the representatives of the firms heading to campus that fall, cautioning them that a reporter would be roaming around campus and interviewing the very students they were looking to hire. Overall, the faculty and staff at Wharton proved to be valuable resources and were extremely helpful in making me familiar with the school and its annual recruiting frenzy. They guided me through the Wharton curriculum, provided campus tours, invited me to career fairs and workshops and allowed me to observe without interfering.

My personal experience also proved helpful. Throughout my career as a business journalist, I had interviewed many of the CEOs and bankers who most Wharton students aim to work for and emulate. Meeting Wharton's students was like turning back the clock and tapping into what these executives were like before they were awarded stock-option packages, bought private jets and, in some cases, became famous. Having met many of Wharton's future business leaders of America, I can say that Wall Street in the twenty-first century is in good hands.

Reflecting on Wharton's Class of 2004, I am confident that at least one of these students is going to make a name for him- or herself. It's just a matter of how many it's going to be, and in which section of the *Wall Street Journal* I will read about them. Such is the nature of Wharton and its students. For them, this is just the first part of their story.

SELECTED SOURCES

BUSINESS RESOURCES:

A lot of information about investment banks comes from the banks themselves, whether in the form of press releases or on their Web sites. For information on which investment banks are the most powerful on Wall Street, Thomson Financial puts out quarterly reports called "league tables," which rank the banks by the types of deals they have done and the size of those deals. The league tables can be located at *http://www.thomson.com/financial/investbank/fi_investbank_league_table.jsp*. Below is a selected list of articles and resources that proved helpful in my research.

Duca, John V. "The Democratization of America's Capital Markets." *Economic and Financial Review*, April 2001. Federal Reserve Bank of Dallas.

"Firms Churn the Dynamics of Turnover on Main Street and Wall Street." Research Department, Federal Reserve Bank of Dallas. December 9, 1999.

Gandel, Stephen. "Women Losing Out in Wall Street Downsizing: 20% Job Drop, Top Execs Disappearing." Crain Communications Inc. Oct. 14, 2002. New York.

Leonhardt, David. "Buy! Sell! Have a Beer! Dueling Gurus (and Pals)." *The New York Times*, September 2, 2001.

Securities Industry Association. "SIA Survey: Representation of Women, Minorities Increases in Key Industry Positions As Diversity Initiatives Expand." Securities Industry Association. November 6, 2003. Link to press release: *http://www.sia.com/press/ 2003_press_releases/html/pr_survey_results.html*

Ward, Vicky. "Lazard's Clash of the Titans." *Vanity Fair* No. 536, April 2005. The Conde Nast Publications. New York.

CAREER RESOURCES:

Career guides from Vault, Inc. and WetFeet, Inc. detail what a person can expect in situations such as walking into an investment banking interview or starting out as a consultant. Books such as *Goldman Sachs: The Culture of Success* written by Lisa Endlich, a former Goldman vice president, as well as corporate Web sites provide insights about the histories and cultures of the banks and consulting firms that Wharton students want so desperately to work for. To gain a better sense of the lifestyles that the students would be adopting, I interviewed bankers and consultants and read Michael Lewis's *Liar's Poker* and John Rolfe and Peter Troob's *Monkey Business*, both firsthand accounts of what it's like to be in the trenches.

Alsop, Ronald. "How to Get Hired." *The Wall Street Journal*, September 22, 2004. p. R8.

Butcher, Sarah. "Interview Insiders: Do Not Make These Mistakes." eFinancial Careers Ltd. January 20, 2005. *http://news.efinancial careers.com/HOW_TO_ITEM/newsItemId-18500000000060304*

Endlich, Lisa, *Goldman Sachs: The Culture of Success*. New York: Touchstone, 2000.

Glater, Jonathan D. "Management: Business Students Do an

About-Face; Recruiters for Banks and Consultants Have Regained the Upper Hand." *The New York Times.* February 14, 2001.

Knowledge@Wharton. "Speculate on This: What Motivates Investment Bankers?" (Based on a study by Peter Cappelli and executive search firm Spencer Stuart.) February 13, 2002. Philadelphia.

Vault, Inc. *Career Guide to Investment Banking.* New York: Vault Inc., 2004. Fourth Edition.

——. Fick, J. Hollie. "What's So Great About the Bulge Brackets?" New York: Vault Inc. May, 30, 2000.

——. Lott, Tom. "Corporate Finance–The Deal Team." Excerpted from Vault.com *Career Guide to Investment Banking.* New York: Vault Inc., Sept. 1, 2000.

WetFeet Insider Guide. *Careers in Management Consulting, 2005 Edition.* San Francisco: WetFeet Inc., August 2004.

——. *Careers in Investment Banking, 2005 Edition.* San Francisco: WetFeet Inc., 2005.

——. *McKinsey & Company: WetFeet Insider Guide 2005 Edition.* San Francisco: WetFeet Inc., 2004.

EDUCATION, SCHOOL RANKINGS, AND EMPLOYMENT INFORMATION:

Penn's Career Services department has an impressive array of information, including interviewing tips and practice questions for specific types of companies, career survey reports, upcoming events, as well as job listings and other information. The site can be accessed at *http://www.vpul.upenn.edu/careerservices/*.

Some of the most useful sources of information for this book were the surveys compiled by Wharton's Career Services department on students' career plans and internships. Barbara Hewitt, the associate director of Career Services for Wharton undergrads, prepared the data from these surveys, which track the average number of interviews students had, the salary and bonus statistics, what industries they took jobs in, or what other postgraduate plans they may have.

Merritt, Jennifer. "The Best B-Schools." *BusinessWeek*. October 18, 2004.

———. "Concerning BW's B-School Survey." *BusinessWeek*. April 6, 2004.

National Association of Colleges and Employers. "Year-End Report Shows Salary Gains for Class of 2004." press release. Bethlehem, Pa., September 15, 2004

National Association of Colleges and Employers. "Hiring of New College Graduates to Increase 13.1%." press release. Bethlehem, Pa., September 8, 2004

National Center for Education Statistics, a division of the U.S. Department of Education. *Digest of Education Statistics, 2003*. Washington, D.C., August 2003. *http://nces.ed.gov//programs/digest/d03_tf.asp*

U.S. Census Bureau. "Facts for Features: Back to School." July 6, 2004. *http://www.census.gov/PressRelease/www/releases/archives/facts_for_features_special_editions/002263.html*

U.S. News & World Report. "America's Best Colleges 2005." Retrieved April 5, 2005 from U.S. News.com Web site.

GENERAL INFORMATION AND NEWS ABOUT THE UNIVERSITY OF PENNSYLVANIA AND THE WHARTON SCHOOL:

The University of Pennsylvania Web site has extensive information on admissions statistics, curriculum information and programs, geographic distribution of students, the community, and more. The site is located at *http://www.upenn.edu/*

Alsop, Ron. "Wharton Changes with the Times." *The Wall Street Journal Online's College Journal.* September 17, 2003. *http://www.collegejournal.com/bschool04/articles/20030917-alsop-wharton.html*

——. "Wharton School Moves to Top Spot." The Wall Street Journal Online's *College Journal.* September 17, 2003. *http://www.collegejournal.com/bschool04/articles/20030917-alsop-lede.html*

Byrne, John A. and Lori Bongiorno. "The Best B-Schools: Move over, Northwestern–This Time, Wharton Is No. 1." *Business-Week.* October 24, 1994.

Chan-A-Shing, Kevin. "Financial Times Ranks Wharton #1 Again." *The Wharton Journal,* Philadelphia: Wharton School of the University of Pennsylvania., February 9, 2004.

Conway, Terry. "Wharton: On Top and Determined to Stay That Way." *Philadelphia Business Journal.* Philadelphia: American City Business Journals Inc., August 9, 1999.

Han, Peter. "Deconstructing Wharton's Own Death Star." *The Wharton Journal,* Philadelphia: The Wharton School of the University of Pennsylvania, November 18, 2002.

"Judith Rodin: An Enduring Legacy." University of Pennsylvania Web site. June 20, 2003. *http://www.upenn.edu/pennnews/rodin_legacy/*

Key, Peter. "Connected Campuses: Area Universities Wire Classrooms, Update Facilities to Keep Up with High-Tech Curve." *Philadelphia Business Journal.* Philadelphia: American City Business Journals, Inc., October 18, 2002.

McCartney, Gerry. "Technology Q & A: The Uses of Technology in Huntsman Hall with Wharton CIO Gerry McCartney." The Wharton School of the University of Pennsylvania. 2004. *http://www.wharton.upenn.edu/huntsmanhall/tour/facts_q1.html*

Thomas, George E. and David B. Brownlee. *Building America's First University: An Historical and Architectural Guide to the*

University of Pennsylvania. Philadelphia: University of Pennsylvania Press, 2000.

Thorpe, Francis N. "The University of Pennsylvania." *Harper's New Monthly Magazine,* Vol. 91 No. 542. July, 1895. New York: Harper & Brothers.

Sandrik, Anthony. "Fall at Wharton: The Resume Chase Resumes." *First Call,* Vol IV No. 2. September 22, 2003.

HISTORICAL INFORMATION:

The University of Pennsylvania's extensive online archives allowed me to not only read the words of the school's famous founder, Benjamin Franklin, but also learn about the fascinating history of Wharton and the University of Pennsylvania as a whole. To access this information, go to *http://www.archives. upenn.edu/.* For a tour of Wharton's past, there's "Wharton a History of Leadership: A Selective Timeline of the Wharton School" with commentary from Management professor Daniel Raff, an avid historian. The site can be found at: *http://www.wharton. upenn.edu/huntsmanhall/timeline/.* There's also another comprehensive history called "Wharton–A Century of Innovation," which can be found at *http://www.wharton.upenn.edu/innovation/ index.html.* Below are some other helpful historical references.

Addison, Agnes. "Benjamin Franklin (1706–1790)." University Archives and Records Center University of Pennsylvania, 1940.

Franklin, Benjamin. "Proposals Relating to the Education of Youth in Pensilvania." A pamphlet from 1749. Hypertext version created by Derek Smith available from the University Archives and Record Center University of Pennsylvania at *http://www. archives.upenn.edu/primdocs/1749proposals.html.*

Geisst, Charles R. *Wall Street: A History from Its Beginnings to the*

Fall of Enron, revised and expanded edition. New York: Oxford University Press, 2004.

Lehrer, Eli. "Nerds on Wall Street." American Enterprise Institute for Public Policy research. July–August 2002.

Mintz, S. (2003). *Digital History.* Retrieved January, 2004, from *http://www.digitalhistory.uh.edu.*

Renner, Michael. "Corporate Mergers Skyrocket." *Vital Signs 2000.* Washington, D.C.: Worldwatch Institute, May 2000.

Sahlman, Rachel. "Benjamin Franklin" *SPECTRUM Home & School Magazine.* Arizona: K.B. Shaw, March 7, 2004.

ACKNOWLEDGMENTS

Writing a book can be a very solitary pursuit, but it takes a whole community of people to truly make it all happen. Of utmost importance are those who make the book come to life, and for that reason I am greatly indebted to the Wharton students who gave their precious free time and met me between job interviews, midterm exams, group projects and personal commitments, when they could have been spending their time catching their breath. Of special note are the students, who—in great detail—shared their triumphs and defeats with me, namely Jon Gantman, Jessica Kennedy, Shreevar Kheruka, Anthony Sandrik, Regi Vengalil, Shimika Wilder and Grace Yoon. The pleasure has been great and it has truly been all mine.

I would also be remiss not to mention the dozens of other Wharton students, alumni and MBA students who provided their insights, including, but definitely not limited to, Christopher Albergo, Tony Huang, Rob Jawl, Gregg Johnson (who introduced to me by Josh Renfree), Judy Kawaguchi, Ayo Omojola, Father James Martin, Nitin Rampat, Sharleen Sun and Valerie Wong. There were also several bankers and consultants who took time out of some very busy schedules (usually late at night or early on a Saturday morning) to teach me about the industries they worked in. I greatly appreciate their generosity and candor.

I could not have met many of the students found in this book without the help of Wharton's faculty and administration. Not only did they allow me to wander around campus and poke my head into information sessions, but they also offered me their time and their knowledge. Peter Winicov, the Associate Director of Communications for Wharton, took my call out of the blue and set the ball rolling. Barbara Hewitt at Career Services (one of two full-time people on staff who works for the Wharton undergrad program's Career Services) shepherded me through the ins and outs of the recruiting process, even as the campus overflowed with recruiters and her office was overwhelmed by anxious students worried about ruining their chances to get a job with their dream firm. Patricia Rose, the director of Career Services, was extremely diligent in letting recruiters know that I was there. Suzanne Kauffman Depuyt and Anita Henderson patiently explained the school's curriculum to me, while Beth Hagovsky candidly shared with me the school's efforts to build a Wharton community that went beyond grading curves and GPAs. Peggy Curchack also from Career Services graciously allowed me to sit in on her interviewing workshops, and Wharton's Chief Information Officer Gerry McCartney gave me an inside look at Wharton's incredible emerging technologies.

The folks at *Forbes* magazine, especially Mary Ellen Egan, Kasia Moreno and Stewart Pinkerton, were not only incredibly supportive, but they also allowed me to take the time off that I needed to write this book. I can't thank them enough for being so understanding and patient.

Throughout my time in Philadelphia there were two things I desperately needed: a bed and a form of transportation. For the former, I am indebted to Allison and Michael Golden for opening their home to me and being so incredibly generous. And to Cole, who always made me smile. My family has also been a source of great support and enthusiasm, in particular Michelle, Roddy and Abby Morrison. My incredible mother, Connie Ridgway, and my stepfather, Jim Smith, have not only supported me throughout my life, but even more so while I was researching and writing this book. They made my life much easier by giving me the means to get from here to there on my own time. I am eternally grateful to have them in my life.

Joe Veltre at the Artists Literary Group and Kevin DiCamillo at Paulist Press allowed me to tap into their valuable insights and expertise. Michael Maiello was one of my most thoughtful critics. I had an endless supply of cheerleaders and supporters in Nancy Beiles Dorsch, Vanessa Cunningham, Peter Gilligan, Lea Goldman, David Miller, Cyrus Roxas, Beth Spielman and Michael Uy. And from hundreds of miles away, Corina Lindley, Cullen Meade and Burke Drane. Their optimism was contagious when I needed to catch it the most. Joe Tantalo not only lent me his computer when mine went berserk, but he made sure I had a great home-cooked meal every once in a while, and I can't thank him enough. And, of course, my dog Piper was my constant companion throughout long nights in front of the computer and always gave me a reason to stretch my legs and throw a ball around. She is truly a best friend.

None of this would be possible without the talented group over at Gotham Books, in particular my publisher William Shinker, editor Brendan Cahill, and his right-hand man Patrick Mulligan. I will always be grateful to Brendan for giving me this opportunity. He was the beginning of this book, and it seems fitting that he be the ending, as well. Not only did he trust me with his idea, he had enough faith in me to let me run with it. His patience and support were unending, and his talents inspiring. This is not only a book because of Brendan, it's a *much better* book because of him.